PEOPLE
WHO MADE
HISTORY

WITHDRAWN
GEORGE W. BUSH

Cheryl Fisher Phibbs, *Book Editor*

Daniel Leone, *President*
Bonnie Szumski, *Publisher*
Scott Barbour, *Managing Editor*
David M. Haugen, *Series Editor*

GREENHAVEN
PRESS ®

THOMSON

GALE

San Diego • Detroit • New York • San Francisco • Cleveland
New Haven, Conn. • Waterville, Maine • London • Munich

THOMSON

━━━━✳━━━━ ™

GALE

WITHDRAWN

LIBRARY OF CONGRESS CATALOGING-IN-PUBLICATION DATA

George W. Bush / Cheryl Fisher Phibbs, book editor.
  p. cm. — (People who made history)
Includes bibliographical references and index.
ISBN 0-7377-1847-1 (pbk. : alk. paper) — ISBN 0-7377-1846-3 (lib. : alk. paper)
  1. Bush, George W. (George Walker), 1946– . 2. Presidents—United States—Biography. 3. Presidents—United States—Election—2000. 4. United States—Politics and government—1993–2001. I. Phibbs, Cheryl Fisher. II. Series.
E903.G46 2004
973.931'092—dc21   2003040860

Printed in the United States of America

CONTENTS

FOREWORD

In the vast and colorful pageant of human history, a handful of individuals stand out. They are the men and women who have come variously to be called "great," "leading," "brilliant," "pivotal," or "infamous" because they and their deeds forever changed their own society or the world as a whole. Some were political or military leaders—kings, queens, presidents, generals, and the like—whose policies, conquests, or innovations reshaped the maps and futures of countries and entire continents. Among those falling into this category were the formidable Roman statesman/general Julius Caesar, who extended Rome's power into Gaul (what is now France); Caesar's lover and ally, the notorious Egyptian queen Cleopatra, who challenged the strongest male rulers of her day; and England's stalwart Queen Elizabeth I, whose defeat of the mighty Spanish Armada saved England from subjugation.

Some of history's other movers and shakers were scientists or other thinkers whose ideas and discoveries altered the way people conduct their everyday lives or view themselves and their place in nature. The electric light and other remarkable inventions of Thomas Edison, for example, revolutionized almost every aspect of home-life and the workplace; and the theories of naturalist Charles Darwin lit the way for biologists and other scientists in their ongoing efforts to understand the origins of living things, including human beings.

Still other people who made history were religious leaders and social reformers. The struggles of the Arabic prophet Muhammad more than a thousand years ago led to the establishment of one of the world's great religions—Islam; and the efforts and personal sacrifices of an American reverend named Martin Luther King Jr. brought about major improvements in race relations and the justice system in the United States.

Each anthology in the People Who Made History series begins with an introductory essay that provides a general overview of the individual's life, times, and contributions. The group of essays that follow are chosen for their accessibility to a young adult audience and carefully edited in consideration of the reading and comprehension levels of that audience. Some of the essays are by noted historians, professors, and other experts. Others are excerpts from contemporary writings by or about the pivotal individual in question. To aid the reader in choosing the material of immediate interest or need, an annotated table of contents summarizes the article's main themes and insights.

Each volume also contains extensive research tools, including a collection of excerpts from primary source documents pertaining to the individual under discussion. The volumes are rounded out with an extensive bibliography and a comprehensive index.

Plutarch, the renowned first-century Greek biographer and moralist, crystallized the idea behind Greenhaven's People Who Made History when he said, "To be ignorant of the lives of the most celebrated men of past ages is to continue in a state of childhood all our days." Indeed, since it is people who make history, every modern nation, organization, institution, invention, artifact, and idea is the result of the diligent efforts of one or more individuals, living or dead; and it is therefore impossible to understand how the world we live in came to be without examining the contributions of these individuals.

GEORGE W. BUSH: AN APPOINTMENT WITH HISTORY

George W. Bush has been a strong leader in every aspect of his presidency. He has held history-making presidential approval ratings, healed a grieving nation through one of its darkest hours, led the world in a fight against terrorism, instigated the largest restructuring of government in seventy years, and proved to be a successful campaigner not only in his own election but in helping to garner Republican control of the House of Representatives and the U.S. Senate during his first midterm elections in 2002. For a man who almost did not become president, Bush has proved a powerhouse in office.

GROWING UP A BUSH

Growing up in the shadow of a successful family and spending most of his earlier years struggling to find his way, Bush learned to take advantage of the chances life offered and to approach situations placed before him not only analytically but with a dose of humor. An incredibly accomplished family history put a lot of pressure on Bush to develop within the family context. Although Bush states that his father, George H.W. Bush, never tried to shape him, he had to figure out where he was going and who he was outside of family expectations. Bush's heritage was saturated with Wall Street successes, politics, East Coast prep schools, and the military.

His paternal grandfather, Prescott Bush, was a U.S. senator and served on the boards at Yale, Pan American Airlines, CBS, Prudential Insurance, and Dresser Industries. His paternal grandmother's family developed a national dry goods business and one of the oldest and largest investment houses on Wall Street.

Bush's maternal heritage was in the publishing industry, and his father was a military hero. The elder Bush was successful in the oil business and in the political arena, serving as head of the Republican Party, an ambassador to China, vice president, and the forty-first president of the United States. The weight of the family legacy was always present.

SEIZING OPPORTUNITIES

Bush's life has been shaped not only by high expectations but by personal tragedy as well. Bush's sister, Robin, died of leukemia when he was only seven years old. Her death helped him learn to live his life in chapters and seize opportunities as they came. Bush argues that the source of his personality is more than the scope of one or two events, yet close friends say his sister's death helped mold him and taught him to deal with a world driven by chance.

Bush's philosophy of seizing opportunities as they present themselves is oddly illustrated by a story about the family cat, Ernie. One night, when Bush was fifty-two years old and serving as governor of Texas, he thought his dog Spot had treed a squirrel and Bush went to investigate. According to Bush, in the tree

> was a scrawny, tiny kitty, which had somehow survived the streets of downtown Austin and ended up in a tree in the only backyard for miles, the backyard of the Governor's mansion. The kitty was skittish and afraid at first, but as food was put out the cat gradually warmed up. The kitty has six toes. Its paws look like baseball gloves and the Bush's named it Ernie because Ernest Hemingway had six-toed cats. Ernie became a member of the Bush family. The lesson of Ernie is, no matter what tough circumstances you find yourselves in, never give up. Ernie went from the streets of Austin to the Governor's mansion, all because a dog chased him into a tree.[1]

This philosophy to use every moment, seize opportunities, and make the most of what life offers describes how George W. Bush has tried to live his life.

EDUCATION

Bush's years at prep school and college helped him figure out his own path in life. At the age of fifteen, Bush left his free-spirited life in Texas to attend Phillips Academy, a New England prep school in Andover, Massachusetts. The academy was rigorous, competitive, and elite—quite a scary change for someone who had never left home. Bush, however, was following in his father's and grandfather's footsteps, a pattern he would adopt for much of his early adulthood.

At Phillips Academy, Bush was an average student, and a solid athlete, who played varsity basketball and baseball, but he was never the class star. His friends saw him as a self-assured, larger-than-life Texan and nicknamed him "Lip" because he had an opinion on everything.

When Bush graduated from Phillips Academy in 1964, he headed to Yale. He entered his freshman class as a "legacy," following a long line of Bush alumni. Elsie Walker, one of Bush's closest relatives and friends says he had bitter, uncomfortable moments at Yale. Walker explains, "It was awkward for him, as the son of his father, to be at Yale when there was so much antiwar and so much antiestablishment . . . and he comes from quite an establishment family. He felt real conflict and a real loyalty to his family, and I think it was hard to come from a prominent Republican family."[2] While his classmates were protesting the Vietnam War and the political establishment, Bush took the opposing view. He argued that if the United States was in a war, it should be supported by its citizens.

Bush embraced college, enjoying fraternity parties and football weekends. He was known for his ability to include others in social activities. His friends cite several examples of Bush reaching beyond his social circle to move effortlessly among different college cliques.

MILITARY

As Bush moved closer to graduating from Yale in 1968, his student deferment from military service in Vietnam was about to expire. Distinguished military careers dotted his family history and that of his friends, so twelve days before graduation, at the age of twenty-one, Bush registered with the Texas Air National Guard. During extensive interviews and a battery of tests, Bush told the commander of the 147th Fighter Group that he wanted to be a fighter pilot like his father. There were only ninety-eight officer slots when Bush enlisted, and seventy-two were already assigned. Out of the twenty-six that remained, only five were for pilots. These were assigned based on college degree and the candidate's performance on the written exams. Bush made the cut and headed for training at Moody Air Force Base in Georgia. There, he studied Morse code, aerodynamics, and physiology. In 1969 Bush earned his wings and headed back to Houston to fly night maneuvers as part of the Texas Air National Guard.

When Bush's commitment to the Texas Air National Guard

was completed in the early 1970s, he had not settled on a path in life. With the encouragement of a college friend, Bush applied to Harvard Business School. Bush said completing the application forced him to think about what he had accomplished and what he hoped to achieve. At the time, he was working with an inner-city poverty program known as Project PULL in Houston. Bush recalls,

> My job gave me a glimpse of a world I had never seen. It was tragic, heartbreaking, and uplifting, all at the same time. I saw a lot of poverty. I also saw a lot of bad choices: drugs, alcohol abuse, men who had fathered children and walked away, leaving single mothers struggling to raise children on their own. I saw children who could not read and were way behind in school. I also saw good and decent people working to try to help lift these kids out of their terrible circumstances.[3]

When he received his acceptance letter to Harvard, he was not sure he wanted to give up his work at PULL. Bush's partner and mentor at PULL, John White, encouraged him to attend. "If you really care about these kids as much as I think you do, why don't you go and learn more and then you can really help."[4] So, in 1973, George W. Bush entered Harvard Business School to earn his master of business administration degree. Bush describes business school as a turning point.

> By the time I arrived, I had had a taste of many different jobs but none of them had ever seemed to fit. I had worked as a management trainee for an agribusiness company in Houston, and worked in a couple of political campaigns. One summer I delivered mail and messages at a law firm; I spent another on the customer service and quote desk for a stockbroker. One summer I worked on a ranch, and another I rough necked on an offshore rig. It was hard, hot work. I unloaded enough of those heavy mud sacks to know that was not what I wanted to do with my life. . . . [Harvard] taught me the principles of capital, how it is accumulated, risked, spent and managed.[5]

In March of his final year at Harvard, Bush went to visit a friend in Midland, Texas. He recalls,

> When you step outside in Midland, Texas, your horizons suddenly expand. The sky is huge. The land is flat, with not even the hint of a hill to limit the view. The air is clear and bright. Appropriately, "the sky is the limit" was the slogan in Midland when I arrived. It captured the sense of unlimited possibilities that you could almost feel and taste in the air. You can see as far as you want to see in Midland, and I could see a future. I could smell something happening. This is one of the

few places in the country where you can go without a portfolio and train yourself and become competitive. The barriers to entry were very low.[6]

Bush was immediately inspired by the energy and entrepreneurship of the oil industry.

MIDLAND

Bush began his career in the oil business as a "landman" in Midland. A landman reads the land records in a county courthouse to determine who owns the mineral interests that lie below a piece of property. A landman also determines whether the minerals are available for lease and, in many cases, negotiates a lease for the rights. Bush states,

> I eventually learned to trade mineral and royalty interests with some of the $15,000 left over from an education fund my parents had set up. I began to invest in small pieces of drilling prospects. The first well I participated in was a dry hole. It was disappointing, but I knew the risks and had not gambled very much.[7]

As the energy business flourished during the late 1970s, he built a small, solvent outfit of his own. "I formed my first company, Arbusto (Spanish for Bush), to hold the mineral and royalty interests I had begun trading. Eventually, Arbusto would become the general partner of the limited partnerships that I would form as an investment vehicle for people to participate in the energy business.[8]

MARRIAGE

While Bush was in Midland running his business, Laura Welch had come to Midland to visit her family. She was working on a graduate degree in library science in nearby Austin, Texas. Mutual friends introduced Bush and Welch in the summer of 1977 at a dinner party. "The next night we all went to play miniature golf and the next weekend I visited Laura in Austin. I was scheduled to go to Maine to visit Mom and Dad; I went and stayed one day, then flew back to Austin to see Laura. That's when my mother said she knew I was smitten,"[9] said Bush. Three months later, on November 5, 1977, they were married.

In 1978 Bush campaigned for Congress. "It turned out to be a wonderful way to spend our first year of marriage. We were united on a common mission; we spent lots of time together,"[10] Bush recalls. Friends came over to await election returns. "As soon as the votes from Lubbock came in, I knew that I had lost,"[11] said Bush. Disappointed, he went back to work developing his energy company.

OIL

In 1979, oil prices surged as a result of the Arab oil embargo. Investors like Bush were lured by the high prices. Over the next three years Arbusto invested more than $3 million in U.S. wells. According to Bush, each of the partnerships were returning cash.

In 1982 Bush sold stock in his company to an investor. The capital bought oil and gas leases and enabled him to hire an engineer to oversee drilling operations, several geologists, a vice president of finance, and a landman. Arbusto became a fully operational oil company.

Bush was then introduced to the investors of Spectrum 7. They were "looking to expand with an operating company that could develop prospects and operate wells. I was looking for people who could help raise drilling capital. So the merger that took place in 1983 was a perfect fit."[12] Bush became the chief executive officer, running the business in Midland while the investors raised money and ran their other businesses.

The price of oil plummeted in late 1985 when the Organization of Petroleum Exporting Countries could not maintain discipline among its members and the oversupply of foreign crude made its way to the United States and began to affect oil prices. Midland suffered through its version of the 1929 stock market crash. Bush sought a buyer for his business. The chief investor, Harken Energy, was better able to wait out the crisis, and it wanted Bush's oil and gas reserves. Harken was also a publicly traded company. "We worked out a trade, our assets for Harken stock. This gave the investors in Spectrum 7 a saleable asset. I would serve on Harken's board of directors as a consultant to the company,"[13] Bush recalls. Once his business was sold, Bush took his family and moved to Washington, D.C., to participate in his father's campaign for president.

CAMPAIGNING WITH HIS FATHER

Lee Atwater, a political consultant known as the emerging prince of new politics, was chosen to run George H.W. Bush's campaign. Although Atwater was incredibly talented, he had ties to Bush's rivals for the Republican nomination, and George W. was not sure his father would be favorably served by him. Bush told Atwater, "In our family, if you go to war, we want you completely on our side." Atwater responded with the suggestion that changed young Bush's life: "If you're worried about me, join the team and keep an eye on me."[14] Bush did just that.

He was put in the thick of the campaign, monitoring not just Atwater's activities but also everyone else who worked for his father. "I was a loyalty enforcer and a listening ear,"[15] Bush says, describing his work. He was instrumental in bridging political gaps between the Republican Party and political interest groups. Bush met with everyone from environmentalists to evangelicals and was the liaison for governors, mayors, influential fundraisers, and anyone who needed special attention. He never left a room until everyone was satisfied. Bush was a sounding board, assessor of problems, and a general morale booster. He reminded everyone that their job was to get his father elected, but once his father was in office, he headed back to Texas.

THE RANGERS

When Bush returned to Texas in 1980, he heard about the sale of the Texas Rangers baseball team. "I began reading speculation in the newspapers. Television station owner Ed Gaylord might buy the Texas Rangers; a group of Florida investors was interested. And so was I. If they were selling, I was buying. Of course, I had more determination than money." Bush met with the owner, Eddie Chiles, to convince Chiles to sell him the team if he could come up with the investors. Bush assembled a group of friends that merged with a few Dallas, Texas, businessmen, and a partnership agreement was arranged. "Once all the investors received their original money back, plus a 2 percent return, they would split 85 percent of any profits." One of the partners, Rusty Rose, and Bush were to share in the day-to-day management of the partnership and split the remaining 15 percent of profits,"[16] says Bush. "A lifelong baseball fan, I was about to own a baseball team. I remember thinking, 'This is as good as it gets. Life cannot be better than this.'"[17]

Bush's role as general managing partner of the Texas Rangers became his political springboard. It publicized him, demonstrated that he could manage a complex organization, and gave him financial independence. Fans sought his autograph as eagerly as they did the players'. Baseball made Bush a regular guy, not a president's son from Yale or Harvard, but a neighbor cheering on a ball club with his family.

Those who worked with Bush said he had an uncanny ability to hire the right people and to create consensus and contentment among peers and subordinates.

His most significant achievement as managing partner of the Rangers was getting the Arlington taxpayers to agree to pay for two-thirds of a new stadium for the team. He sold the stadium to the public by speaking at rallies and on television. Bush helped create a desirable image for the Rangers, pitching season ticket sales and corporate sponsors and even winning over the media by building the press boxes at club level. Bush insisted that the Rangers would not have good reviews if they did not have great press boxes. His gift for public relations vastly improved not only the team's image but also its profits.

While his mother was the first lady of the United States, Bush invited her to attend an evening at the ballpark as his guest to throw out the first pitch of the game. Barbara Bush later wrote in her memoirs,

> We started with a reception for the wives of the players, wives of the owners and some key women in the management. We had pictures taken and everyone was darling. On to the game and I was so excited. George knew every living human, almost seemed like all 38,000! He introduced me to the "best grounds keeping in the major leagues," the "finest ticket-taker in any park," and the "fastest hot dog vendor." He knew them all. He had Reading Is Fundamental [RIF] posters everywhere and gave tickets to kids participating in the RIF program and handed out bookmarks with Texas Rangers on one side and RIF on the other to every single person who came. The ball I was to throw out had been signed by all the players and by the coach. Below their names they put their favorite books.[18]

George W. Bush says, "For five years, Laura and I went to fifty or sixty home games a year. We'd talk about baseball, about our girls, about life. It was a time of family and friends. Our girls grew up at the ballpark."[19] Commenting that baseball was a great training ground for politics and government, Bush states, "The bottom line in baseball is results: wins and losses. We succeeded in baseball because we had a vision and a message. I learned to overlook minor setbacks and focus on the long haul. I would find those skills invaluable in my campaigns and tenure as Governor of Texas."[20]

GOVERNOR BUSH

At a political rally in 1993, Bush was introducing Kay Bailey Hutchison, a friend who was running for the Senate. As Bush walked onstage, the crowd started hollering, "Run for governor" and "Governor Bush." Worried about how Texas schools were governed, crime—especially juvenile crime—and the state's business climate, Bush was interested in the idea. He said his wife, Laura, knowing how much he enjoyed their life in baseball, was surprised over the course of the next few months "when all I could talk about was how I wanted to change Texas and become its Governor."[21]

Bush turned out to be a tireless and nearly flawless campaigner when he ran for governor of Texas against the popular incumbent, Ann Richards. She derided Bush as "Shrub," claiming he was just running on his father's name, but voters saw Bush as a substantial candidate and elected him with nearly 54 percent of the vote.

As the chief executive in Texas, Bush let political appointees do their jobs and intervened only when he saw a problem. He had a bold education agenda implementing a controversial plan to end social promotion. It required children to pass reading and math tests in fifth grade and reading, math, and writing tests in the eighth grade.

At his urging, legislators toughened educational standards, and the juvenile justice code. Under his guidance, the legislature passed welfare reform and the largest tax cut in Texas history. Employment increased while juvenile crime and welfare rolls decreased. According to November 1996 statistics, while other states were struggling, Texas had a growing economy and Bush's fiscal stewardship as governor had left a billion dollars in surplus funds in the state budget. Bush saw this as a down payment toward a fundamental tax-cut package.

One of the most controversial issues Bush faced as governor was the decision to uphold the death penalty. Many executions took place during his tenure as governor, including the execution of the first woman in more than twenty years. "Some advocates of life will challenge why I oppose abortion yet support the death penalty; to me, it's the difference between innocence and guilt,"[22] Bush says.

During the reelection campaign for his second term as governor, Bush recalls, he "couldn't get on an elevator or walk through the back of a hotel kitchen on the way to make a speech without someone saying, 'Governor, please run for President.' The question had become a distraction, interfering with my attempts to deliver any other message."[23]

Bush finished his reelection campaign uncertain of whether he would seek the presidency. "It might have affected some votes, but overall, I think most of my fellow Texans were proud to have their Governor considered a potential president."[24] Bush became the first governor elected to two consecutive four-year terms in the history of Texas.

Once reelection was behind Bush, the pressure to make a decision about seeking the presidency mounted as the deadline to enter the race neared. He worried about exposing his family to a national stage. On the other hand he felt the country was at a critical moment in history.

A DEFINING MOMENT

During a private prayer service with the Bush family for his second gubernatorial inauguration, Bush's hesitations about running for president were overcome during a twenty-minute speech by Pastor Mark Craig. Craig spoke on the hunger of people for faithfulness and honesty in government. He retold the biblical story of Moses, who was asked by God to lead his people to a land of milk and honey. Moses had a lot of reasons to shirk the task. As the pastor told it, Moses' basic reaction was, "Sorry, God, I'm busy. I've got a family. I've got sheep to tend. I've got a life. Send some other person. But God did not and Moses ultimately did his bidding."[25] Craig added that people were starved for leaders with ethical and moral courage who would do what is right for the right reasons even if it was not easy or convenient. Later Bush's mother told George that the pastor had been talking about him. Bush responded to her that Craig was calling on everyone to use what power they had to do good for the right reason, but he acknowledged that the sermon had spoken directly to his heart. Bush felt that Craig was personally challenging him to do more. With this conviction, Bush began his national campaign to be president:

> I know that I am seeking an awesome responsibility. I know that serving as Governor of Texas is not anywhere near the same as being President. But if Texas were a nation, it would be the eleventh-largest economy in the world. I've had some success, and I've learned to lead. You cannot lead by dividing people. I am a uniter, not a divider. My campaign will be positive, hopeful and inclusive. I want to show that politics, after

a time of tarnished ideals, can be higher and better, I hope to give our country a fresh start after a season of cynicism.[26]

FAITH IS THE MAN

Bush believes that religious faith changes lives, and he credits his faith with teaching him humility and giving him focus and perspective. Realizing that his faith could be misinterpreted in the political process, Bush said that he tries to live out his faith rather than flaunt it.

In 1986, while the Bushes were on summer vacation in Maine, the Reverend Billy Graham visited them. Bush says he knew he was in the presence of a great man because he could see the Lord reflected in Graham's demeanor. Bush credits Graham with leading him to a path of faith. "It was the beginning of a change in my life. I had always been a religious person, but that weekend my faith took on new meaning. It was the beginning of a new walk where I would recommit my heart to Jesus Christ."[27]

According to Bush, his life is built on a foundation of faith that does not shift. This faith also gives him the freedom to fail. "I believe in a divine plan that supersedes all human plans. My faith frees me to put the problem of the moment in proper perspective and frees me to make decisions that others might not like. It frees me to do the right thing."[28]

THE RUN FOR PRESIDENT

In 1999, as Bush began his presidential race, one of the problems he wanted to fix was the glimpse of hopelessness he saw in the national soul:

> We live in the greatest and freest and most prosperous nation in the world, yet too many of our citizens do not believe their lives have meaning or value. The American dream is a distant offer meant for somebody else. Many people do not believe the fundamentally American conviction that you can be what you want to be and achieve what you want to achieve, so long as you are willing to work hard and earn it. This gap of hope is found in the poverty of our inner cities, where neighborhoods have become urban war zones, a world of barred windows and gang violence and failed schools, a world of shattered glass and shattered dreams. We see glimpses of this hopelessness in schoolyards where children inexplicably, tragically, horrifically murder other children.
>
> I worry that we are being divided into two nations, separate and unequal: one nation with the tools and confidence to

seek the American dream; another nation that is being left behind. We risk becoming two societies; one that reads and one that can't, one that dreams and one that doesn't.[29]

This was the message of Bush's presidential campaign. Bush supported individual accountability, believing that Americans are a single, moral community with obligations to each other, not a society dependent on more government programs as the answer.

Bush ran his presidential race with this conviction and held the lead in the campaign until just before the Democratic National Convention. At the time, opponent Al Gore's lead went up and did not come down until late September when the presidential debates took place. Postdebate polls reported that the American people thought Gore presented a different image of himself at each debate and came across as divisive. This propelled Bush back to the front of the race until the week before the election on November 7, when Gore made a push for the win. The indecision of the American people seemed to strengthen, with neither candidate holding a strong lead. As election day drew closer, more states appeared undecided.

FIVE WEEKS TO VICTORY

Of the dramatic seesaw contest, reporter Jamie Dettmer observed,

> Election day started badly for the Bush campaign. The GOP's [Republicans'] morning exit polls looked ugly and reports of high turnouts in the battleground states of the Northeast and Midwest revived fears about the black vote, (historically strong in the Democratic camp) turning out in droves.
>
> Midday brought relief, say Bush campaign sources. The exit polls started to swing their way and by mid-afternoon, they believed they were ahead in several of the battleground states. Bush and Gore had insatiable last minute campaign appearances, making calls to radio stations, and urging voters to turn out.[30]

By the end of the day, once the polls had closed and actual results began to be reported, two phone conversations took place between Bush and Gore. The first was placed by Gore to concede the race, but a second call from Gore retracted the concession explaining that the state of Florida was too close to call and there would need to be a recount.

Historically close elections have been defined in several ways: by the difference between the candidates in the national popular vote, by their difference in the electoral vote, and by the difference in popular votes that would actually have changed the election outcome. The 2000 election seemed to challenge all three.

This would be the fourth time in American history when a presidential election entered into a disputed phase after initial ballot counts. The outcomes of the previous contests, however, were not determined by a court of law as in the 2000 election. Gore stayed active in the postelection campaign, pushing the election results to be played out in the judiciary system. The Bush campaign preferred the Florida legislature. It was going to take Florida's electoral votes to swing the election one way or another. Additionally, disputes over election inconsistencies in Florida clouded the vote totals. In the end, after a historical five-week battle through political, state, and federal processes, the U.S. Supreme Court upheld the original Bush victory in Florida, making him the forty-third president of the United States.

BUSH'S FIRST YEAR IN OFFICE

Bush spent much of his first few weeks in office implementing his campaign agenda: courting a Democratic-controlled legislature to advance a $1.6 million tax cut. He introduced his education reform bill and his Patient's Bill of Rights for congressional approval.

Surrounding himself with seasoned staff members and one of the most experienced national security teams in the history of the presidency, Bush faced his first foreign policy crisis just three months after he entered the office. In April 2001 an American surveillance plane and a Chinese fighter collided over China. The American surveillance plane made an emergency landing in China, and the Chinese government refused to release the twenty-four grounded Americans. For ten days China held the hostages and demanded an apology from the United States for the incident and for the death of its fighter pilot. The Bush administration took an uncompromising stance, avoided a concession for the surveillance, apologized for the Chinese pilot's death, and used economic interests to negotiate the return of the hostages. Once the China incident was resolved, Bush went back to managing the national agenda, focusing on his education reform package until terrorist attacks on U.S. soil redefined his presidency.

A WARTIME PRESIDENT

On September 11, 2001, as Bush was reading to a group of kindergartners to promote his education reform package, he received a message that both of the World Trade Center towers in New York had been hit by airplanes. Later that same morning, he would join the nation to hear of two other terrorist attacks involving airplane crashes: one into the Pentagon and one diverted to Pennsylvania that was believed to be headed for the White House. America was in shock and grieved the loss of those killed during the attacks. Overnight, these incidents handed Bush a mission as the leader of the free world in a war against terrorism.

To heal the nation, Bush made a strong presence at the rubble of the World Trade Center and the Pentagon disaster areas. He organized a National Day of Prayer and Remembrance for the victims of the tragedy during which he delivered a moving and healing speech to the nation. He also stood before the nation to accept worldwide condolences to the American people and vowed retaliation for these terrorist attacks. Bush's visibility and leadership during the aftermath of the attacks helped him achieve and maintain the highest presidential approval ratings ever recorded. Writing for *Presidential Studies Quarterly*, Fred Greenstein noted that a Gallup poll completed a day before the terrorist strikes found only "51 percent of the public expressed approval of his presidential performance. Three days after the attacks, Gallup fielded the first of an extended run of polls in which Bush registered approval levels in excess of 85 percent."[51]

A major challenge for Bush after September 11, 2001, was to respond to the urgent need to protect America. He chose to model a new Homeland Security office after the National Security Council. The Security Council was a White House department responsible for coordinating the various operating agencies and getting them to work as a team. Bush put a good friend, Tom Ridge, governor of Pennsylvania, in charge. Creating this office was the largest reorganization of the federal government in seventy years.

Additionally, as a president called into war, Bush made specific demands of Afghanistan. Bush stipulated that terrorist training camps be closed; leaders of al-Qaeda, a religious terrorist group behind the September 11 attacks, be turned over to authorities; and illegally detained foreign nationals be released. When these demands were not met, Bush ordered military campaigns against al-Qaeda terrorist training camps and military installations of the Taliban regime.

Bush argued that his actions were justified in a world in which the moral choice was obvious. "Every nation, in every region, now has a decision to make. Either you are with us or you are with the terrorists,"[32] Bush declared on September 20. Three months later, in December 2001, the Taliban was gone and Afghanistan was stable enough to install an interim form of government in which its 26 million people would have the opportunity to be politically represented.

THE WAR AGAINST IRAQ

One year after the terrorist attacks, Bush addressed the nation and reminded Americans that September 11, 2001, was a milestone passed but that the mission against terrorism would go on. The next day, at the General Assembly of the United Nations (UN), Bush asked the world to unite and end the danger posed by Saddam Hussein of Iraq. As a condition to end the Persian Gulf War in 1991, Iraqi leadership pledged to reveal and destroy all weapons of mass destruction, cease repression of its people, renounce all involvement with terrorism, and prove its compliance through rigorous inspections. Bush claimed that Hussein had broken every aspect of these promises and had shown contempt for the UN by ignoring his previous commitments to the world. Bush further argued that twelve years of defiance by the Iraqi regime to the 1991 UN resolutions was a threat to peace. He asked the UN to require the Iraqi regime to honor its previous commitments as a sign of accountability. "If Iraq's regime defies us again, the world must move deliberately, decisively to hold Iraq to account. . . . The purposes of the United States should not be doubted. The Security Council resolution will be enforced—the just demands of peace and security met— or action will be unavoidable."[33]

Bush also claimed that Iraq was building and hiding weapons that would enable Hussein to dominate the Middle East and intimidate the civilized world, stating further that the safety of America depended on ending Hussein's direct and growing threat. "We must stand up for our security and for the permanent rights and the hopes of mankind. By heritage and by choice, the United States of America will make that stand."[34]

Before the United Nations would honor Bush's request

and vote for a military solution, it decided to give Hussein one final chance to disarm. A new team of inspectors was sent into Iraq to perform weapons inspections and determine Iraq's compliance.

For four and a half months the United States and its allies worked with the Security Council to enforce its twelve-year-old demands. In the interim, while weapons inspectors worked in Iraq, Bush was rallying an international coalition to help disarm the Iraqi regime militarily. Acknowledging Hussein's threat to world security, the U.S. House and Senate authorized President Bush the use of military force in Iraq if it became necessary.

On March 16, 2003, the Security Council extended compliance deadlines for the Iraqi regime. Frustrated with UN inaction, Bush and allied countries held a summit in the Azores as a last resort for a political solution to this conflict. Feeling every measure to avoid war had been taken, Bush gave Hussein forty-eight hours to leave Iraq. Three days later, Bush ordered the coalition forces of forty countries to begin military action in Iraq.

People from around the world argued that this was a historical operation, claiming the United States had never participated in a preemptive attack on another nation. But Bush's presidency had been filled with historical records: a president whose father had also been president, a historical post-election campaign and victory, organizing the most experienced presidential staff ever assembled, implementing the largest tax cut and educational restructuring in American history, survival of the most tragic terrorist attacks on American soil, and the establishment of a Homeland Security Department, and leading his first midterm elections in 2002 to usher in the strongest change in political power in the House of Representatives and the U.S. Senate since the formation of America. Bush continued to seize opportunities and lead America with courage through challenging times during his appointment with history.

NOTES

1. George W. Bush, *A Charge to Keep*. New York: William Morrow, 1999, p. 89.

2. Quoted in Bill Minutaglio, *First Son George W. Bush and the Bush Family Dynasty*. New York: Random House, 1999, pp. 107–108.

3. Bush, *A Charge to Keep*, p. 58.

4. Bush, *A Charge to Keep*, p. 59.
5. Bush, *A Charge to Keep*, p. 60.
6. Bush, *A Charge to Keep*, p. 56.
7. Bush, *A Charge to Keep*, p. 62.
8. Bush, *A Charge to Keep*, p. 62.
9. Bush, *A Charge to Keep*, p. 80.
10. Bush, *A Charge to Keep*, p. 82.
11. Bush, *A Charge to Keep*, p. 82.
12. Bush, *A Charge to Keep*, p. 63.
13. Bush, *A Charge to Keep*, p. 64.
14. Bush, *A Charge to Keep*, p. 179.
15. Bush, *A Charge to Keep*, p. 180.
16. Bush, *A Charge to Keep*, p. 199.
17. Bush, *A Charge to Keep*, p. 198.
18. Barbara Bush, *A Memoir.* New York: Charles Scribner's Sons, 1994, pp. 290–91.
19. Bush, *A Charge to Keep*, p. 206.
20. Bush, *A Charge to Keep*, p. 208.
21. Bush, *A Charge to Keep*, p. 26.
22. Bush, *A Charge to Keep*, p. 147.
23. Bush, *A Charge to Keep*, p. 223.
24. Bush, *A Charge to Keep*, p. 224.
25. Bush, *A Charge to Keep*, p. 8.
26. Bush, *A Charge to Keep*, p. 241.
27. Bush, *A Charge to Keep*, p. 136.
28. Bush, *A Charge to Keep*, p. 6.
29. Bush, *A Charge to Keep*, p. 136.
30. Jamie Dettmer, "A Wild and Crazy Election Night," *Insight on the News*, December 4, 2000.
31. Fred Greenstein, "The Contemporary Presidency: The Changing Leadership of George W. Bush: A Pre- and Post-9/11 Comparison," *Presidential Studies Quarterly*, June 2002.
32. George W. Bush, speech to the nation, September 20, 2001. www.whitehouse.gov.
33. George W. Bush, speech to the United Nations, September 12, 2002. www.whitehouse.gov.
34. Bush, speech to the United Nations.

CHAPTER 1

EARLY
INFLUENCES

PEOPLE
WHO MADE
HISTORY

GEORGE W. BUSH

Midland Influence

Nicholas D. Kristof

Steeped in optimism and embedded with values, the community of Midland, Texas, gave George W. Bush life lessons and a character that brought him to the White House. He has commented that if you want to understand him, you must understand the attitude of Midland. Midland offered Bush a world of right and wrong, dreams, opportunity, respect for tradition, faith, and the acceptance of risk as a way of life. Self-reliance was also a part of the community's character. When the people of Midland needed a theater or hospital they worked hard to raise the funds themselves without governmental help or intrusion. Because of the lifestyle growing up in Midland provided, Bush believes that people can do anything if they work hard enough. Nicholas D. Kristof, a staff writer for the *New York Times*, explores this foundational period and how it shaped George W. Bush in the following article from May 2000.

Many of the roots of Mr. Bush's political philosophy as a presidential candidate . . . seem to go back to his childhood. Midland, a conservative, up-from-the-bootstraps town that has grown from 25,000 when he was a little boy to almost 100,000 today, mirrors Mr. Bush's optimism, his faith in business and his doubts about an activist government. While playing Little League baseball, running for class president, or even sobbing in the principal's office, George W. Bush absorbed West Texas values that many old friends say are central to understanding who he is today.

"I think his political philosophy comes completely from the philosophy of the independent oil man," said Joe O'Neill, a fellow rapscallion in childhood. "His homage to his parents, his respect for his elders, his respect for tradition, his belief in religion, his opposition to abortion—that's the philosophy he grew up with here."

27

Mr. Bush himself, in a long interview about his roots, made a similar point. "I don't know what percentage of me is Midland," he said, "but I would say people, if they want to understand me, need to understand Midland and the attitude of Midland."

It is in the soil of Midland that Mr. Bush has said he would like to be buried when he dies, and it was to Midland that he returned in the 1970's to marry and start a family. It gave him an anchor in real America.

AN ORDINARY UPBRINGING

Mr. Bush has often said that "the biggest difference between me and my father is that he went to Greenwich Country Day and I went to San Jacinto Junior High." That may be an exaggeration of the younger Mr. Bush's populist credentials, because he is also a product of Andover, Yale and Harvard. But there is still something to it.

The father, chauffeured to and from private school in Connecticut in a black sedan, suffered politically because of the perception that he was a blue blood who could not relate to ordinary people. The younger Mr. Bush also has been tainted by the idea that he was born into privilege with a visa to effortless wealth and prominence. Yet George W. Bush actually had a rather ordinary childhood, and his years biking around small-town streets in jeans and a white T-shirt left him with a common touch that is among his greatest assets as a politician.

"He understands Bubba because there is more Bubba in him," Karl Rove, the longtime political adviser to the Bushes, told a reporter in 1992, when Mr. Bush's friends were still carefree enough to say colorful things about him. "He is clearly the wild son—even today. Part of it is rooted in Midland, where he grew up in an ordinary neighborhood, where houses are close together and risk was a way of life.". . .

Midland, impatient with ideas and introspection, was a world of clear rights and wrongs, long on absolutes and devoid of ethical gray shades. It may be the source of some of Mr. Bush's greatest political strengths, the unpretentiousness and mellow bonhomie that warm up voters, and also of his weaknesses, including an image of an intellectual lightweight that is underscored whenever he mixes up the likes of Slovenia and Slovakia. . . .

A CONSERVATIVE TOWN

Oil made Midland a boomtown, attracting ambitious businessmen like the elder Mr. Bush and many other out-of-staters as well. These people made for a conservative town but not a redneck one; Midland had a large proportion of geologists, engineers, lawyers and accountants, and Ivy League college graduates were everywhere.

Mr. Bush recalls it in Norman Rockwell pastels, and so do many other residents. Children bicycled everywhere on their own, crime was almost nonexistent and if anyone suspicious—say, someone with a beard—showed up in town, then-Sheriff Ed Darnell (known as Big Ed) would stop him, escort him to the edge of town, and tell him to "get out."

Yet what no one volunteers is that it was also rigidly segregated in those days, like most places in the South. Black children went to their own school rather than to Sam Houston Elementary with George Bush. The bus station and train station had separate waiting rooms for blacks and whites, and there were separate, dilapidated drinking fountains marked "colored" at the stations and at the courthouse.

The Bushes' first encounter with West Texas racism came when they casually invited a black man, working for the National Association for the Advancement of Colored People, to come by their temporary home in neighboring Odessa. The man had the tact to stay away, but neighbors heard about this and warned the elder George Bush to stop these invitations unless he wanted to be tarred and feathered.

Racial slurs were routine, and young George picked up the words from neighbors. Once when he was about 7 years old he used one in the living room in front of his mother, Barbara.

Michael Proctor, who lived across the street and was playing with George at the time, remembers watching as Mrs. Bush grabbed her son by the ear and dragged him into the bathroom. She washed his mouth out with soap as he spluttered indignantly.

"His family was probably the only one around that didn't use racial slurs," Mr. Proctor said. "I probably didn't realize it was wrong until I saw that."

Alongside the racism directed at blacks, there was a measured respect for the Mexicans who came over the border to work in the oil fields. As a boomtown, Midland needed laborers and welcomed Mexican immigrants, who were regarded as hard-working and thrifty. Some old friends find an echo of that attitude in Mr. Bush's efforts to push the Republican Party to reach out to immigrants.

"We saw these people cross the border and just wanting a good job," recalls Randall Roden, a neighbor boy and best friend. Mr. Roden recalls going out with George and his father to an oil well and spending the night sleeping in the back of the Bushes' station wagon as the crew—Mexicans among them—struggled to get the well going.

"I formed the very strong impression, and I think George has the same one, that these people came for economic opportunity and worked very hard," Mr. Roden said. "If you wanted a Mexican worker to have a new pair of boots, you'd have to buy it for him. Because if you gave him money, he'd send it home."

GAINING A FOOTHOLD IN TEXAS

George W. Bush, though born in 1946 in New Haven, Conn., while his father was still an over-achieving student at Yale, moved to West Texas when he was not quite 2 and grew up in this nurturing environment. These days, as the son of a president and scion of a wealthy family, he is often perceived as a child of privilege, but neighbors in those days insist that in the 1950's that was not the case.

The Bush family in the Northeast had money, but the elder George left all that behind to make his own fortune in West Texas. Equipped with connections but initially without seed money, George and Barbara Bush and little George, their firstborn, settled in a tiny apartment in the hard-driving oil town of Odessa, where they shared a bathroom with a mother-daughter team of prostitutes living next door.

Local people say that you raise hell in Odessa but raise a family in nearby Midland, a much more respectable place. So, after a one-year interlude in California, the Bushes moved to Midland, living in a bright blue 847-square-foot bungalow on a newly built street in which every home was identical—but painted bright colors to make them seem different. It was called Easter Egg Row, because the houses looked like colored eggs.

The family prospered in the oil business and moved into a series of nicer houses in Midland, culminating in one with a swimming pool. But this was not as much of a draw as it might have been. Just down the street lived Peggy Porter, one of the cutest girls in school, and because she had a pool as well, it was in much greater demand than the Bush family's.

Occasionally George W.'s grandfather, Senator Prescott S. Bush of Connecticut, would visit and cause a mild stir of interest in the neighborhood. But for the most part, the Bush family was regarded as fairly typical of the out-of-staters. . . .

Young George was not some country hick, and he also learned to fit into the world of his Connecticut grandparents. The family regularly spent part of the summer at the family retreat in Kennebunkport, Me., and in 1954 the father took George and his best friend, Randall Roden, to Washington to see the White House, the United States Capitol and a baseball game with the Washington Senators (whose later incarnation would move to Texas and become the Rangers, owned in part by George W. Bush).

They had lunch at the senator's home in Georgetown, and a thirsty Randall promptly demonstrated the distance from Midland to Georgetown by drinking from his finger bowl.

When they are tracked down, the boys and girls who once played dodgeball at Sam Houston Elementary School, while now scattered around the country, offer recollections that are very similar: Midland was an idyllic place in which to grow up, and George W. Bush was a very typical child. In contrast to other recent presidential candidates, Mr. Bush in childhood is remarkable primarily for his ordinariness. . . .

As a boy, Mr. Bush's ambition was to be another Mickey Mantle.

"All George ever wanted to be was a Major League baseball player," recalled a buddy, Terry Throckmorton. "That's all he ever talked about."

A STUDENT OF BASEBALL

No one has ever accused Mr. Bush of being an intellectual, and the indifference to books started early. Childhood friends recall Mr. Bush reading only two sets of books for pleasure—the Hardy boys and a series of mystery books about baseball. As one asks about his reading habits, there are a few snickers.

"Did we sit around in those days reading books?" asked Mr. McCleskey, smiling broadly. "No."

George and Barbara Bush led a drive to build a school library (the school did not previously have one), but books were not a major part of a boy's childhood in Midland. Erstwhile acquaintances, while deeply admiring of the Bushes' goodness and decency, have trouble recalling early signs of greatness in the son.

"Well, no, I never did think about what he might do in life," said Austine Crosby, his third-grade teacher. "He was just a good, well-rounded young man, and he did his work."

And academically? "He was O.K.," Mrs. Crosby said, a bit defensively. "He was O.K."

So was he in the top quarter of his class academically?

"Well, in the upper half, anyway."

Even if he did not distinguish himself as a student, former classmates describe him as smart and blessed with an excellent memory. He had a passion for baseball statistics, a first-rate collection of baseball cards and a reputation as such a shrewd trader that boys were careful not to agree to a trade with George Bush without thinking it over very carefully.

In the mid-1950's, George came up with a scheme that showed remarkable ingenuity and helped make his collection of baseball cards the best around. He began sending baseball cards to famous players, enclosing return postage and a cheery good-luck message, and asking the players to autograph the cards and send them back.

This way, he got autographed cards from Mickey Mantle, Willie Mays and other famous players. Some of those cards are now worth thousands of dollars.

Mr. Bush's lifelong adoration of baseball began when he and other neighborhood boys would go early to school to play ball. Mr. Bizilo, the principal, would take off his jacket, loosen his tie and hit balls for the boys to field.

George was a good ballplayer, friends say, a bit on the small side but making up for it with enthusiasm and aggressiveness. He played catcher for the Cubs, a Little League team, and made it to the town's Little League All-Star team. . . .

BECOMING A TEXAN

"There's an assurance that you have growing up in a place like Midland, a self-confidence and a real genuine interest in connecting with people," said Marge Petty, the other politician in the group (a Democratic state senator in Kansas).

In particular, it was in Midland that Mr. Bush first learned to fit in, even if his parents were Yankees and his grandfather a senator. That ability to adapt and bridge groups has never left him.

Moreover, Midland values were remarkably unshaken by the 1960's. Some Midland alumni say they let their hair grow a bit longer, but—like George W. Bush—they mostly stood with the establishment instead of rejecting it. Very few seem to have protested significantly against the Vietnam War, seriously used drugs, thought of police as "pigs," denounced their parents as oppressors or picked up a copy of [philosopher Karl Marx's] *Das Kapital.*

"It's a town of embedded values," Mr. Bush recalled, adding that it had "a heavy dose of individualism and fairly healthy disrespect for government." Asked if his own skepticism about the role for government is a product of Midland attitudes, Mr. Bush paused and finally nodded, saying: "I think there's a parallel there, I do."

Midland was steeped in optimism, and for many people growing up here in the 1950's, the moral of childhood was that the system worked, that anyone who struggled enough in that baking desert had a good chance of finding oil and striking it rich. The trajectory of the Bush family itself, from the apartment with the shared bathroom to the sprawling house and pool, underscored the point.

"The lesson lasted with George W. for years," said Bill Minutaglio, a Texan who has written a biography of Mr. Bush. "I think he truly believes that people can win the lottery if they work hard, that if they put their nose to the grindstone it'll all work out without government help or intrusion."

The antipathy for government seems a little odd, from afar, because in those days the oil business depended heavily on quirks in the tax code to encourage investments. Still, when the people of Midland sought a theater, a hospital and a new baseball diamond, they did not ask the government but raised money themselves and turned out on the week ends to do much of the work on their own.

When Mr. Bush talks about "compassionate conservatism" or "faith-based initiatives," he evokes what old classmates remember as the spirit of Midland of the 1950's. Asked if that is what he has in mind, Mr. Bush interrupts half-way through the question. "Yeah, absolutely," he said.

Those who know Midland are convinced that Mr. Bush is sincere when he preaches compassion and calls for a "responsibility era." But some also admit that it is fair to question the relevance of lessons from a town where raw capitalism made so many people rich and where community spirit wove such a strong safety net. . . .

Mr. Bush's political debut appears to have come in the seventh grade, although both he and his wife, Laura, (who was in the same seventh grade but barely knew him) say they have no recollection of it. Classmates recall that he ran for seventh-grade class president against Jack Hanks. . . .

George was elected by a narrow margin.

"I voted for George because he was cuter," recalled Peggy Porter Weiss, "and in the seventh grade that's what counted."

Tragedy Binds Mother and Son

George Lardner Jr. and Lois Romano

The death of his younger sister helped deepen a powerful link between Bush and his mother. According to his brother Marvin, Bush was intuitive and spontaneous, yet when his four-year-old sister Robin died of leukemia, it became necessary for Bush to fill life with humor. Bush made it his personal responsibility to make his mother and father smile again, using his outspokenness and wit to heal his grieving parents. In the following essay from 1999, George Lardner Jr. and Lois Romano portray Bush with his father's looks and his mother's spirit. As a mother deeply involved in her son's development, Lardner and Romano describe the powerful influence Barbara Bush had on her eldest son. Both writers are staff writers on the political team for the *Washington Post*.

On a fall day in 1953, George and Barbara Bush drove their green Oldsmobile up the gravel driveway at Sam Houston Elementary School in Midland, Texas, looking for their oldest child. George W. Bush and a friend from second grade were lugging a Victrola from their classroom to the principal's office when he spotted his parents' car. He was sure his little sister was in the back seat.

"He went running back to the teacher and said, 'I've got to go. My mother and father and Robin are here,'" Barbara Bush, the former first lady, recalled in a recent interview.

"I run over to the car," said George W., remembering the same moment, "and there's no Robin."

"That's when we told him," his mother said. "In the car."

Two days earlier, Pauline Robinson Bush—"Robin"—had died in New York of leukemia, two months shy of her fourth birthday. Her big brother had known she was sick but never dreamed she was dying. "Why didn't you tell me?" Bush repeatedly asked his parents, and for years the question would resonate in the Bush family.

INDELIBLE SCARS

At age 7, Bush found himself surrounded by bewildering grief. His parents were not even 30 years old, trying to move past a devastating loss while raising George W. and his baby brother Jeb.

The death left indelible scars on the Bushes. Barbara Bush still has trouble talking about her daughter's death. Her husband would cite the experience when he ran for president and was asked if he had ever known hardship. George W.'s eyes welled with tears when discussing his sister in an interview in May [1999].

A child's death reverberates in a family in unexpected ways. For the Bushes, among other consequences, the loss of Robin helped to establish and deepen an enduring and powerful link between Barbara Bush and her oldest son. It was during his childhood in Midland and Houston, the years he spent at home before going to boarding school at age 15, that George W. in many ways became his mother's son.

When Robin had become sick, it was Bush's father who wore his anguish openly, who had to leave the room at Memorial Sloan-Kettering cancer center each time Robin had another transfusion. And it was Barbara Bush who stayed resolutely at their daughter's side in New York, her strength belied only by her hair, which at age 28 began to turn white.

After the couple returned to Midland, Barbara plunged into despair. Her husband tried his best to cheer her up. But he was pulled away by the demands of building an oil business, working long days and traveling frequently. That left Barbara alone with her two children for long stretches. Of the two boys, only George understood what had happened.

As the gloom began to lift from the Bushes' three-bedroom frame house on West Ohio Street, it was their ebullient cutup of a son who, despite his own pain, helped drive it away—joking, playing, working hard to make his mother smile again. Time helped salve Barbara Bush's pain, but so did "Georgie."

Barbara Bush once said it didn't dawn on her what was

happening until one day when she heard her son tell a friend that he couldn't come out because he had to play with his mother, who was lonely. "I was thinking, 'Well, I'm being there for him,'" she recalled. "But the truth was he was being there for me."

Elsie Walker, a Bush cousin who lost one of her own sisters, put it this way: "You look around and see your parents suffering so deeply and try to be cheerful and funny, and you end up becoming a bit of a clown."

As part of a family famously allergic to engaging in public introspection, Bush is reluctant to talk about the forces that shaped him. He acknowledges, of course, that his sister's death was profoundly sad for him and his parents, but he also sees the sources of his personality as "more complex than one or two events." Few would argue with that assessment.

Yet some close to the Bushes do see the death of his sister as a singular event in George W.'s childhood, helping to define him and how he would deal with the world. Life would be full of humor and driven by chance. And it would be something approached with a certain fatalism. Even as an adolescent, Bush would tell his friends, "You think your life is so good and everything is perfect; then something like this happens and nothing is the same," recalls John Kidde, a high school classmate.

This attitude would ultimately liberate Bush to live his life in the present, "in chapters" as his brother Marvin would say, seizing opportunities as they came without fretting about what tomorrow might bring.

THE SPIRIT OF BARBARA BUSH

From his mother he would pick up a verve that echoes in the traits that have made Bush a more lively and comfortable politician than his father. His large-sized personality, his blunt outspokenness, his irreverence and readiness with a joke drew friends and allies to him long before he sought office, then became an important source of success once he entered politics.

From the time he was a boy, the intuitive, spontaneous son seemed very different from his guarded, dignified, over-achieving father. When members of the extended Bush family gathered in Maine in the summers of George W.'s youth, the physical resemblance they noticed was to George, but the spirit was all Bar, headstrong and quick-witted. Mother and son, as one relative put it, were "always in your face."

"I don't think George W. would ever be sassy or sarcastic with his father and if he was, it would be within the foul lines," said cousin John Ellis. "But Bar will say to George W. something like, 'Oh, don't be ridiculous,' and they're off to the races."

Nor have George W. and his mother ever gotten out of each other's faces. Even when her son was married and in his forties and on the cusp of his political career, Barbara did not hesitate to let him know what she thought.

Bush spent hours thinking and talking about running for governor of Texas in 1990, encouraged by the enthusiasm of his friends. Barbara Bush thought he should stick to running the Texas Rangers, the baseball team he had just bought with a group of other investors. "When you make a major commitment like that, I think maybe you won't be running for governor," she told a group of reporters at the White House in 1989, who lost no time relaying her remarks to her son.

As he fielded calls from the reporters, Bush tried to make light of his mother's remarks. But he was privately irked, according to a source who saw him that day. As it happened, it would be four years before he ran for governor.

A relationship of affectionate tension and banter, it has its origins in the Texas of the 1950s, when George W. was a boy coming of age and Barbara a young mother coping with the unexpected trials of early adulthood. . . .

NIGHTMARES AND TRAGEDY

It was just a few weeks after Jeb was born in February 1953 that the Bushes began to realize something was wrong with Robin. She had been strangely exhausted, telling her mother one morning she couldn't decide what to do that day—lie down and read or lie down and watch cars go by outside. Blood tests showed she had advanced leukemia—a disease that today might well be curable.

Leaving their sons with friends, the Bushes immediately took Robin to New York, where an uncle, John Walker, was a renowned surgeon and president of Memorial Sloan-Kettering cancer hospital.

The ensuing months were a blur of cross-country trips and sadness. George W.'s father flew back and forth to New York on weekends while working long hours at Zapata [Petroleum Corp.]. Barbara Bush remained in New York.

By October, Robin was dead.

Even after all these years, Barbara Bush still questions the decision not to tell her son that Robin was dying. "I don't know if that was right or wrong. I mean, I really don't, but I know he said to me several times, 'You know, why didn't you tell me?'" she said. "Well, it wouldn't have made a difference."

She and her husband feared that the young boy might inadvertently let Robin know she was gravely ill, but mostly, she said, they didn't want to burden him. "We thought he was too young to cope with it," she said.

After Robin's death, the pain that hung over the house was often unspoken, according to Randall Roden, a childhood friend of George W. Once, while Roden was spending the night, Bush had a bad dream and his mother rushed in to comfort him.

"I knew what it was about— he had nightmares for some period of time," said Roden. "It was one of the most realistic experiences I have ever had about death and I am certain it had a profound effect on him because it had a profound effect on me."

It bothered Barbara Bush that friends never mentioned Robin, no doubt because they wanted to spare her and her husband's feelings. But the silence rankled. Finally, as she tells the story, George W. helped break the ice, when one day at a football game he told his father that he wished he were Robin.

Friends who were sitting with Bush and his father froze in embarrassment, and his father asked him why he said it. "I bet she can see the game better from up there than we can here," his son replied.

BARBARA BUSH SETS THE RULES

Even as a young man, George W.'s father had an exalted place in his family. Graced with good looks, athletic ability and proper ambition, "Poppy" Bush—a nickname bestowed because his grandfather George Herbert Walker was called "Pop"—was held up as a role model. Barbara Bush treated her husband with similar deference, insulating the first man she had ever kissed from the nagging and tiresome issues that naturally consume a growing family. Two more sons were born—Neil in 1955 and Marvin in 1956—and finally, in 1959, Dorothy, filling a void left by the daughter her husband so deeply missed.

It was Barbara Bush who set the rules and became the authority figure, while her husband was held up as a much-revered statesman-like figure among the children. It was Barbara who drove the car pools, supervised the homework and piled five kids in a car with a housekeeper for the grueling cross-country trips to Kennebunkport for summer vacation.

It was a time when fathers had relatively little to do with raising their children, so George W.'s father was hardly conspicuous among the other Midland oilmen by his frequent travel and hard work. Joe O'Neill, a boyhood friend, recalls that some weekends George W.'s father, the former Yale baseball captain, would help coach the neighborhood boys, impressing them mightily by leaning forward to catch fly balls with his glove behind his back.

But, said Mike Proctor, another childhood friend, "The one who was always there was Barbara Bush.". . .

THE ENFORCER

In 1959, the Bushes finally pulled up stakes from Midland and moved to Houston. George W. had just finished the seventh grade at San Jacinto Junior High, where he played quarterback, ran for class president—and won. Bush has often invoked the school as proof of his Texas pedigree, compared to that of his father. "He went to Greenwich Country Day and I went to San Jacinto Junior High," Bush likes to say. What he doesn't say is that he spent just one year at the school—his last year in public education.

The Bushes enrolled their oldest son at the Kinkaid School, a private academy in one of the nation's wealthiest suburbs, an exclusive Houston enclave called Piney Point Village. The newly arrived eighth-grader made an easy transition. He was quickly elected a class officer and made the school football team. One classmate remembers him as a "classic good old boy type"—easygoing and swaggering, with a gift for making friends.

Even though Bush would live in Houston full time for only two years, he managed to amass a large group of friends who would carry him through holidays and summers. Sundays were the big socializing day, when the Bushes would open their home to neighborhood families for hamburgers and hot dogs and endless backyard softball games.

Barbara Bush always had a jigsaw puzzle going at the end of the living room, which she brilliantly used to rope her children—and the children of others—into conversation. "Come on down here, and help work on this," she would say to an awkward teenager who stumbled into the house.

"Before you knew it," a family friend recalled, "you were working on the puzzle, then talking about the puzzle and then telling her all your problems."

But she was also "the enforcer," as her children described it, the parent most concerned with discipline and rules. Barbara Bush never subscribed to the "wait till your father gets home" school. "I don't think that's any good," she said. "I don't think your husband comes home, exhausted from work, and you say, 'Well, go sock Marvin.'"

More often than not it was her oldest son who was the offender. "I think one of the things I'm most grateful to George for is that he certainly blazed the path for those of us who followed," said his brother Marvin.

Obnoxious behavior on Bush's part drew swift retribution, according to Douglas Hannah, an old friend. When the three of them played a round of golf one summer in high school, Barbara Bush admonished her son to stop swearing—and then banished him from the game after he ignored her warnings. Hannah and Barbara Bush played out 16 holes while Bush cooled his heels in the car.

Bush's friends recall his father being present mostly on weekends, frequently running the grill. But as his father's career became all-consuming, the oldest son—only 20 years younger than his parents—came to function as a third adult in the household, and something of a young uncle to the other children. . . .

ON THE EDGE

To his much younger brothers and sister Bush seemed his own force of nature, an exciting, unpredictable hurricane who could make any family gathering an event. "We all idolized him," said sister Doro Bush Koch. "He was always such fun and wild, you always wanted to be with him because he was always daring. . . . He was on the edge."

"We'd go out in the boat at night [in Kennebunkport] and that was always an adventure. Now, if we went out in the boat at night with Neil, you know that was fine because he's a boatsman, my brother Neil, and he knew everything about it—and still does. George, on the other hand, it was more of a kind of a wild risky thing because we're not sure that he, you know, could manage the boat as well."

As the handsome son of a rising business and civic figure in Houston, George W. was always on the list for holiday balls and the social rituals of what was essentially a traditional southern town. But those who remember him from his early teen years recall a young man devoid of polish and pretense, spurning "snobs," sneering at anything that resembled ostentation.

"It was almost a reverse snobbery," recalled Lacey Neuhaus Dorn, Bush's neighbor in the early '60s. "He just hated the glitz. . . . If someone had a fancy car, he'd make a comment that it was too fancy for his blood."

But as George Herbert Walker Bush's first-born, there were some privileges that he could not turn down. Ninth grade would be his last year at Kinkaid. His parents decided that in the fall of 1961 he should continue his education at Phillips Academy in Andover, Mass., one of the nation's most exclusive and rigorous prep schools and his father's alma mater.

For the first time, Bush would feel the full weight of his father's illustrious past.

Failures in the Oil Business

Joe Conason

Growing up close to money and political power, George W. Bush used both to start his own oil-drilling venture only three years after receiving his Harvard MBA. In the 1980s, oil prices were down and interest rates were skyrocketing. Bush needed one financial savior after another to rescue him from a multitude of business failures until 1988, when he organized a partnership to purchase the Texas Rangers baseball team. In this February 2000 article, Joe Conason details Bush's difficult history in the oil business, outlining the successes and failures that haunt Bush's past. Conason writes for *Harper's Magazine.*

From the outset of his career, George W. Bush exhibited an impatience that would have embarrassed his father, who underwent a long apprenticeship in the oil business. In 1978, only three years after graduating from Harvard Business School and returning home to Midland, Texas, he incorporated his own oil-drilling venture.

Almost simultaneously, he made an even more startling announcement. Again unlike his father and grandfather, who established their fortunes and reputations before running for public office, George W. declared his candidacy for Congress in 1978 from the district that included Midland. His name was his only political credential, aside from a year as president of the Delta Kappa Epsilon fraternity at Yale.

His candidacy seemed almost plausible, however, when he defeated a far more seasoned opponent in the Republican primary. He went on to lose badly in the general election to a Democrat who had mocked Bush's pretentious description of himself as an independent oilman. Actually, Bush didn't commence any operations of his oil firm, Arbusto Energy, until early in 1979.

SAVED BY INVESTORS

With assistance from his uncle Jonathan Bush, a personable Wall Street financier, George W. assembled a limited partnership of two dozen investors. The Arbusto partners included George W.'s grandmother Dorothy Bush; Rite Aid drugstores chairman Lewis Lehrman, then a rising force in New York Republican politics; William Draper III, a corporate executive and family friend who was later appointed to head the Export-Import Bank; and James Bath, a mysterious Houston aircraft broker who appears to have been fronting for several Saudi Arabian sheiks.

About $3 million poured into Arbusto, producing little oil and no profits but expansive tax shelters. In 1982, George W. changed his company's infelicitous name to Bush Exploration Oil Co. His father by this time was vice president of the United States, but the new company name didn't improve the son's luck or alter the fact that petroleum prices were sinking while interest rates were rising. More than once, Bush's venture was near ruin when wealthy benefactors suddenly appeared with fresh cash. The most generous was Philip Uzielli, an old Princeton buddy of James Baker III, the family friend then serving as chief of staff in the Reagan White House. For the sum of $1 million, Uzielli bought 10 percent of the company at a time in 1982 when the entire enterprise was valued at less than $400,000.

Soon Uzielli's million was gone, too. But just as his company was heading toward failure, George W. met William DeWitt and Mercer Reynolds, a pair of Ohio investors with their own small oil firm, called Spectrum 7. DeWitt, who had graduated from Yale a few years earlier than Bush, happened to be the son of the former owner of the Cincinnati Reds, and he shared Bush's passion for baseball. After a quick courtship the Spectrum 7 partners agreed to merge with Bush Exploration, naming George W. as chairman and CEO and awarding him a substantial share of stock. Although the vice president's son helped Spectrum 7 to raise additional money, catastrophic losses continued. During a six-month period in 1986, Spectrum 7 lost $400,000, and the partners feared creditors would foreclose their remaining assets.

Once more George W. attracted a financial savior. That September, Spectrum 7 was acquired by Harken Energy Corporation, a medium-sized, diversified company. After Bush joined Harken, the largest stock position and a seat on its board were acquired by Harvard Management Company, the private firm that invests the university's endowment. The Harken board gave Bush $600,000 worth of the company's publicly traded stock, plus a seat on its board of directors and a consultancy that paid him up to $120,000 a year. His partners understood perfectly what had happened. As Spectrum 7's former president, Paul Rea, recalled later, the Harken directors "believed having George's name there would be a big help to them."

Thus ending his years as an oilman with a substantial income and minimal corporate duties, George W. in the spring of 1987 moved his family from Texas to Washington, where he served as "senior adviser" in his father's presidential campaign. Intense and sometimes volatile, he made appearances at fund-raisers and rallies, acted as an emissary to major campaign donors and leaders of the religious right, and occasionally bullied reporters whose publications he disliked. Those confrontations injured his own reputation, but his father rolled to victory over Democrat Michael Dukakis in one of the nastiest elections in decades.

TEXAS RANGERS

Toward the end of the 1988 campaign, George W. heard from his former Spectrum 7 partner Bill DeWitt that the Texas Rangers were on the market. To make a successful bid, DeWitt would need Texas backers, and the son of the incoming president was perfectly situated to find them. George W. also had a powerful advantage in dealing with the team's owner, an aging Midland oil millionaire named Eddie Chiles, who had been a Bush friend since the 1950s.

For George W., an ardent lifelong fan with no real job, DeWitt's proposal was a providential opportunity. His duties as a director of Harken Energy, though undemanding, offered little chance to improve his resume. His hopes of running for governor in 1990 had been squelched by incredulous party insiders, who complained that he had never "done anything." To acquire the Rangers and thus keep the franchise in Texas would be to do something of profound significance to Texans.

Baseball commissioner Peter Ueberroth was eager to help the son of the new president, but he was not so eager when George W. said the biggest investors in the proposed Rangers syndicate were his old Yale frat brother Roland Betts and

Tom Bernstein, Betts's partner in a film-investment concern. Betts and Bernstein were from New York, not Texas.

The indispensable local money came from Richard Rainwater, formerly the chief financial adviser to the Bass brothers of Fort Worth. Little known to the general public, Rainwater was famous on Wall Street for growing the Bass inheritance from around $50 million in 1970 to more than $4 billion by the time he left in 1986 to manage his own investments.

Both Bush and Ueberroth met with Rainwater in early 1989 to persuade him to join the Rangers syndicate. Rainwater then took effective control of the deal, bringing along Edward "Rusty" Rose, a well-known Dallas investor, to oversee the franchise. Under an agreement worked out by Betts and Rainwater, the title of "managing partner" would be shared between Rusty Rose and George W.—but the president's son would operate under a tight rein. He would function as the new ownership's friendly public face while Rose ran the business.

Bush's stake in the team, just under 2 percent, was among the smallest. He purchased his shares with a $500,000 loan from a Midland bank of which he had been a director and eventually scraped together another $106,000 to buy out two other limited partners. Rainwater, Rose, and their associates put up $14.2 million, while Betts and Bernstein invested about $6 million; the balance came from smaller investors, loans, and the equity of minority partners in the old Chiles partnership.

Two months after his father's inauguration, George W. Bush called a press conference in Arlington to announce that the Rangers sale had been successfully completed for a price that was later reported to be $86 million. Proclaiming that the new owners would share a "civic dividend" with Texas, he began to promote himself along with the team. While Rainwater, Rose, and all the other partners remained in the background, George W. behaved as if he were "the owner" of the Rangers. He attended every home game and even printed "baseball cards" bearing his own picture to hand out from his box.

Meanwhile, George W. maintained a financial interest in Harken Energy. He had been granted enough additional stock options, at a generous discount, to increase his holdings by more than half. By 1989, however, those shares were falling in value. A series of questionable decisions by chairman Alan Quasha had jeopardized the company's future, and its losses reached $40 million in 1990. Even the company's CEO admitted that its financial statements were "a mess."

BAHRAIN

Once more, however, the Bush name seems to have provided sudden deliverance—this time in the form of a contract with the emirate of Bahrain. Until 1989 the Bahraini oil minister had been negotiating an agreement for offshore drilling with Amoco, a huge energy conglomerate with decades of worldwide experience. Those talks were abruptly broken off, supposably because the Bahrainis had decided that a smaller firm would give their project more attention. The Bahraini officials were put in touch with Harken through a former Mobil Oil executive named Michael Ameen. At the same time, Ameen also happened to be working as a consultant to the U.S. State Department, which had assigned him to brief Charles Hostler, the newly confirmed American ambassador to Bahrain (a San Diego real estate investor who had given $100,000 to the Republican Party for the 1988 election).

These several events culminated in a January 1990 announcement that astonished oil-industry analysts: the government of Bahrain had awarded exclusive offshore drilling rights to Harken. "It was a surprise," one top analyst told *Time* magazine with dry understatement. Quite apart from Harken's shaky financial condition, the company had never drilled a well anywhere but Texas, Louisiana, and Oklahoma, and had never drilled undersea at all. So depleted of cash and so deeply in debt was Harken that the company was forced to bring in the more experienced and solvent Bass brothers as equity partners, so that construction on the $25 million project could begin.

Only the presence of President Bush's oldest son could explain Bahrain's extraordinary decision. There was no question that the rulers of Bahrain were aware of his role. In addition to his Harken directorship, George W. sat on the company's "exploration advisory board," which meant that his name had been mentioned at least twice during initial discussions with Bahraini officials. "They were clearly aware he was the president's son," said Monte Swetnam, a former Harken executive who conducted the talks with the emirate's oil ministry.

George W. flatly denied any part in Harken's bid. "Ask the Bahrainis," he replied flippantly when journalists asked whether they had been enticed by his name. Harken has said that Bush was not involved in the Bahrain deal. Later, Bush claimed he had opposed the project because Harken was not "prepared."

However it was procured, the Bahrain contract pushed up the price of Harken stock from $4.50 to $5.50 in a matter of weeks. And on June 22, 1990, six months after the contract was announced, George W. quietly sold off 212,140 shares, or two thirds of his interest, which grossed him $848,560. He used most of the proceeds to pay off the bank loan he had taken a year earlier to finance his portion of the Texas Rangers deal. A few weeks later, in early August, Iraqi dictator Saddam Hussein invaded Kuwait. Saddam's aggression drove down the share prices of every oil company doing business in the Gulf, including Harken, whose shares fell to $3.12.

SELLING HARKEN STOCK

By the time George W. unloaded his Harken stock in late June, diplomatic alarms had been sounding in the Bush White House about Saddam's aggressive intentions. Although there is no evidence that the president's son was tipped off about the impending Gulf crisis, he certainly had reason to know that Harken was still in trouble. He served on the company's three-member audit committee and also on a special "fairness committee" appointed that spring to consider how a corporate restructuring would affect the value of the company's outstanding shares. Two months after Bush sold the bulk of his Harken holdings, the company posted losses for the second quarter of well over $20 million and its shares fell another 24 percent; by year-end Harken was trading at $1.25.

When Bush's stock dumping was first reported by the *Houston Post* in October 1990, there were no accusations of insider trading. Then in April 1991 the *Wall Street Journal* revealed that the Securities and Exchange Commission had not been notified of his timely trade until eight months after the legal deadline. The regulatory agency commenced an investigation that concluded in 1991 with no action against George W. It was hardly a surprise. The SEC chairman at the time, Richard Breeden, was an especially ardent Bush loyalist, and the agency's general counsel was the same Texas attorney who had handled the sale of the Rangers baseball team for George W. and his partners in 1989. Bush has insisted that he didn't know about the firm's mounting losses and that his stock sell-off had been approved by Harken's general counsel.

Although no wrongdoing was proved, the suspicions surrounding Harken Energy and other dubious enterprises associated with the president's sons—particularly Neil Bush's directorship of a crooked Colorado savings-and-loan—caused the family severe embarrassment during the 1992 election. George W. described the twelve months he spent on the futile Bush-Quayle reelection effort as "the most miserable year of my life."

BUILDING A BALLPARK

But that unhappy interlude scarcely stalled his own quest for success. Soon after buying the Rangers, he and his partners realized that the franchise would never make money unless they replaced the team's old ballpark, badly outmoded in an era of luxury skyboxes. With the backing of billionaire Rainwater they could have built a new stadium themselves, of course, but that would have violated an important tenet of major league economics. The construction costs of new sporting facilities are provided by taxpayers, not club owners. But because few municipalities accept such fiscal burdens without coercion, Rangers management began to hint unsubtly that unless the city government of Arlington provided land and financing on favorable terms, they would have to move the team to nearby Dallas or Fort Worth.

Major league baseball's negotiating advantage almost invariably leads to "public-private" deals, in which public funds subsidize private profit with the justification that the presence of the team will stimulate wider economic activity. Even by those standards, however, the capitulation of Arlington mayor Richard Greene was uniquely abject. In October 1990, Mayor Greene signed a contract that guaranteed $135 million toward the stadium's estimated price of $190 million. The Rangers put up no cash but financed their share through a ticket surcharge. From the team's operating revenues, the city would earn a maximum of $5 million annually in rent, no matter how much the Rangers reaped from ticket sales and television (a sum that rose to $100 million a year). The most remarkable provision, however, permitted the franchise to buy the stadium after the accumulated rental payments reached a mere $60 million. The property acquired so cheaply by the Rangers included not just a fancy new stadium with a seating capacity of 49,000 but an additional 270 acres of suddenly valuable land.

This scheme predictably generated local opposition to "corporate welfare." But together with Mayor Greene, George W. convinced an overwhelming majority of Arlington voters to approve a sales-tax hike that would back the stadium bonds in January 1991. The referendum must have left an impression on Governor Ann Richards, who quickly signed legislation creating the Arlington Sports Facilities Development Authority—with power to issue bonds and exercise eminent domain over any obstinate landowners.

Never before had a municipal authority in Texas been given license to seize the property of a private citizen for the benefit of other private citizens. That is exactly what happened to a recalcitrant Arlington family that refused to sell a 13-acre parcel near the stadium site for half its appraised value. Their land was condemned and handed over to the Rangers. The ensuing lawsuit revealed that well before any of the enabling legislation had passed, the Rangers management had planned to wield condemnation as a weapon to drive down the price, and an outraged jury awarded more than $4 million to the Arlington family whose land had been expropriated.

Long before that verdict came down, however, the shiny new structure George W. had christened The Ballpark in Arlington was finished. It may have been no accident that the arena's outer walls were clad in reddish brick and pink granite that subtly echoed the appearance of the beautiful old state capitol in Austin. On November 8, 1993, with the stadium being readied to open the following spring, Bush announced that he would be running for governor. He didn't blush when he proclaimed that his campaign theme would demand self-reliance and personal responsibility rather than dependence on government.

CHAPTER 2

THE MAKING OF A PRESIDENT

PEOPLE WHO MADE HISTORY

GEORGE W. BUSH

Team Player

Joe Nick Patoski

George W. Bush was managing general partner of
the Texas Rangers baseball team for five years. It
was during this time that Bush managed to build a
reputation. The management skills he exhibited and
fine-tuned with the Rangers enabled Bush to become
a successful businessman. While in the public eye,
he used creative financing, exceptional negotiating
skills, and political finesse to make the Rangers one
of the most successful clubs in the league. Besides
winning him friends and supporters, his success also
guaranteed him and his partners a positive return on
their investment.

In the following 1999 article, Joe Nick Patoski reviews Bush's career with the Rangers and the successes that eventually enabled him to secure the job
of governor of Texas. Patoski is a senior editor for
Texas Monthly magazine.

The Ballpark is the legacy of Bush's five-year stint as managing general partner of the Rangers, a time in which he
built up both the franchise's bottom line and his own, along
the way honing many of the skills he draws upon in politics.
Fundraiser Bush shook out $46 million from various in-
vestors during the depths of Texas' last economic bust in the
run-up to buying the team. Consensus-builder Bush got the
Ballpark referendum passed in Arlington when similar
measures were being nixed by voters elsewhere. Manager
Bush ran a business efficiently in the glare of the public eye.
People-person Bush nourished the egos of the famous and
the anonymous, from Juan Gonzalez to the groundskeepers,
always addressing them by name. After all that, running the
free world might seem like T-ball.

Privilege, pedigree, and personal relationships were the
reasons Bush hooked up with the Rangers in the first place.

Joe Nick Patoski, "Team Player: George Bush's Career Running the Texas Rangers,"
Texas Monthly, vol. 27, June 1999, p. 113. Copyright © 1999 by *Texas Monthly*. Reproduced by permission.

His name surfaced as a possible major league owner in the weeks after his father was elected president. "George had spent most of 1988 campaigning and then on the transition team, but he decided he didn't want to be in Washington— he wanted to go back to Texas," says one of his fraternity brothers, Roland W. Betts, a movie financier who'd been looking for a pro sports team to buy. "In December he called me and said the Rangers were in play. The Macks [a venerable baseball family] wanted to buy the team from Eddie Chiles, but there was growing concern that they wanted to move the team to Florida."

FINDING INVESTORS

Chiles, the Fort Worth oilman who achieved notoriety with his "I'm Mad" radio spots, had known George W. as a kid. A friend of the Bush family, he flew George's sister Robin to hospitals in his private plane when she was diagnosed with leukemia. He'd bought the Rangers in 1980, but at age 78 he was ready to call it quits—a fact Bush was made aware of by William De-Witt, Jr., his oil-business partner in Midland in the eighties. DeWitt, whose father had owned the St. Louis Browns and the Cincinnati Reds, wanted a piece of a team himself.

Bush got cash commitments from several sources. Betts signed on, but only after receiving assurances that his friend wasn't going to run for office anytime soon. Also ponying up were Connecticut real estate whiz Craig Stapleton, Bush cousin through marriage; former Marriott Corporation executive Fred Malek, who had been a member of Richard Nixon's inner circle; and three Cincinnati investors: produce wholesaler Bob Castellini, oilman Mercer Reynolds, and broadcasting executive Dudley Taft. Chiles was so impressed that he signed a letter of agreement with the Bush group.

But baseball commissioner Peter Ueberroth wasn't satisfied. Although he wanted Chiles to find a buyer who would keep the Rangers in Texas, a top ten media market, he thought Bush's investors didn't have enough local ties. At Ueberroth's urging, Bush went to see Fort Worth financier Richard Rainwater, the money man behind the Bass family. Subsequently, Rainwater met with Bush, Betts, and Stapleton at the Highland Park home of Edward "Rusty" Rose, a financier known as the Mortician for his ability to squeeze profits from falling companies acquired through leveraged buyouts. "We talked about the possibility of owning the team together," Betts recalls. "At the end of the day Rainwater said if he was going to do it, he wanted Rose as general partner because he liked and trusted him. I said the same thing about George. Rose and George met, and after a few lunches they agreed to run the team together." The publicity-shy Rose made one stipulation: Bush would be the managing general partner, meaning he'd deal with the media and the public, while Rose would serve as chairman of the board.

Rose threw in $3.2 million and raised another $9 million from other investors, including Rainwater and cable television mogul Jeff Marcus. Bush rounded up $14 million, contributing $606,000 of his own—the smallest amount of any major investor. All told, seventy investors representing 39 limited partnerships bought a piece of the team. Betts and fellow film financier Tom Bernstein paid the most money ($7 million) and received the largest share (18 percent).

Once those initial arrangements were hammered out, Bush approached several other investors. Among them were Schieffer, a former state representative from Fort Worth, and Comer Cottrell, the CEO of a Dallas hair products firm. Edward Gaylord, the Oklahoma City media magnate, reduced the one-third piece of the team he'd bought from Chiles in 1986 to 10 percent. Other small shareholders from the Chiles era, including Arlington realtor Mike Reilly, held on to a total of 4 percent.

The Bush-Rose group was formally incorporated as BR Rangers. No decision would be made without the approval of the two general partners. "Neither of us has the responsibility to make any decision without consulting with the other," Bush would later explain. "On a certain task, he may lead on it or I may take the lead. The buck stops on our desks." For his efforts, Bush was paid an annual salary of $200,000; Rose's company would reportedly receive a retainer of $120,000. In addition, once all the investors were repaid with accrued interest, both Bush and Rose were to be compensated for putting the deal together with a bonus, or promote fee, of 10 percent and 5 percent, respectively. The $86 million deal was officially approved by baseball's executive committee in April 1989. But the real work had only just begun.

LEARNING THE BUSINESS

To put it kindly, the Rangers were a beaten-down franchise. Since relocating to the Dallas–Fort Worth area from Washington, D.C., in 1972, they had consistently performed poorly on the field and at the ticket office. They were finally drawing fans (they passed the 1.5 million mark in attendance in 1986, 1987, and 1988) and cultivating talent (pitcher Nolan Ryan, a bona fide star; Ruben Sierra, an outfielder with Hall of Fame potential) but they were playing in a jerry-built stadium that was originally intended for minor league competition. "The first time I went down there, I was just shocked," says Betts, and he wasn't alone in his assessment. "At our first meeting, that was the mantra: To turn this thing around and add value to our investment, we were going to build a new stadium."

Most of the 1989 season was devoted to learning the business of baseball. Quickly adapting to his role as the public face of the owners' consortium, Bush was as much of a fixture at the old Arlington Stadium as John "Zonk" Lanzillo, Jr., the drum-beating superfan. He was always in his seat next to the dugout, boots up on the railing, munching peanuts, watching the game, signing more autographs than most of the players. His parents got involved too. In 1989 their springer spaniel Millie gave birth to Spot Fletcher, who was named in honor of Rangers shortstop Scott Fletcher. Two years later the president broke tradition and threw out the first pitch of the season in Arlington instead of Baltimore, the closest city to Washington with a major league club.

Behind the scenes, George W. set to mending fences, improving the team's image, and winning over critics like Jim Reeves of the *Fort Worth Star-Telegram*, who covered the sale of the Rangers and had few kind words for the Bush group. "I had an early built-in grudge against George in particular," says Reeves. "I thought he was a failed politician and obviously a guy who was playing off his dad's name because he wasn't putting much money in." Bush went out of his way to win over Reeves, even inviting him to play a round of golf, and the reporter gradually came around. "I found him to be a very personable, direct, very informed general partner. The more we were around him, the better the team's relationship with the press would be. You could believe what he told you."

He was good at other things as well: He was instrumental in neutralizing the agendas of various personnel, marketing Ryan aggressively, and broadening the team's appeal by instituting Spanish-language broadcasts. Baseball details, however, were left to the baseball people. "They went out of their way to let us know they weren't going to be hands-on owners," said Tom Grieve, then the Rangers' general manager. "They made it clear from the start they did not buy the team because they wanted to brag to their friends that they owned a baseball team. They told me, 'We're business people and expect to be profitable, and we expect our baseball people to be accountable.' But never did they come in and say, 'When are you gonna get rid of this guy?'"

By the end of the first year the initial plan that had been in the back of everyone's mind was formalized. If the Rangers were going to make the transition from a have-not franchise to one of the haves and maximize their value, they would have to play in a new stadium—ideally, a state-of-the-art facility that looked old and traditional but had all the requisite sky boxes and other modern bells and whistles. The partners looked around for someone who could manage a large public project, considering both Tom Luce and Bush himself at one point before designating Schieffer the stadium czar in July 1990. He was charged with selecting a site, developing a strategy, and getting the project under way despite a seemingly impossible obstacle: The partners didn't want to have to pay for the new park themselves.

BUILDING THE BALLPARK

Schieffer looked around the Metroplex for a few months before concluding that Arlington was the best site and that a halfcent local sales tax was the best way to pay for it. He then got busy winning over voters to raise the $135 million in bonds it would take to build a new home for the home team. Tarrant County judge Tom Vandergriff, who was instrumental in luring the Rangers from Washington, and Arlington mayor Richard Greene were enlisted to spearhead the three-month effort. Both Schieffer and Bush were actively involved. At one point both men spoke from the pulpit of the Mount Olive Baptist Church in Arlington, with Bush declaring, "A vote for the tax would be a vote for contracts for African American businesses."

With minimal opposition—Arlington's economy is based on tourism and entertainment, and a large percentage of its sales taxes are paid by out-of-towners—the bond issue passed in January 1991 by a two-to-one margin. Nearly 34,000 voters went to the ballot box—more than in any election in Arlington's history. Under their agreement with the city, the Rangers would chip in $30 million from revenues of ticket sales, surcharges, and luxury-box leases, and pay for any additional costs, which added up to another $26 million. The team would assume full ownership of the stadium when the bonds were paid off. "This eventually will give us the ability to compete on a payroll level that will put us with a whole new echelon of ballclubs," Bush said after the referendum passed. "We'll be able to pay the market price to keep our talent and, at the same time, keep ticket prices down." Following the vote, Schieffer shifted his focus to the Texas Legislature, which passed a bill that would ratify the arrangement, then he took the lead in getting the park built, soliciting designs from architects—nineteen submitted bids—before hiring David Schwartz of Washington, D.C., a Bass family favorite.

Back home, two flaps surfaced around the construction of the stadium. The first involved the condemnation of thirteen acres of land owned by the Curtis Mathes family, for which the city offered $1.375 million and the Matheses wanted $2.1 million. A state district court eventually declared the condemnation illegal and ordered that the Mathes group be paid the full amount they asked for, plus damages, which ultimately came to more than $11 a square foot, far higher than the $2.67 per square foot maximum that the city paid for any other single parcel during the land acquisition. The Rangers eventually worked out a payment plan to pay off the difference. The second snag was the awarding of minority contracts. The Rangers were criticized by the Arlington chapters of the NAACP and LULAC, the Arlington Hispanic Advisory Council, and even one of their own partners, Comer Cotrell, for not throwing enough business to black and Hispanic firms.

In the end, of course, the problems got resolved and the Ballpark got built. Much of the credit went—correctly—to Schieffer, who demonstrated he could orchestrate and delegate and was rewarded by being named the team's president. But Bush's behind-the-scenes involvement—in managing Schieffer, troubleshooting, and going public when necessary—was crucial, people familiar with the situation say. "The bond election, the ballpark, the financing technique, that was all George's deal," says Mike Reilly. "He quarterbacked the whole thing, but he never took the credit."

LEAVING THE TEAM

Bush took a leave of absence from the team before the 1994 season to run for governor, missing much of the Ballpark's inaugural season. The venue's classic lines and distinctively Texan look—from the native granite and red brick to the Longhorns in the facade—were an instant hit, drawing almost 3 million fans. A museum, sports bar and restaurant, luxury boxes, and a four-story office building outside the outfield fence bumped up the final cost to $191 million, but those additional revenue streams led *Financial World* magazine to rate it as the most profitable facility in baseball.

During the election, [governor of Texas] Ann Richards tried to make the public-private arrangement for financing the stadium an issue in the governor's race, a means of showing Bush as a beneficiary of corporate welfare, but it didn't take. After he won, Bush put his assets—including his share of the Rangers—in a blind trust and resigned as managing general partner. (His timing couldn't have been better: A players' strike cut short the 1994 season, caused the World Series to be canceled, and alienated many fans.)

Bush's official parting with the team came four years later, in June 1998, when buyout king Tom Hicks snapped it up for $250 million. By the time of sale, Bush's 1.8 percent share of the ownership had ballooned to 11.3 percent, and he pocketed almost $15 million: $2.7 million as a return on his investment and a $12.2 million "general partner interest"—his 10 percent "promote fee" for putting the ownership group together back in 1989. Not surprisingly, he was widely criticized by the usual suspects—the *Texas Observer* among them—for earning so much while seemingly doing so little, but his fellow owners sprang to his defense. "To me and to everyone in the partnership," Schieffer says, "it was not unusual to get a percentage on the back end like that for putting the deal together."

In any case, what Bush really got out of the deal was something more important than money: After years as Junior, he finally became his own man. "Before the Rangers, I told him he needed to do something to step out of his father's shadow," says Roland Butts. "Baseball was it. He became our local celebrity. He knew every usher. He signed autographs. He talked to fans. His presence meant everything. His eyes were on politics the whole time, but even when he was speaking at Republican functions, he was always talking about the Rangers."

Running for Governor

Skip Hollandsworth

Bush's success in running the Texas Rangers ball-club helped boost him into the governor's mansion. Bush's big struggle during the gubernatorial campaign was how voters perceived him. Separating himself from his family history and focusing on his own achievements was a constant battle. Bush ran on the platform that he had the guts to shake things up and make changes for the good of Texas. Sincere in his concerns about the deteriorating state of education and the widespread fear of crime in the state, Bush ran an issues oriented, energetic campaign to put him into the governor's seat. In this May 1994 article, Skip Hollandsworth, executive editor for *Texas Monthly* magazine, captures Bush the campaigner and reviews his successful unseating of a popular incumbent. Hollandsworth is the winner of the 1998 Texas Institute of Letters O'Henry Award for Journalism and the 1990 Charles E. Green Journalism Award.

Bush is keenly aware that a lot of people, even those who swear allegiance to him, don't know a thing about him as a politician except that he is the former president's boy. George the Younger, he's called. The First Son. The Shrub. Regardless of how much George W. Bush wants to talk about issues, the decisive factors in many voters' minds are likely to be how they perceive him to be like his father and how they perceive him to be different—whether they believe he has his father's strengths or his weaknesses.

[Incumbent Texas governor] Ann Richards' most piercing attack against Bush is that he has done nothing to prove himself as a leader. Yes, he ran an oil company and then helped put together the group of investors that bought the Texas Rangers baseball team, of which he is the managing

Skip Hollandsworth, "Born to Run: What's in a Name? How About the Republican Nomination for Governor," *Texas Monthly*, vol. 22, May 1994, p. 112. Copyright © 1994 by *Texas Monthly*. Reproduced by permission.

general partner. But until his gubernatorial announcement, he had only taken a cursory interest in politics: an impulsive 1978 run for Congress and work in his father's presidential campaigns. Bush's critics claim he is little more than an untested candidate who hides his ignorance of government behind a wall of self-confidence—and behind his last name. "If his name was George Smith," snorts a Richards aide, "no one would take him seriously."

CAMPAIGNING FOR GOVERNOR

Bush's friends and supporters, however, portray him as an articulate, quick-witted leader, a far better debater than his father, and surprisingly, a savvier politician. Nor is he timid about matching his personality against that of the legendary wisecracking Richards. "Don't underestimate this guy," says Fred McClure, a former senior legislative aide to President Bush in Washington and now a Dallas financier and neighbor of the younger Bush. "He's no doubt the biggest political animal in the family—and clearly more competitive than his father."

Demonstrating that he has indeed learned from the mistakes of his father, Bush is trying to paint Richards exactly as Bill Clinton painted the elder Bush during the 1992 presidential campaign: as a likable but ineffectual incumbent, a defender of the status quo. Bush has already positioned himself as the candidate of change in this campaign. He has introduced proposals to overhaul the state's public education, welfare, and juvenile justice programs. He uses phrases— "the landscape for change," "a startling new vision"—that surpass normal Republican lingo. "Believe me," says Bush, "I'm not afraid to shake things up. Otherwise, we're stuck with more of the same problems no one has ever had the guts to fix."

In his office, Bush sighs again. He knows he is embarking on a grueling personal journey to step out of the shadow of his beloved old man. "All that I ask," he says, giving me another glare, "is that for once you guys stop seeing me as the son of George Bush. This campaign is about me, no one else."

"If the election was held on Southwest Airlines," Bush tells me, "I'd win in a heartbeat." We are on a morning flight from Dallas to Midland for a campaign appearance, and he has already signed half a dozen autographs on cocktail napkins for other passengers. On a Southwest flight a few days earlier, sixteen people sitting in the eight rows behind him handed him a sheet of paper that they had signed, promising to vote for him. Before boarding a flight on another day, he ran into Roger Staubach, a former Dallas Cowboys quarterback and avid Republican who is rumored to be a future political candidate himself. . . .

Like his father, Bush gets an adrenaline rush when he's out campaigning, shaking hands with strangers, saying "Nice-ta-mee-cha," and cheerfully telling them, if they are unsure of how to reply, that they should come out to watch the Rangers play in their new stadium. He also has his father's gift for remembering names. Often he travels with only one young aide, Israel Hernandez, who gives him a schedule of the day's events and hands him breath mints—about a dozen a day. "Hand me a mint there, Israel," Bush says when he shows up at a campaign stop, then he's out of the car with jackrabbit speed, jaw-boning with everybody. There is no one whispering into his ear the names of his bigger supporters. Bush knows them.

Casual Style

Unlike his father—who startled voters with his inane asides . . . —George W. has the ability to win over strangers. On the Midland flight, he sees a boy wearing a Rangers hat and says, tongue in cheek, "Listen, kid, work hard at baseball and you too can get a $45 million contract like Juan Gonzalez." Pause. "But if you can't hit the curve, please try to make a nice income when you grow up so you can buy lots of Rangers tickets." The passengers chortle and hand him more napkins to sign.

While the elder Bush has always been known as an unfailingly polite man, George W. takes pride in his own irreverence. He loves to needle his friends. He can cuss like a sailor. And he tells stories with great good humor, even the embarrassing ones about himself. If his dad, as the *Washington Post* once wrote, really is a slight bore, like "every woman's first husband," then George W. is the wild boyfriend every woman dated in her youth. His closest pals, who all say he can act brash and cocky, have nicknamed him the Bombastic Bushkin. . . .

Bush does have a casual style that's rarely seen in his patrician parents. When he strides into his office in Dallas, he throws his inexpensive Haggar sport jacket on the floor—he has no coatrack—and eats from a bag of popcorn as he answers phone calls and shouts at his secretary through the always open door. His office is decorated like a dorm room. Baseball gloves and baseball bats and replicas of Bowie knives are scattered about. A Texas flag lies on top of a counter, half buried under some books. A personalized Texas license plate—reading BUSH—is on another table. The Baseball Encyclopedia is near his chair. . . .

Something Bush has inherited from his father is a kind of manic energy. He ran a marathon in Houston after the 1992 presidential race (finishing in a respectable 3 hours and 44 minutes). He prefers to spend his lunch hour running and sometimes lifting weights at Dallas' tony Cooper Aerobics Center. At the end of the day, in his comfortable one-story North Dallas home, Bush sits at his desk in an office just to the right of the front door, simultaneously talking on the phone, flipping through television channels with his remote control, and helping his daughters, who attend Hockaday, the most exclusive private girls' school in Dallas, with their homework. Sometimes he leaps up and heads out to the front yard with his springer spaniel, Spot (a daughter of the former first dog, Millie), and throws a tennis ball for her to chase. . . .

Laura initially felt reluctant about Bush's entering the governor's race. "She wanted to be sure I was running for all the right reasons," Bush tells me, "and that I wasn't running because I felt I had something to prove." It is a striking admission, for it suggests that even those closest to Bush have wondered about his need to become governor. Ambition, of course, is a tricky matter: All politicians are motivated to run for office through some mixture of private needs and public desires. But because Bush is the son of a famous man, and especially because he is trying to prove he can succeed at his father's profession, his drive to become governor is perhaps a little more perplexing. Is this campaign his grand attempt to win his father's approval? Is George W., the loyal son, running out of spite against Ann Richards, who has never hesitated to take potshots at the Bush family, as in her famous 1988 Democratic Convention speech, when she said that the elder Bush was born with a silver foot in his mouth? Or is it because he has a plan, as he says in every campaign speech he gives, to turn Texas into "a beacon state, a place where other people say, That's what I want my state to be"?

Bush makes a point to tell me, over and over, that he has

never had long-range political ambitions. "I've never been a long-term planner about anything," he says. "I have lived my life with more of a short-term focus—on the theory that other interesting things would come up for me to do." If there is a theme that runs through Bush's adult life, it's that of a man who quickly, sometimes impulsively, seizes the opportunities that are put before him. He admits he never considered becoming an oilman until the day he stopped in Midland for a brief visit in 1975 and decided to stay there. He says he never planned to buy a major league baseball team until a friend gave him a tip in late 1988 that the Rangers were for sale. And he swears he didn't make up his mind to run for governor until June 1993, "when everything began to feel right and when everything that Ann Richards was doing, or not doing, began to feel so wrong."

SINCERE CONCERNS

All of his friends say in interviews that Bush is sincere in his concerns about the deteriorating state of education and the widespread fear of crime in Texas. But, they add, to understand the candidacy of Bush, it is important to understand what it means to be a Bush in Texas, a member of Texas' most famous political family. Congenial and closeknit, the Bushes are far from a tortured clan like the Kennedys, with their scandals and their obsessive drive toward power. The Bushes obviously feel imbued, however, with an invincible sense of self-confidence, a kind of family faith, a conviction that they are the right people to lead. . . .

George W. Bush has often joked that the key difference between him and his father is that "my dad went to Greenwich Country Day School in Connecticut and I went to San Jacinto Junior High in Midland." The elder Bush was raised in a home with three maids and a chauffeur. He went to tea dances. At home, he had to wear a coat and tie to the dinner table. George W. grew up in a nice but unpretentious neighborhood with a bunch of brash, rough-and-tumble oilmen's sons—and he fit right in. Early photographs of George W. show a boy with a rakish gleam in his eye, an amused look on his face—"A wonderful, incorrigible child," says Barbara, "who spent many afternoons sitting in his room, waiting for his father to come home to speak to him about his latest transgression."

Perhaps because the elder Bush felt it so difficult to shake loose from the influence of his own stern father, U.S. senator Prescott Bush, he never played the role of the fierce disciplinarian with his own children. "I can't exaggerate to you what wonderful parents George and Barbara Bush were," George W. says. "They were liberating people. There was never that oppressiveness you see with other parents, never the idea that their way was the only way. My dad went out of his way to make sure that I felt accepted by him.". . .

When Bush talks about "the family as the backbone of Texas" and "Texas as a wonderful way of life" in his gubernatorial campaign speeches, what he's referring to is his own Midland childhood. This is not the Midland that Clayton Williams, the last Republican gubernatorial candidate, described during his 1990 campaign. Williams' Midland was a world of flamboyant wildcatters and cowboys. Bush's Midland, however, was a world full of people like his parents, Ivy Leaguers who had come to West Texas to make their fortunes. The families got together for golf at the country club. They had backyard barbecues in their neighborhood—a neighborhood no different, really, than any upscale neighborhood in Houston or Dallas. They went to First Presbyterian and joined the board of the United Way and sent their kids off to private schools back East. Although the younger Bush saw his parents mingle with poor people, theirs was a world devoid of hardship. . . .

GOING POLITICAL

[Bush] shocked his friends—and, of course, his parents, who once again had no idea of his plans—with his announcement that he was entering the 1978 race for the House of Representatives in a West Texas district that stretched from Midland-Odessa past Lubbock. After 34 years, the incumbent Democratic officeholder, George Mahon, had decided to retire, and Bush, after just two years in Midland, saw another opportunity. If his father's political ambition was shaped by the idea of noblesse oblige, the obligation of public service among those born in high places, George W.'s was shaped by the idea of carpe diem: Seize the day. Close the deal. Make something happen. . . .

"George did sort of leap into it," says Laura, "but even back then he was smart enough to know that a lot of politics was simply timing. You know, there are a lot of would-be governors of Texas sitting around today who never took the opportunity to get into a race when the time was right. If George is good at anything, it's timing."

In what seemed to be a largely amateur effort, Bush

"HE IS GOOD, THIS BOY OF OURS"

George H.W. Bush included a letter in his memoirs describing George W. Bush on election day in 1998 when young George was running for governor. In the letter to friend Hugh Sidey, the elder Bush speaks of his son's popularity and charisma and says with pride that George had the right reasons for wanting to serve.

Yesterday we attended George's final Houston rally. He was the rock star—Mr. Charisma. The rest of the ticket and some congressmen were all on stage when George entered. Then came Laura and Jenna, then Bar[bara] and me. The rest of the ticket became mere strap hangers. George was in command.

He is good, this boy of ours. He's uptight at times, feisty at other times—but who wouldn't be after months of grueling campaigning.

He includes people. He has no sharp edges on issues. He is no ideologue, no divider. He brings people together and he knows how to get things done. He has principles to which he adheres but he knows how to give a little to get a lot. He doesn't hog the credit. He's low on ego, high on drive.

All the talk about his wild youth days is pure nuts. His character will pass muster with flying colors.

Yesterday I told him—"George, on November 4th things will be very different." He knew exactly what I meant. And, Hugh, it will be different. Though the national press has already focused on his potential and though the polls look good he will be in a different league come tomorrow. He is strong though—tough enough, too, to withstand the pressure. . . .

Tomorrow I might well be the Dad of the Governors of the second and fourth largest states in the union. But there will be no feeling of personal vindication, no feeling of anything other than pride in two honest boys who, for the right reasons, want to serve—who fought the good fight and won.

People will call to congratulate us, but they will never begin to know the true depth of my feeling towards my sons. It will be what life is really all about for me right now.

Six years ago I was president of the United States of America. Tonight, maybe, the father of two governors. How great it is!

But then tomorrow a whole new life begins.

George H.W. Bush, *All the Best, George Bush: My Life in Letters and Other Writings.* New York: Scribner, 1999.

recruited his buddies, all political novices, to act as his campaign advisers. He never asked his father for help (although his mother did send out a letter to the people on her Christmas card list, asking them to contribute to the campaign).

Bush's opponent in the Republican primary called him a carpetbagger, a Connecticut Yankee, and a member of the Rockefeller-controlled Trilateral Commission which, according to the opponent, was trying to take over the world. "I didn't even know what the Trilateral Commission was," says Bush, who won the primary anyway. He then lost 53 percent to 47 percent in the general election to the popular Democratic state senator Kent Hance of Lubbock. Near the end of the campaign, the easygoing Bush lost votes when he was accused of loose morals because he had served beer at a meet-the-candidate party for Texas Tech students.

Bush's strong showing gave him his first taste of the power of the Bush name in Texas. But for the next decade, he barely mentioned politics again. It was as if his congressional campaign had been just another one of his impulsive ventures. . . .

Bush did consider running for governor in 1990, but he decided the timing wasn't right while his father was still president. (Another story has it that the White House vetoed a George W. race because it would be too embarrassing to the father if the son lost.) But the political bug had returned. In late 1991 the elder Bush asked George W. to visit Washington to interview members of the Cabinet about the upcoming 1992 campaign. George W. got the message that White House chief of staff John Sununu needed to go. After talking to his father, George W. spent the night at the White House and the next morning walked into Sununu's office and came out with his resignation. Some White House staff members were stunned that the coup de grace was administered by such an outsider. But George W. was proving himself to be a savvy political player, the type who would confront people and take stands in a way his father wouldn't.

POLITICAL LESSONS

In retrospect, George W. says he learned two lessons from his father's 1992 defeat: Baby boomers were looking for a generational change in leadership, and if you campaign on the status quo, you lose. "People don't care what you did for them last year," says Bush. "They want to know what next year is like. Richards is telling people that we're all getting better because the level of crime has gone down a few percentage points. No one cares about that. Everyone is still scared to leave their homes."

He also recognizes that Richards, despite her national stardom, is vulnerable simply because Texas is increasingly becoming a Republican state. Republican leaders still believe the only reason Richards won in 1990 was because Clayton Williams turned out to be such a stereotypical good old boy who infuriated many Republican women. . . . "George W. Bush is too smart to screw up like that," says state Republican chairman Fred Meyer. "If you look at results of the 1990 Williams-Richards race [in which Williams lost by less than 100,000 votes], all George has to do is get back the upscale Republican female voters from Houston and Dallas who abandoned us last time—and he wins." It's a hopeful analysis: In the past four years, Richards has probably won back her share of Democrats who crossed over to vote for Clayton Williams, and she still has a great following among women, Republican and Democrat.

Nevertheless, George W. Bush, the master of timing, sees the 1994 gubernatorial election as his greatest opportunity of all. He has bought four new suits from the Culwell and Son men's store in Dallas. He has paid visits to many older GOP [Republican Party] fat cats, former supporters of his father's, some of whom have been skeptical of his candidacy. A few privately say they aren't sure they appreciate the idea of a Kennedy-like dynasty emerging among Republicans. But supremely confident that "they'll like me if they just get a whiff of me," Bush has persuaded the old fat cats to come through. Of the first twenty donors who gave $20,000 or more to the Bush campaign, seventeen were contributors to his father's presidential campaign.

Most importantly, he has made it to the general election without a primary. . . . Without a primary opponent, Bush had time to develop his platform, which was nonexistent. He also spared himself a bruising fight with an opponent who could have forced him to debate such social issues as abortion or gun control, which might have isolated Republicans on the far right or given Richards more fodder to use against him in the general election. As Bush began delivering his first campaign speeches in November, he told audiences that he was not running because he was the son of George and

Barbara Bush; he was running because he was concerned for the future of his own children. It was a great line. The only problem was that his brother Jeb was also using it in his own Florida gubernatorial campaign. George W. Bush was proving himself to be a terrific campaigner, but a critical listener couldn't help but wonder if, deep down, Bush was truly prepared for this race.

It's a morning meeting of criminal justice officials in the northeast Texas town of Sherman, and Bush has arrived to pass on his vision of Texas: a state where everyone is, to use one of his favorite words, "accountable." A state where people alone are responsible for making their lives better. A state with a drastically reduced welfare program, in which benefits are cut off after two years and the recipients forced to go to work. There will be no guilt-ridden Yalies in Bush's Texas. . . . The kind of government Bush says he prefers is one that creates "negative reinforcement" to make people change their behavior. "A governor can't pass a law to make you love," he says. "But he can pass a law to protect the innocent, law-abiding citizens from thugs."

BUSH AND CRIME

To that end, he is sharing with these Sherman officials his seventeen-point plan to stop juvenile crime, which includes sending especially violent juvenile criminals, even those as young as fourteen, to adult prisons (though segregated from the adult population) for mandatory sentences. "It's always been normal, when a child turns into a criminal, to say that it's our fault—society's fault," Bush says. "Well, under George W. Bush, it's your fault. You're going to get locked up, because we aren't going to have any more guilt-ridden thought that says that we are somehow responsible."

A juvenile probation officer challenges him. "We need more juvenile detention facilities," she says. "We need more rehabilitation for these kids to help them change."

"Wait a minute," says Bush, his temper rising—he does not respond well to criticism—"In order to win the war, we've got to make these criminals realize we mean punishment. They'll start changing once they realize they're going to get punished every time they screw up."

While Governor Richards . . . proposes that juveniles undergo more counseling, including heavy counseling for drug addiction, which she calls the major root of crime, Bush wants quick results. He doesn't think much about the roots of crime. He also doesn't put much stock in open-ended rehabilitation programs. At Richards' urging, the Legislature initiated a policy establishing drug treatment in prison—a program that criminal justice experts almost unanimously agree is long overdue in Texas—but Bush will have none of it. He proposes to take $25 million from drug-treatment programs in the adult prison system to build more local detention centers for juveniles. "The first priority is building more prisons and getting these criminals off the streets," he says.

Bush's approach to crime is indicative of his strengths and weaknesses as a politician. On the stump, his lock-'em-up attitude has great appeal to voters, but it's naive for him to think the high recidivism rates for criminals will ever drop significantly unless there are strong rehabilitation programs for prisoners used to a life of crime.

As a political newcomer who has spent little time studying government policy, Bush is having to learn as he runs. During a tour of a boot camp in Austin one afternoon, a boot camp official was giving an in-depth report on the variety of vocational classes offered to the young inmates. "Hey," interrupted a curious Bush, firing a question out of left field, "what happens when one of these fellows decides he wants to punch you?"

Depending on your point of view, it is either refreshing or a little unnerving that a man who might be governor in November is still working out his ideas about what a governor should do. In a meeting earlier this year, he told his group of education advisers . . . that he wanted to hear some proposals that would completely undermine the top-heavy Texas Education Agency (TEA) that controls local school districts. The advisers met among themselves a few times, then came back to Bush. After a one-hour meeting, Bush pulled the trigger and chose the most radical option presented to him: a "home rule" plan that would allow a locality's voters to declare the locality completely independent from the TEA and set up its own school system, using whatever teaching methods and curricula it chooses. . . .

EDUCATION

Bush envisions schools being run by local school boards that care about education, but it's at least equally likely that the home-rule plan could lead to endless debate among newly autonomous local school boards over whether to include sex education and school prayer in the classroom. Bush doesn't seem to have thought much about this. He says he threw out the idea, in part, to get voters to begin thinking more deeply about various ways to reinvigorate public education. In a frank confession, he also tells me he went public with such a plan early in the campaign "because I knew I needed to show myself to be something other than what people project me to be, which is a nice and decent person but maybe not too substantive, maybe a guy who just floated through Yale as opposed to being a leading-edge intellectual." He adds, "I wanted people to know I cared about ideas and that I was willing to think differently."

Bush does not deny that there are still gaps in his policies. He talks about increasing the share of state spending for education—thereby shrinking the inequitable funding through local property taxes—but he cannot exactly say where that funding will come from. (The cost of raising the state's share of education spending from the current 45 percent to, say, 50 percent, would send state spending soaring from $7 billion a year to $8 billion a year.) He says he wants to use his personal persuasive skills as governor to encourage localities to build "tough love" academies for unruly school kids and start mentoring programs for disadvantaged youngsters—but he doesn't say exactly how he can talk financially over-burdened city councils into spending more of their own money without receiving assistance from the state. He vows to overturn a federal court's infamous Ruiz ruling that has made the cost of operating prisons excessively high—but he doesn't know yet what his arguments in court would be. . . .

On March 2, Texas Independence Day, the former president made a rare appearance for his son. He and Barbara were featured guests at a private $1,000-a-person fundraising dinner at Dallas' Loews Anatole Hotel. It was a glorious evening to be a Republican from Texas. Around the tables, the crowd was giddy from U.S. senator Kay Bailey Hutchison's recent acquittal. They talked about how strong she and Bush would look at the top of the Republican ticket in November. The ballroom was filled with polished, professional-looking women in their thirties and forties, exactly the kind of supporters Bush needs to beat Richards. . . .

"This race is really not about me. It is about the desire of everyone in this room to see to it our children can live in prosperity. I'm just the messenger," [said Bush].

But George W. wanted to make sure this audience knew this race was really all about him. When he got to the line in his prepared text that read, "As sure as I'm standing here, I know we're going to win," he said instead, "As sure as I'm standing here, I know I'm going to win." Even at that moment, he was still fighting to be his own man, someone other than his father's son.

The Republican Front-Runner

Ramesh Ponnuru

As governor of Texas, George W. Bush fulfilled campaign promises in his first one hundred days in office. He promoted adoption and parental rights, signed legislation recognizing Texans' right to carry concealed weapons, and reformed the legal and juvenile justice system lowering crime rates.

One of Bush's most successful efforts of involving faith-based institutions in welfare provisions drew rave reviews. His first priority, education, was reformed when Bush passed sweeping school legislation.

In this 1997 article, Ramesh Ponnuru, a reporter for the *National Review*, takes a look at Bush's history as governor of Texas. Noting Bush's need to find a strong agenda, Ponnuru claims the governor's discipline, personal charm, moderate temperament, and conservative record would give him the best odds of winning the Republican presidential nomination in 2000.

He [Texas governor, George W. Bush] is the latest in a long line of establishment candidates who have been conservative enough to succeed in a Republican Party that was moving right. So, for instance, Gov. Bush seems more conservative than Bob Dole, who ran a more conservative campaign in 1996 than Bush's father did in 1988. And the elder Bush [President George H.W. Bush] was to the right of Jerry Ford. . . .

For all the similarities, one thing Gov. Bush isn't is a clone of his father. For one thing, nobody doubts that he's a Texan. He used to own a controlling interest in the Texas Rangers, and, as he often says, he went to San Jacinto Junior High.

Nor is his famous name what's causing national Republi-

Ramesh Ponnuru, "The Front-Runner: Is It George W. Bush Already?" *National Review*, vol. 49, December 22, 1997, p. 52. Copyright © 1997 by National Review, Inc. Reproduced by permission.

cans to take notice. When Bush ran for governor in 1994, there were those who considered him a lightweight trading on his father's name. He had had a wild frat-boy reputation, and a wholly justified one, as he freely admits in speeches. And he's still irreverent, given to needling and a talented mimic. Writes *Texas Monthly*'s Paul Burka: "His enthusiasm for his job is that of a child who has just been let loose in the greatest playground in the world."

But he has also discovered discipline. He married librarian Laura Welch and they had twin girls, now teens. Laura reportedly got him reading the Bible and attending a Methodist church. . . . [Texas] Republican State Senator David Sibley remarks, "He's maniacal about exercise. He used to drink and he just quit. When he latches on to something, he's like a pit bull."

INTENSIVE FOCUS

As his predecessor, Democrat Ann Richards, learned too late. Gov. Richards had achieved national stature in 1988, when she ridiculed Republican presidential nominee George Bush for having been "born with a silver foot in his mouth." On the face of it, she was in a strong position to win re-election in 1994. As former Democratic consultant Mark McKinnon recalls, "In '94 the economy was in great shape, the incumbent governor was one of the most popular in state history, every Democrat on the ticket won that year—except Richards. Despite everything, George Bush beat her like a red-headed stepchild."

He did it by sticking like rubber cement to a short agenda: tort reform, juvenile justice, education, welfare. He never took the bait when she attacked him. While he talked about the next term, she defended the last one. . . . Says McKinnon, "He tipped his hat to the lady and said, You've done a terrific job, but I'm a conservative Republican alternative. He had a strategy and stuck to it. In old political-consultant parlance, this guy gets it. He really gets it."

He has kept the same focus as governor. The official powers of the governor are quite limited: Lieutenant Governor Bob Bullock and Comptroller John Sharp arguably wield more power, and both are Democrats. But Bush has deftly used his weak office to become a political powerhouse. He's insanely popular in Texas. According to the Harte-Hanks poll, 71 per cent of Texans think he deserves re-election;

even in the Democratic stronghold of El Paso, he has 92 per cent approval. He has no gender gap. (One adviser half-jokingly remarks that female voters must like the idea of a former wild man domesticated by a good woman.)

Democrats spent the summer debating whether even to field a candidate against him: doing so could raise turnout and endanger Democrats lower on the ticket. National Democrats, on the other hand, want to raise his negatives. That's because they fear him as a presidential candidate. If the polls are right, Bush would narrowly beat [Democratic front-runner] Al Gore if the election were held tomorrow.

ON THE ISSUES

Bush can face the voters with a solid, if uninspiring, record of moderate conservatism. He has promoted adoption and parental rights. He has signed legislation recognizing Texans' right to carry concealed weapons. He delivered on his promises on tort reform and juvenile justice; and, under Bush, Texas performs a third of the nation's executions. Gov. Bush can take credit for the fact that the decline in crime rates that began under Gov. Richards has continued.

On welfare, Bush's performance has lacked luster. Texas's welfare caseload is falling, but no faster than the rest of the country's. Bush might have had more success had he won his public fight with the Clinton Administration over his proposal to privatize the system.

But conservative welfare expert Robert Rector is skeptical: "Why privatizing the administration of the liberals' welfare system is a big deal is something I've never understood at all. The problem with welfare is not that it's administered badly. It's that it rewards idleness and illegitimacy." Indeed, the governor's idea of creating centers where those on welfare could do "one-stop shopping" for state services could expand the reach of that system.

Similarly, though the governor's efforts to involve faith-based institutions in welfare provision have drawn raves from religious conservatives, it is not clear whether their main effect will be to reform welfare or to corrupt those institutions. States like Wisconsin, where welfare rolls have fallen at twice the rate of Texas, have instead focused on work requirements. Texas doesn't have serious sanctions for shirkers, and as a result it failed to meet the federal requirement that 75 per cent of two-parent households on welfare work.

Gov. Bush can claim more success on education, his "number one priority." He has passed sweeping charter-school legislation. Respected education guru Chester Finn says he's "pretty impressed" by the governor: "He seems to believe in what I believe in." On standards, he says, "most states are in so much worse shape that Texas gets a B."

Bush's limited voucher program, however, has been a failure, with few parents aware of it and fewer public schools cooperating. Bush's rhetoric on standards has been conservative: he focused public attention on the need for all third-graders to be literate before President Clinton adopted the theme, and lately he has taken to touting the advantages of phonics. But critics complain about his lack of follow-through: conservatives on the state board of education have been fighting other Republicans—including the Bush-appointed heads of the Texas Education Agency and board of education—on behalf of higher standards, and consequently taking abuse from the press for being Christian fanatics, with nary a peep from the governor. . . .

School finance led Bush to his biggest political defeat—and, worse yet, on taxes, which are still the glue that holds the Republican coalition together. In 1989, the state Supreme Court held the state's school-funding system, based on local property taxes, unconstitutionally inequitable. The legislature's solution was to redistribute tax revenues from rich districts to poor ones. Suburban Republicans saw their tax bills skyrocket under the "Robin Hood" system. So when Gov. Bush saw the prospect of a $1-billion surplus, he jumped at the chance to solve the problem.

He proposed to use the surplus to cut property taxes. But he also proposed a tax reform: a shift from property taxes, which he called "a tax on the American dream of home ownership," to an array of consumption taxes and business taxes.

The substantive objection to the plan was that it would, over time, change the political landscape in a way that would make conservative policy goals harder to achieve. The proposal that the state provide the majority of school funding could only weaken local accountability. It's no accident that the states with high-achieving schools, like New Hampshire, rely on local funding. Yet Bush, in his 1997 State of the State speech, endorsed the key finding of the Supreme Court: that "relying too much on local property taxes . . . is inherently unequal and unfair." He thus conceded the framing of the issue as how to spend "everybody's" money on "everybody's" children.

A similar structural defect beset his tax policy. The highly visible, and therefore hard-to-raise, property tax would be cut; an array of less visible, and thus easy-to-raise, taxes would pick up the slack. Anti-tax activist Grover Norquist, who ran $120,000 worth of radio ads attacking the plan, says that though it was a net tax cut, using "a political dynamic analysis, taxes would have been higher in ten years."

The Democrat-run State House promptly hijacked Bush's plan; Norquist's Americans for Tax Reform itemized 75 different tax hikes in the resulting bill. Gov. Bush lobbied for its passage anyway, arguing that the State Senate would fix it. The Senate tried, but no compromise was reached. So the governor settled for a straight property-tax cut of $1 billion, which works out to about $150 per household. That surplus could have been spent instead, and so Gov. Bush effectively blocked any resumption of his predecessor's spending spree. Not a bad final result—if it is final; Bush let the tax-reform genie out of the bottle, and Democrats may have more than three wishes in the next legislative session. . . .

Conservatives have had other disappointments. Bush's administration has been the loudest in claiming a right to tax any commercial transaction on the Internet that has some connection to the state. He supported the creation of the "Texas Healthy Kids Corporation," which will probably receive federal funds under the Hatch-Kennedy kidcare bill. Like his father, Bush eschews partisanship: Republicans have complained about some high-profile Democrats he has appointed, and conservatives about the "movement types" he hasn't. . . .

READY FOR THE NATIONAL STAGE?

Some of Bush's fans wonder whether he's ready for the national stage. Oratory doesn't seem to run in the family, and the younger Bush reportedly tends to mispronounce words. His last two appearances in the national spotlight cast him in an unflattering light. The audience at the Midwest Republican conference in Indianapolis in August was underwhelmed by Bush's speech. And at the dedication of the Bush presidential library in November, the governor's remarks about how his father had "brought dignity and character and honor to the White House" were taken as an ill-timed rebuke to the man who beat his father. Bush's communications director, Karen Hughes, denies any such intent—an explanation that at least suggests a tone-deafness toward the media. Which raises another issue: Gov. Bush doesn't have to deal in Texas with a press as liberal or as nasty as that in Washington, or indeed with as entrenched a liberal culture. How would he handle it in a national campaign, or in national office?

And how would he deal with his father's legacy? Norquist wants Republicans to hold the line on taxes: "Bush's son cannot be a national figure until he has repudiated his father's tax increase, and demonstrated to the world that he has zero intention of doing anything so stupid and destructive." But by the next primary season, almost ten years will have passed since that tax increase. Memories may have faded. On the other hand, if Gov. Bush wastes time trying to rehabilitate his father's Administration, control of the past would become an independent reason for conservatives to oppose him.

If Bush decides to run for President, though, perhaps his biggest challenge will be to explain why he wants the job. So far, he has no signature issues. His self-description as a "compassionate conservative" is the same as that of his potential rival Rep. John Kasich (R., Ohio)—and in Bush's case, it inevitably recalls his father's much-mocked promise of a "kinder, gentler" nation. Anything else? Bush often speaks of a "cultural crisis" and says, "We need a spiritual renewal in America.". . .

Bush is pro-life, with the standard exceptions for rape, incest, and the life of the mother. He failed in his effort to get a parental-notification bill through the legislature, but he succeeded in blocking a pro-euthanasia bill. Yet he wouldn't divide Republicans: Ann Stone of Republicans for Choice calls him "a bridge-builder" and takes comfort from his feud with [chairman of the Texas Republican Party Tom] Pauken, "who was the great Satan to a lot of moderates."

If he won the nomination, Bush would be a strong candidate in the general election. His personal charm is not to be underestimated. . . . Republican strategists also think that Bush's support for welfare for legal immigrants and the public education of the children of illegal immigrants, and his opposition to official-English laws would make it harder to tag him with the anti-Hispanic label.

Indeed, Gov. Bush is probably the strongest, and most conservative, candidate the Republican establishment is likely to produce. As such, how conservatives evaluate Bush in 2000 will depend on the extent to which they believe their movement has been absorbed by the Republican establishment. If they think it has largely been ensconced, many of them will go with Bush. What the country needs now, they will conclude, is the implementation of an existing center-right consensus rather than the creation of a new, more conservative one. In that case, they will find the combination of substantive conservatism and temperamental moderation quite attractive.

Progressive Politics

Dana Milbank

Dana Milbank paints a clearer picture of what George W. Bush stands for in the areas of economics, taxation, and international affairs. Leaning toward private sector solutions, Bush prefers a limited role for government and welcomes church and state co-operation on contending with social ills such as drugs and crime. As a governor untouched by Republican constituencies, Bush also gravitated toward progressive thinking on taxes, prescription drugs, poverty, and education. Many commentators have likened Bush's "concern for the underclass" rhetoric to ideals traditionally espoused by liberals. Milbank's 1999 article focuses on the ideology of Bush as the governor of Texas and highlights the themes and political agenda Bush would later bring to his bid for the presidency. Milbank is a writer for *New Republic* magazine and has authored books on politics.

To get a clearer idea of what Bush is about, one must leave the governor's mansion and drive 20 minutes north to the improbably named Austin suburb of Jollyville. There you will find Mrs. Gutierrez's second-grade class in the middle of its weekly character-building lesson. A boy named Tray raises his hand to compliment Philip for "trying not to hurt people's feelings." Pint-sized Jessie pipes up to compliment Pamela because "when I had no friends at recess she came over and played with me." But then a boy complains about some naughty behavior. "Is that responsible?" Mrs. Gutierrez asks. "No!" the class says in unison. "Is that compassionate?" "No!" "What should we be doing at all times?" the teacher asks. "Personal best," the tots respond. Thus do the happy children of Jollyville, under a public school program championed by Governor Bush, learn how to become "good citizens for Texas." In December, they studied perseverance;

Dana Milbank, "What 'W' Stands For," *New Republic*, vol. 220, April 26, 1999, p. 66.

in March, self-reliance. Those with exemplary character get a seat at the "VIP Honor Table" in the lunchroom.

Still don't grasp George W.'s philosophy? Then drive north for another hour to Waco, the town David Koresh and his radically anti-government Branch Davidian sect put on the map. Here, in another public school program backed by Bush, a Baptist seminary student named Brandon Barnard is warning a group of sixth-graders at Midway Intermediate School about genital warts "the size of my fist." Such warts are tough to remove, he adds. "You do what you want," Barnard says, as the children squirm. "I don't want anybody cutting, burning, or freezing that part of my body." Barnard flashes a slide on the screen listing the consequences of premarital sex: cancer, AIDS, death, pain, emotional scars, infertility. Then he shows a slide listing the consequences of abstinence: self-control, self-respect, self-discipline. "Virginity is a gift," Barnard declares, holding up a package in purple wrapping paper. "I'm proud to be a virgin."

The two scenes, and hundreds like them playing out across Texas, encapsulate the Bush ideology. It is, at first glance, a conservative message, based on the notion that traditional values will help prevent poverty and other ills. But, deeper down, Bush's approach, warts and all, should sound familiar—and possibly comfortable—to some liberals. He assumes that government can be a force for good and that it has a responsibility to help the weak. Bush's stances so far on national issues such as Kosovo and abortion have been full of ambiguity and obfuscation, seemingly dictated more by tactic than by principle. Still, beneath Bush's mush is some evidence that he's trying to introduce a government-friendly conservatism to a party often hijacked by harsh and selfish ideology.

Bush's own label for his philosophy, "compassionate conservatism," is a tired phrase and easy to ridicule. Bob Dole used it to great effect in his 1988 presidential campaign. But, in Bush's case, it appears to imply a more activist style of conservative governance. Instead of demanding anti-abortion laws, he seeks alternatives, such as abstinence and adoption programs, which will reduce abortions. Instead of the usual Republican lock-'em-up-and-throw-away-the-key line on criminal justice, he has fostered a faith-based rehabilitation program for prisoners. He has demanded increases in education funding and opposed anti-immigration measures. Instead of a flat tax, he talks of modest cuts and reducing regressivity. "What he understands about conservatism that many conservatives don't is that, at its core, it's caring about the poor, the underclass," says Al Hubbard, an old business-school classmate of Bush's who has helped him line up advisers. "The biggest problem facing our country is the underclass and the lack of opportunity for the underclass." And the answer, says Hubbard, "is not about saying, 'Lower taxes, reduce regulation, and everybody will be fine.'" It is, rather, about a host of government interventions that Bush and his advisers have proposed: mentoring programs, literacy programs, welfare-to-work programs in which church volunteers offer both skills training and Bible study, cuts in sales taxes that disproportionately affect the poor, tax incentives to aid poor neighborhoods, and substantial increases in public education spending.

These ideas may sound more Jesse Jackson than Ronald Reagan, but they are common in Bush circles. Typical is Mark McKinnon, who worked for Democrats . . . before agreeing to be Bush's media strategist. "He's willing to step out on issues that have long been contrary to the interests of the Republican Party," McKinnon says. "He's figured out a way for Republicans to actually be for something." Several conservative Democrats in the Texas legislature, likewise, backed Bush's reelection. Even Texas Democratic Party spokeswoman Liz Chadderdon admits: "When you look at Bush's agenda, you could plug in Clinton's name and it would be the same."

NEW COALITION

More of such words from Democrats would make Bush a formidable challenger to Vice President [Al] Gore. On the other hand, the very things that make Democrats embrace Bush will irk the GOP's conservative primary voters. The Bush strategy appears to be a calculation that the hard right of the Republican Party, after two presidential defeats, may be willing to take half a loaf—much as liberal Democrats accepted the more centrist Clinton in 1992 after twelve years in the wilderness. Bush may also be gambling on support from independents, who can vote in Republican primaries in some states. It's a plausible strategy, particularly because so many Republican candidates are already vying for the far right's backing.

But, while Bush's philosophy may have a ring of familiarity to some Democrats, they would be mistaken to think he is one of them. "It sounds like liberalism because there's concern for the poor, but it doesn't come out of liberalism," says Marvin Olasky, a University of Texas professor who advises Bush. "He's a throwback to one of the conservative strains of the nineteenth century." Bush doesn't come from the economic conservative/social Darwinist school but neither does he side with the fundamentalists/moralists.

So what is Bush? Some conservatives have argued that he is reunifying the Reagan coalition of fiscal conservatives and the religious right that fell apart under Bush's father. But those wishful thinkers will be disappointed. First, Bush isn't fleeing from his old man. Many of young Bush's top advisers—Larry Lindsey, Michael Boskin, John Taylor, Martin Feldstein, Al Hubbard, Paul Wolfowitz, Condoleezza Rice, Bob Kimmitt, and Josh Bolten—also served in or gave advice to his father's administration.

More significantly, the coalition Bush is assembling is in some ways the opposite of Reaganism. Reagan's alliance was in large part libertarian, and young Bush's is communitarian. The communitarian movement, known also by its "civil society," "social capital," and "quality of life" buzzwords, is vaguely defined, but it's based on the idea that too much Hobbesian individualism has created an atomized, selfish, and disconnected society. Government, by encouraging private and nonprofit efforts to restore community, and by tempering individual rights with responsibility to society, can help to restore the purpose. But, in truth, the philosophy's roots go much further back, to Aristotle, who believed that government could help to engineer an ideal society. It's the kind of conservatism championed by Edmund Burke, and it claims such historic figures as Disraeli and Bismarck, who were pioneers of the welfare state. A few modern conservatives, including Olasky and columnist George Will (whose 1983 book *Statecraft as Soulcraft* was an anti-individualist tract), have taken this view, but they were oddballs until now.

"It's a new coalition," Olasky says. "That's why some people on the right are so uncomfortable" with Bush. In Bush's way of thinking, the individual-rights champions on both sides—the civil libertarians on the left and the antigovernment, leave-us-alone right-wingers—are on the outside. They'll be replaced by a mixture of incentive-based conservatives and good-government liberals. "He could bring a lot of communitarian Democrats with him," Olasky says. If liberals were willing to give up some federal control, Bush and likeminded conservatives would be content to spend more money on the poor and other government pursuits. "Let's throw away the budget cutters," Olasky says. "I see that coming with Bush. I see that as part of a governing alliance."

Some still suspect that Bush is a moderate, establishment Republican in his father's image. But they, too, are mistaken. President Bush, with a sense of noblesse oblige, saw himself as a duty-bound steward with little ideological passion. But his son, a baby-boomer and a product of the 1960s, is more activist than caretaker.

In this sense, his outlook is somewhat like Al Gore's, and the two are largely vying for the same governing coalition. Gore's "livability" agenda, proposals to rescue communities from urban sprawl, are part of the same quality-of-life genre that inspires Bush. Young Bush and Gore, of course, are both scions of powerful political fathers, educated in prep schools and the Ivy League. Both men are correspondingly cautious and tend to favour small initiatives to sweeping change. Gore also grasps the "limited government" philosophy that is a pillar of Governor Bush's thought. In fact, Bill Bradley, taking a more traditional Democratic view, contrasts himself from Gore by promising to "cultivate ten strong oaks rather than sprinkling water on a thousand house plants." Former Clinton official Lanny Davis, a fraternity brother of Bush's at Yale (and a Gore backer), says: "Among all the Republicans running, [Bush] comes closest to the centrist Democratic philosophy." Bush, says Davis, is "as close to Bill Clinton and Al Gore as he could be politically. George Bush is on the forty-seven yard line in one direction, and Al Gore is on the forty-seven yard line in the other direction."

Bush aides, not surprisingly, bristle at the Clinton-Gore comparison, which they see as an attempt to make their candidate appear too liberal to Republican primary voters. "Sorry, Lanny," says Karen Hughes, Bush's press secretary. "Governor Bush is not on the same field. The Democrats are trying to make comparisons that will hurt him in the Republican primary. It's ridiculous, and they know it's not true." Hughes, for her part, calls her boss an "activist conservative." "He's not anti-government," she says. "He believes there is a role for government, but it should be limited."

Emerging Philosophy

Hughes, in many respects, is correct. Though their coalitions overlap and their philosophies intersect, there will still be plenty to separate Bush and Gore. Bush leans toward private-sector solutions, while Gore errs on the side of government intervention. Bush backed legislation allowing Texans to carry concealed firearms; Gore is a strong gun-control advocate. Gore is famously green, while Bush, backed by business and oil men, has been advised by the Competitive Enterprise Institute's Fred Smith, who wants public land privatized and says that the "EPA is a massive mistake." Their differences on abortion and organized labor are equally stark. The two men also will be forced to placate the hardcore interest groups in their parties: Gore and labor, Bush and fundamentalists. If they are nominated, the choice for many voters may come down not to the men but to their fellow travelers: Bush's Bob Barr or Gore's Ted Kennedy?

Virtually none of this Bush philosophy has emerged yet, and that's just fine with the governor's advisers. "He gains in the polls every week by doing nothing," says one. Even Bush has been marveling at his good fortune. "I held a press conference on the drought, and it rained the next day," he told the Texas Daily Newspaper Association at a recent luncheon. "Now my mother's calling up for tips on the lottery." The reception for Bush is, as always, adoring. The governor, after a round of handshakes, gets a fawning introduction and a standing ovation from the newspaper executives. His speech is full of progressive-sounding themes—research and development tax credits and references to his sales tax cut for diapers and over-the-counter medicines. He calls education "by far the most important thing a state does," vowing to hold schools accountable, a favorite theme of New Democrats.

Pioneering a Vision

After the session, the Texas press tries to trap Bush into stating positions. They pepper him with abortion questions ("I'm pro-life, and I've had a consistent position"), gay rights ("I believe we should never discriminate against anybody"), and hate-crime legislation ("All crime is hate"). Three times, Bush falls into a reporter's trap and begins to elaborate on his philosophy but then catches himself. "I've stated my position," he says. Then he returns to his preferred subjects:

limited government, local control, strong families, personal responsibility. The governor chats with the reporters about his latest fishing trip in his familiar, locker-room manner. His banter is friendly. . . . The reporters are charmed. And, when they return to their typewriters, they will find, once again, that deft Governor Bush has told them nothing new.

But, while Bush continues to be cleverly opaque in public, he has been meeting in Austin with a steady procession of policy advisers. Bush is far from devising a specific agenda, but his advisers paint a surprisingly unified vision of the philosophy he would adopt as president.

The Russian kitsch industry specializes in matryoshka, hollow wooden figures of the country's leaders. Inside a Yeltsin shell is a Gorbachev egg, which surrounds a Brezhnev egg right down to a solid Lenin core. If one were building such a toy to explain Bush's domestic policy, the first layer inside the Bush shell would be Indianapolis Mayor Steve Goldsmith. Inside Goldsmith would be Harvard Professor Robert Putnam.

Goldsmith, a Republican, is Bush's chief domestic policy adviser. He is by necessity a pragmatist, and he has been a pioneer in the civil-society movement also championed by the likes of New York Mayor Rudolph Giuliani. His idiosyncratic policies in Indianapolis have a streak of concern for social justice running through them—and Bush's will, too. "I think the governor is articulating a new vision for the Republican Party," Goldsmith says. "You can't miss the idea that the marketplace operates unevenly. . . . Prosperity ought to have a purpose. We're talking about the poor in a very serious way." Among the proposals that civil-society conservatives favor is a large charity tax credit for those who volunteer to help the poor. "I do think he's seriously conservative," Goldsmith says of Bush, but he doesn't think conservatism should be "an excuse to ignore people who are without opportunity."

Goldsmith's website lists a profusion of good-government proposals: reinventing government, more police, fatherhood initiatives, high-tech incentives, neighborhood empowerment, worker retraining. That agenda may well turn out to be Bush's, but it also happens to summarize Al Gore's. "A legitimate observation," Goldsmith says with a chuckle. To be sure, the similarity is more in nomenclature than in policy. But, Goldsmith adds, "As the New Democrats have moved to the center to some extent and as the Republicans recognize the need to be compassionate to the poor, the distinction narrows." The mayor lists among the civil-society thinkers who influence him Harvard's Putnam, a left-leaning thinker who worked in the Carter administration.

Putnam, whose "bowling alone" theory seeped into national political discourse, sees promise for the left in the direction Bush and Goldsmith are taking. "Civic reengagement is a fundamental prerequisite for a new progressive era," he says. Though Goldsmith and Putnam disagree on the role of government in such efforts, Goldsmith's community programs are just the kind Putnam favors. "That's what worries the far right about Bush," he says.

PROGRESSIVE POPULIST

Bush often seems to be torn between progressive instincts and Republican constituencies. In other words, he waffles. This year, for example, the Texas legislature has been debating a federally authorized expansion of health care to children living at 150 percent of the poverty line, or even 200 percent. In February, Bush said, "If you get up to one hundred and fifty percent, we are going to be covering a lot of children that aren't covered today," according to the *Austin American-Statesman*. But two weeks later he softened, and the same paper quoted him as saying, "I'll take a definite position at the appropriate time." On affirmative action, similarly, both opponents and supporters have claimed him. He says he's for "goals" but against "quotas," a vague distinction further complicated by his support for "affirmative access" (the awarding of spots in state universities to high school students who finish in the top ten percent of their graduating classes). Some say that's affirmative action by another name—or that it's little different from Clinton's "mend it, don't end it" fudge.

On policies at the core of his civil-society philosophy, though, Bush hasn't been ambiguous. He admires such programs as "Turn Around Texas," in which local residents and police harass drug dealers in their neighborhoods. Like Giuliani, he's a tough law-and-order guy who has presided over expanded police powers. And he welcomes church-state cooperation. When a faith-based drug rehab group got into trouble with a state agency, Bush called off the regulatory dogs, saving the program. "The state has been our advocate, our boosters," says Gerry Phelps, a Methodist minister who founded a welfare-to-work program that offers job training, life-skills lessons, and Bible study.

Bush's economic policy, like his social policy, has a peculiar preoccupation with the poor and working class. Some of his friends and advisers hear echoes of Jack Kemp. "In a funny way, you can almost call him a populist," says James Langdon, a Democratic lawyer and an old friend of Bush's. When the two men discussed foreign policy, Langdon recalls that Bush declared: "I want to know how it's going to affect American workers." Thought Langdon: "That's a strange thing for a Republican to say."

Bush's economics chief, Larry Lindsey, a former Fed governor, has strong supply-side credentials. But Lindsey says times have changed. "The country doesn't need another revolution," he told me. "In my view, we need to refine. One group that particularly needs conservative help are those with low and moderate income." That sounds like the old liberal complaint about income inequality. Lindsey, who has described himself as a populist, would cut taxes but keep the charitable contribution and mortgage-interest deductions and the capital gains tax. To offset tax cuts that favor the wealthy, he would cut regressive taxes like the telephone excise tax or offer a higher percentage cut to those in lower brackets.

Missing from Bushian thinking is the voodoo-economics idea (as Dad put it) that tax cuts pay for themselves. "The governor would think that's silly," says Glenn Hubbard, a Columbia University economist who is advising Bush on taxes, budget, and health care. "I don't think he's ideological at all," says Hubbard. "He has strong principles, but they're at the big-picture level. He wants market solutions wherever possible, but he also recognizes a role for government in helping markets work." Bush's record in Texas, a boom-time combination of modest tax cuts and small spending increases, confirms this. His latest budget includes a $2 billion property tax cut, $1.5 billion more for teachers and schools, and plans to cut sales taxes on diapers and medication.

The anti-tax Republicans, already suspicious because of President Bush's tax-raising budget deal in 1990, seem to be acquiescing to the son, but not without some difficulty. Grover Norquist's Americans for Tax Reform spent $120,000 on radio ads protesting a tax shift Governor Bush proposed early in his administration. Bush wanted to relieve the tax burden by shifting it in part onto small businesses. Conservatives were sure that the creation of new taxes would eventually make taxes higher. Bush retreated in favor of a straight cut. "He sinned in thought but not in action," Norquist says. Norquist, who has made the pilgrimage to Austin, says Bush backs his view on all major issues: school choice, tort reform, and a supermajority for raising taxes. He's not a purist, of course. "He will be a creature of what's around him," Norquist says. Still, unlike purists such as Forbes, Bush can win. "There are ideologues, icebreakers who open new paths," Norquist says. "But you get your head beaten in when you do that."

INTERNATIONAL AFFAIRS

In international affairs, Bush comes closer to being his father's son. This shouldn't be surprising. He is a typical governor, meaning he hasn't had to worry about foreign events. And he grew up with a foreign-policy-obsessed father, so something was bound to rub off. Young Bush doesn't care as deeply about the international scene as his father, who served as CIA chief and ambassador to the United Nations and China. He would, advisers say, follow the Clinton model of a domestic policy presidency.

Bush is surrounding himself with a hawkish crowd: Wolfowitz, of the Johns Hopkins School of Advanced International Studies (and a sometime contributor to the *New Republic* magazine), Stanford Provost Rice, and Dick Cheney. Others include Donald Rumsfeld, Kimmitt, and Richard Perle, committed internationalists who have no patience for [ultraconservative Pat] Buchanan's protectionist line. His foreign policy advisers say Bush would be determined to project a more muscular presence overseas and pursue an aggressive missile defense system at home. He is determined that GOP "rivals won't out-tough him," as one adviser puts it. "He strikes me as tougher-minded in some ways than his father," says Perle. And, says Perle, Bush is likely to take the internationalism displayed by Clinton and Gore even further: "There will be sharp differences on almost every foreign and security issue."

So far, however, there's been precious little evidence of this. For instance, while his rival John McCain has taken a detailed and forceful stance on the unfolding Kosovo crisis [in the former Yugoslavia]—stating that, if he were president, he would "intensify the bombing campaign to a very significant degree" and that, in contrast to Clinton, he would "consider the option . . . of ground troops"—Bush has shied away from offering any opinions at all. "As governor of Texas, I do not have access to all the information and military intelligence available to the commander-in-chief," he explained to reporters at a March 25 press conference—one of the few times he's actually commented on Kosovo. Having thus excused himself from coming up with any answers of his own, Bush contented himself with asking questions instead. "Will the [NATO air strikes] lead to the goal of ending the conflict and bringing peace and stability to the region? I fervently hope so, although, I share the concerns and misgivings of many Texans and Americans.".

On matters of international economics, Bush is an ardent free-trader, his advisers say, even less inclined than Clinton to engage in trade wars. George Shultz, the former Reagan secretary of state who has been coaching Bush, sees him developing a trade-based foreign policy emphasizing overtures to Mexico and a stronger emphasis on our own hemisphere. Other than his free-trading inclinations, Shultz doesn't believe Bush has an overarching worldview. "Obviously we need to have a sense of strategy, but we need to realize things we do along the way add up," he says.

But, as in the Clinton White House, Bush's aggressive foreign policy could at times conflict with his free-trade stance. The GOP, for example, plans to hammer Gore over the Chinese security issue, arguing that the administration's engagement policy has given away too much to China. But this won't work well for Bush, because his father had much the same policy and because he may have a weak spot of his own for a troublesome foreign country, if his overtures to Mexico as governor are any indication. Like China, Mexico is a country where the U.S.'s interest in fostering trade often conflicts with its other interests—for example, in fighting the drug trade and supporting efforts to clean up the corrupt and anti-democratic tendencies of the Mexican government. The question then is whether Mexico could be to Bush fils what China was to Bush pere. And, notes one adviser, "it would be a tricky dance for Bush" to try to tar Clinton with the China-appeasing brush.

In his talks with advisers, Bush has confessed his ignorance of foreign policy details. But, at the same time, he seems almost cocky. A couple of months back, at a meeting on the defense budget, Bush cut off his advisers who were reciting the minutiae of Pentagon budgeting. "Shouldn't we back up?" he asked, requesting a discussion on military strategy. "If you get that right, the budget will take care of itself." At another meeting, Bush started the discussion with a bold assertion. "I'm going to be the next president of the United States," he said. "I need your help, not to become president—I'll take care of that—but to be a good president."

CHAPTER 3

THE ELECTION
OF THE CENTURY

PEOPLE
WHO MADE
HISTORY

GEORGE W. BUSH

The Presidential Race

Lee Edwards

Thirty days after the 2000 election George W. Bush
finally accrued the 271 electoral votes need to secure
the U.S. presidency. Lee Edwards, senior editor at
the *World & I*, claims that the election was not as
close as it seemed. Bush won twenty-nine out of fifty
states and three-fourths of the counties in America.
Bush also carried small towns and rural areas with
60 percent of the vote. Edwards evaluates the 2000
presidential race using five areas of a campaign:
funding, organization, issues, the media, and the
candidates as campaigners to determine the
strengths and weaknesses of Bush and his political
rival, Democrat Al Gore. According to Edwards's
analysis, Bush clearly matched or bested Gore in all
of these key areas of the 2000 campaign.

A presidential election is usually a referendum on continuity or change, but in 2000 the American people seemed to
vote for continuity and change.

The public's desire for change frustrated Vice President Al
Gore, who should have been able to win the presidency by
promising to continue the unquestioned peace and prosperity of the Clinton-Gore years. But President Bill Clinton was
so personally unwelcome in the living rooms of most Americans that Gore kept Clinton at arm's length throughout the
campaign, insisting again and again, "I am my own man."
Gore strove to negate the wish for change by emphasizing the
"dangerous" nature of his opponent's reforms, such as tax
cuts for the "rich" and partial privatization of Social Security.

The desire for continuity hampered Gov. George W. Bush,
who had to be careful not to criticize too harshly the popular record of the Clinton-Gore administration. He instead
promised to solve the problems that had not been addressed
by Clinton and Gore while using nonthreatening rhetoric
such as "compassionate conservatism." Bush was unable to

Lee Edwards, "The Closest Presidential Election Ever—Bush Won, Barely, by Offering a
Slightly to the Right, Limited-Government Presidency," *World & I*, vol. 16, February 2001,
p. 20. Copyright © 2001 by News World Communications, Inc. Reproduced by permission.

use the character issue as much as he had planned after Gore successfully decoupled himself from Clinton at the Democratic convention.

CLOSEST CONTEST SINCE 1960

The ambivalent mood of the electorate produced the closest presidential contest since 1960 when John Kennedy defeated Richard Nixon by only two-tenths of one percent of the popular vote—about the same margin by which Gore apparently topped Bush in 2000. But Kennedy won both the popular and electoral contests, while Gore narrowly won only the popular vote on November 7. Bush won the electoral vote and therefore the presidency, accruing 271 electoral votes (one more than needed) to Gore's 267. Or did he?

Bush was preparing to announce some of the more prominent members of his cabinet (Colin Powell as secretary of state, etc.) when Florida with its 25 electoral votes suddenly became too close to call. The nation was plunged into a protracted political and legal battle over whether a majority of Florida's voters had voted for Bush or Gore that ended more than one month later.

And yet, depending upon your measuring stick, the election was not close. Bush carried 29 out of 50 states and over three-fourths of the counties in America. The disparity is even greater when you note that the Bush counties covered some 2.4 million square miles of the country, the Gore counties only about 580,000 square miles.

On the other hand, according to *National Review*'s Kate O'Beirne, Gore carried voters in the largest cities by a three-to-one margin. In cities with populations between 50,000 and 500,000, Gore's margin was three to two. The suburbs split evenly between the candidates, and Bush carried smaller towns and rural areas with 60 percent of the vote.

This geographic divide, says O'Beirne, "reflects a cultural split over the role of government." Federal subsidies and mediation are valued in the cities, but in less densely populated areas government and its benefits are "best kept at arm's length."

From the viewpoint of political science, the 2000 presidential race was amazingly close because the two aspirants were so evenly matched in the five essential areas of a campaign: money, organization, the candidates as campaigners, issues, and the media.

MONEY

A shrewd and successful politician once remarked, "Money is the mother's milk of politics." In our modern media society, a political campaign cannot survive without it. And because the stakes were high (control of the White House and the Congress) and the economy was booming, the 2000 federal elections were the most expensive in U.S. history, with analysts estimating that as much as $3 billion was raised and spent on the presidential and congressional races.

The two major presidential candidates each received $67.6 million in public funds. But that funding was easily exceeded by the soft money [private donations] the two parties spent to promote their presidential contenders—an estimated $236 million. Another $300 million was spent by various groups, including single-issue organizations, trade unions, and corporations, on issue ads on behalf of all federal candidates, with most of the advertising appearing on television.

Although Republicans raised more money than Democrats as usual—an estimated $505.5 million to $371.6 million—the gap between the two parties was not as wide as in the past, and liberal groups held their own with conservative groups in political fund-raising. In the crucial area of money in the 2000 race, therefore, Bush had an advantage over Gore by a surprisingly small margin.

ORGANIZATION

Democrats have always depended on the trade unions to deliver the vote on Election Day. The AFL-CIO delivered "big time" in 2000, with union households accounting for 26 percent of all votes, up from 19 percent in 1992. In Michigan, one of the battleground states that Gore carried, union members provided 43 percent of the votes as auto workers got Election Day off.

Black voters, another key Democratic voting bloc, were also a prime objective of organized labor and groups like the NAACP. Although the national black voter turnout was the same in 2000 as four years ago, the turnout by blacks in pivotal states such as Florida and Illinois increased dramatically. Gore benefited enormously: 93 percent of Florida's black voters backed the vice president, compared with 86 percent for President Clinton four years ago.

The Christian Coalition is the Republicans' equivalent of the Democrats' AFL-CIO. The coalition distributed 70 million voter guides last November, up from 40 million in 1996, but it had nothing like the unions' voter delivery system on Election Day. Members of the pro-business National Federation of Independent Business were contacted by phone and mail six million times, up from three million times four years ago. But the federation has no organized plan to get voters to the polls.

In all, the Republican Victory 2000 drive spent an estimated $100 million on automated phone-mail messages, a paid and a volunteer phone-bank operation, a massive direct-mail drive, and an Internet and E-mail operation. The Democrats' Election Day drive cost about $30 million and fielded 50,000 volunteers. Although Republicans outspent Democrats several-fold, they did not outorganize their rivals because of the highly efficient and experienced AFL-CIO effort.

In the area of organization, then, Gore had a slight but decisive advantage over Bush.

THE CANDIDATES AS CAMPAIGNERS

With his ready smile and easy way with people, George W. Bush reminded people of Ronald Reagan; Bush was what the polls call a "natural" on the hustings. The governor even strolled back to the press section of his campaign plane to banter with reporters. In the minds of some observers, Al Gore, always prepared, ever-striving, resembled another former but less attractive president: Jimmy Carter. Gore compensated for his admitted lack of charm with a ferocious tenacity—he was still phoning the news media and urging Democrats to turn out the vote late in the afternoon of Election Day.

The early line on Bush was that he was not smart enough to be president, but after his steady performance in the three presidential debates, most Americans agreed that the Texas governor could handle the programmatic and intellectual demands of the presidency. Gore was overly aggressive in the debates—at one point he came so close to his opponent that Barbara Bush later said she feared the vice president would punch her son in the nose. Gore was eager to portray himself as a fighter, while Bush portrayed himself as the healer. TV viewers seemed to prefer healing to fighting.

Bush is a delegator, who approves a strategy and then lets aides implement it. He is enormously disciplined. He stuck to a basic message of tax cuts, Social Security reform, a stronger military, and school choice wherever he went. Gore is an 18-

hours-a-day, hands-on, check-every-nuance administrator. During the campaign, Gore seemed to offer almost as many themes as there are states in the Union, finally settling on a classic Democratic argument—he was the man of the people fighting the evil corporate interests.

The candidates understood that personality matters: they appeared more often on The Tonight Show With Jay Leno than Meet the Press. In the final weekend before election day, both nominees taped self-deprecating cameos for the satirical Saturday Night Live. But the affable Bush topped the uptight Gore in almost every poll. "Gore is smarter, more articulate, more experienced," explained pollster John Zogby, "and yet he's not blowing this election away." Because, said Zogby, "he's just a less likable character than George Bush."

In the category of candidate-campaigner, therefore, George Bush clearly bested Al Gore. Bush's only serious flaw was a tendency to coast when ahead: he took a Sunday off just one week before the election and never stumped as energetically (one could say frenetically) as Gore.

ISSUES

Candidates distill the issues in the closing days of a campaign, and Bush and Gore followed this traditional pattern in late October and early November 2000. Before conservative crowds, Governor Bush stressed cutting taxes, strengthening the military, and promoting school choice (i.e., vouchers). To swing voters, he promised prescription drugs for seniors, Social Security reform, and tax cuts for the middle class and working poor. "My opponent," Bush invariably said, "thinks the surplus is the government's money. I believe the surplus is the people's money."

Before Democratic audiences, Vice President Gore portrayed himself as a Harry Truman–like populist who advocated equal pay for women, housing protection for gays, and an increase in the minimum wage. He consistently attacked his opponent as beholden to millionaires and special interests. He dismissed Bush's tax cut plan as "a massive redistribution of wealth from the middle class to the wealthiest few" and his proposed partial privatization of Social Security as "dangerous." In contrast, Gore offered targeted tax cuts aimed mostly at lower- and middle-income taxpayers and increased federal spending of at least $2.5 trillion over 10 years.

In other words, George Bush campaigned as a slightly to

the right, limited-government Republican while Al Gore campaigned as a slightly to the left, activist-government Democrat. In the 2000 presidential race, Bush was no Reagan revolutionary, Gore no Clinton New Democrat.

Because Americans are divided in their feelings about the role of government—exit polls revealed an electorate wary about Washington's entanglement in their lives but still desirous of federal entitlements—neither candidate was able to dominate in the area of issues.

THE MEDIA

There are two kinds of media in a political campaign— "free" media (what television, radio, newspapers, magazines, and other media report about a candidate and his campaign) and paid media (what the candidates say about themselves in advertisements run mostly on television).

In 2000, both major candidates showed they had studied and absorbed the lessons of the successful Reagan and Clinton campaigns. Bush and Gore usually spoke before enthusiastic crowds with a bank of American flags behind them and a field of placards before them. Their stump speeches were a litany of short, punchy sentences, crafted for sound bites. They wore blue suits and red ties for the TV debates but switched to open-necked shirts at partisan rallies.

Although most Washington journalists lean to the left politically, they did not regard Vice President Gore with the same fondness as they had President Clinton. They conceded Gore his brainpower but mocked his constantly shifting search on the campaign trail for the right-colored suit and the right facial expression.

In contrast, many national reporters personally liked Governor Bush, although they doubted his capacity to be president. They welcomed Bush's relaxed manner, his sense of humor, his willingness to talk informally with them outside staged events. They even came to admit that he was not as dumb as they had suggested he was at the beginning of the campaign.

But when the race narrowed in the last week, many in the media revealed a political bias. On the final weekend, Gore asked churchgoers at a prayer breakfast to support him, saying, "Good overcomes evil if we choose that outcome." And responding to Bush's promise to appoint "strict constructionists" to the Supreme Court, Gore recalled "the strictly constructed meaning" applied to the Constitution when it was written—"how some people [i.e., slaves] were considered three-fifths of a human being." The networks barely mentioned the vice president's highly charged remarks.

In contrast, they went into a frenzy over a 24-year-old story of young George W. Bush being arrested for driving under the influence of alcohol in Maine. ABC's Nightline devoted an entire program to the incident, NBC's Today much of its morning show.

In the area of paid media, Gore and Bush spent millions of dollars a day to keep their campaign messages running and up to date in key markets across the country. Many ads presented a smiling, energetic, concerned candidate, explaining how he would solve the problems of the day. Others—so-called attack ads—critically analyzed his opponent's positions, often by omitting essential facts. A GOP [Republican Party] ad, for example, derided Gore for claiming he invented the Internet, although the vice president admitted he had exaggerated in taking credit.

The TV networks' most egregious and public error came on election night when they declared, just before 8:00 P.M., that Gore had carried Florida, signaling that Bush had probably lost the presidential race, only to reverse themselves six hours later to say that Bush had won the state and therefore the presidency, only to retract that assertion 90 minutes later and admit the state was too close to call. "This syndrome of rushing to judgment," wrote veteran correspondent Georgie Anne Geyer, "has, step by foolish step, been institutionalized into television news."

In the fifth and final area of a presidential campaign, the media, Bush and Gore once again were almost tied, with neither candidate having a clear advantage.

The 2000 presidential election reflected American politics in all its high drama (the presidential debates) and low comedy (butterfly ballots and hanging chads). But Americans did not worry needlessly about the outcome. They knew there would be no military coup, no UN peacekeeping force, no new election. They knew, rather, that in time there would be a winner, a transition, and an inauguration. And they were encouraged by the spirit of bipartisanship that emerged in Washington, led by the man who offered himself as a unifier and not a divider during the campaign—George W. Bush, the forty-third president of the United States of America.

The Predicted Tie

James W. Ceaser and Andrew E. Busch

In the following 2001 article James W. Ceaser and
Andrew E. Busch examine the political climate of the
United States that culminated in the closest and most
controversial election in a century. Ceaser and Busch
note that Republican and Democratic voters had
reached parity in numbers during the 2000 election,
leaving little doubt that a race between George W.
Bush and Al Gore would be close. The authors then
trace the events of election night in which a see-saw
contest for electoral votes left neither candidate a
clear winner. James W. Ceaser is professor of government and foreign affairs at the University of Virginia.
He is the author of several books on American politics
and American political thought. Coauthor Andrew E.
Busch teaches American government at the University
of Denver where he is an associate professor. He has
also authored several books on American politics.

Compared to the results of other general elections in American history, the contest in 2000 ended with the closest possible division of seats between the parties in the Senate (50
senators from each party), the fourth closest division of seats
(by percentage) in the House, and the second closest presidential race by the electoral vote. . . . It is by far the closest
election in American history. . . .

Trouble began on election night with the collapse of the
television network's vote projection system, which is relied
on today, informally, to declare presidential winners. Trouble spread next to disputes about the accuracy and reliabil-
ity of election and balloting machinery in Florida, and by
implication in the nation as a whole. It then finally moved
on to confusion over Florida's election laws and, more omi-
nously, to controversy over the rightful powers of state judi-
cial and political institutions.

James W. Ceaser and Andrew E. Busch, *The Perfect Tie: The True Story of the 2000 Presidential Election.* Lanham, MD: Rowman & Littlefield Publishers, Inc., 2001. Copyright
© 2001 by Rowman & Littlefield Publishers, Inc. Reproduced by permission.

In the end, the nation's political system held up. Or at least it held up in the sense that a president of the United States, George W. Bush, was finally chosen, albeit more than five weeks after election day. . . . It took a highly controversial decision by the U.S. Supreme Court (determined by a five to four vote) overruling a highly controversial decision by the Florida Supreme Court (determined by a four to three vote) to issue George Bush his election. Bush assumed the presidency with the formal blessings of almost everyone in the political class, and with general support from the American people. . . .

The last disputed presidential election [was] the Hayes-Tilden contest of 1876, when a close national election result led to a revisiting of the votes in a few of the reconstruction governments in the southern states, including Florida. . . . [In the 2000 election] it was the exceptional way the vote was distributed around the country, coupled with an unexpected technical challenge that by chance occurred in the state of Florida, where the difference in vote totals between the two main candidates was smaller than the margin of error that the electoral mechanisms could handle. . . .

PREDICTING THE TIE

Could the improbable results of the election of 2000 have been foreseen? . . .

Political scientists in the middle of the last decade began to suggest that the general electoral condition of our era made a perfect tie conceivable. Even to think in such terms, it must be said, required a conceptual breakthrough in the study of elections. Historical patterns had led analysts to conclude that "normal" electoral alignments consisted of one party gaining a clear long-term advantage over the other, as the Democrats had managed to do for the two or three decades following the elections of 1932 and 1936. Electoral observers in the 1990s were therefore on the lookout for one of the parties to establish clear dominance. . . . Repeated observations in the middle 1990s [showed, however,] that Democratic and Republican partisans were fairly evenly balanced in the electorate. . . . According to a well-known political scientist, Paul Allen Beck, Democrats . . . are about a third of the electorate (perhaps a bit more) and Republicans also about a third. The large remaining slice of the modern electoral pie contains the grouping of non-partisan voters, also roughly a third of the electorate, therefore equal to each of the two partisan slices.

This segment floats between the two parties and is easily attracted to independent candidates and third parties. Modern elections accordingly display a good deal of volatility from one contest to the next. . . .

Successful presidential candidates have been those who have found a way to maintain the enthusiasm and support of their core supporters, while managing to appeal to a larger portion of this floating vote.

Now imagine an election in which almost all of the partisans stick by the candidate of their own party and in which the short-term factors pressure the floating voters equally in different and ultimately offsetting directions. Given the basic shape of the modern electorate, the result would approach parity. This is just about what happened in 2000. Party adherents voted overwhelmingly for "their" candidates, a result that probably had less to do with any extraordinary appeal of Gore and Bush among the candidates' own supporters than with their inability to generate much cross-partisan interest. Whatever the cause, partisan faithfulness in 2000 reached the highest level for any modern election and netted each candidate a roughly equal number of votes by partisans. Next, the net effect of short-term forces split the nonpartisan or floating voters about down the middle. In some instances these forces pressured different groups of voters in opposite directions, though in approximately equal amounts. In other instances these forces pulled and tugged the same people in different directions, causing cross-pressured voters, by far the greatest number of whom were women, to swing greatly back and forth between the candidates. . . .

There are two basic ways of measuring relative party strength, one . . . that looks at how people respond in *surveys* to the question of which party they identify with (Democratic, Republican, or Independent), and the other that looks at which party's candidates people actually vote for in real *elections*. By this last measure, as we have seen, the results in 2000 show the two parties at near parity for each of the national institutions. It is also important, of course, to consider how people vote for the three major political offices at the state level: governor, the state Senate, and the state House. The results here are striking. For the state legislative chambers, Democrats in 2000 control 25 state Houses to 24 for the Republicans, while Republicans control 24 state Senates to 21 for the Democrats. Four Senates are tied between the two parties. There is, however, one office today where one of the parties holds a clear advantage. Among the governors, 29 are Republican and 19 are Democrats. And therein lies a tale. It is surely no accident that the president, George Bush, not only came from the ranks of the Republican governors, but also was nominated with their support and campaigned for the presidency, conspicuously, with their help.

These figures make clear that an important change in relative party strength has taken place over the past decade. At the beginning of the decade, the Republican Party was predominantly a presidential party. Republicans held the presidency (as they had since 1980), but both houses of Congress were in the hands of the Democrats. In the states, the Democrats had the edge in governors (30D-20R) and the decided advantage among state Senates (38-11) and state Houses (40-9). By 1994 the contours of partisan control had begun to change. Democrats now held the presidency, while Republicans captured the House and Senate. Republicans in 1994 gained their large advantage among governors (30R-19D), and had pulled almost even among state Senates (25D-24R) and close among state Houses (26D-22R). The elections of the 1990s therefore did indeed realign American politics. But they did so not by placing a single party in control, but by bringing one of the parties (the Republicans) from an overall minority status into a position of parity. . . .

As the [2000] campaign entered late October, forecasters with help from the hot new instrument of daily tracking polls became even more deeply impressed with the sustained closeness of this race, constantly calling it a "dead heat." And what a peculiar kind of dead heat it was—not just close, but oscillating. The Gallup tracking poll showed the lead changing no fewer than nine times over the course of the fall campaign. Although similar data are not available from past elections, the best guess is that previous close races have tended to follow the pattern of a horse race or marathon, in which one candidate is consistently in the lead, and at the very end the trailing candidate makes a single upward bid, either managing to pull ahead or ending up just short. But the 2000 race continually moved back and forth in September and October, with George W. Bush generally maintaining an ever so slight lead in the final week or so of the campaign. At the last possible moment in early November, however, the polls began to close with momentum swinging in the direction of Al Gore.

Final results of four of the most respected polling firms were as follows: Zogby/MSNBC (Gore plus 2), Gallup (Bush plus 2), Washington Post (Bush plus 1), CBS (Gore plus 1). All of these results, of course, were well within the margin of error that allowed victory for either candidate. And averaged together, they just happen to make a Perfect Tie. . . .

ELECTION NIGHT 2000

[On election night in 2000,] the television commentators, who were privy to the early returns of the national exit polls, let it be known at 7 P.M. that this election was going to be close—very, very close. And to eliminate any suspicions that this claim was just media hype or feigned impartiality, some took the unusual step of saying that they really meant it. If this was disappointing news for Bush supporters, things shortly would return much worse. Just before 8 P.M. the networks declared Al Gore to be the winner in Florida. Within the next hour and a half, Gore was also awarded Pennsylvania and Michigan. Bush had thus lost all three of the big battleground states. Almost every scenario for a Bush victory depended on his carrying at least one of them. What hope remained now for Bush was the slim prospect of winning almost all of the remaining states where the outcome had been considered doubtful. That, or else the miracle that only George Bush himself had predicted: winning California. . . .

Under these circumstances, a good many sensible citizens, with jobs to attend the next morning and with children to awaken for school, took the cue and went off to bed. . . .

[But George Bush] questioned the networks' call of Florida. His sources on the ground, he insisted, were reporting something very different. Viewers no doubt regarded this statement as understandable spin, designed to buoy supporters in the West, where voting was still going on. The networks, as the anchors assured viewers, make calls only when they are certain. As [CBS news anchor] Dan Rather put it, "If we call a state, you can take it to the bank. Book it!" But to everyone's astonishment, Bush's claim, not Dan Rather's, proved correct. The networks soon discovered that they had miscalled Florida, based, so it was later explained, on important errors and miscalculations made from their combined pool source of information, the Voter News Service. Shortly before 10 P.M. EST the networks pulled Florida from Gore's column and placed it back among the undecideds.

Viewers were now witnessing a near television equivalent of the famous media debacle of 1948, when major newspapers declared Dewey the victor over Truman. Only this time there were real consequences to the error. A wrong call had been made not only before voters in other states had voted, but also—contrary to general network policy—while some of Florida's own polls were still open. The western part of the Florida panhandle lies in the central, not the eastern, time zone. Were some Florida voters discouraged from turning out at the last moment in areas of the state that strongly favored George W. Bush? . . . Bush now actually ahead in the vote count in Florida, CBS News anchor Dan Rather commented at 10:06, "It's beginning to look increasingly like the advantage is going to George W. Bush." By 10:10 he had Gore "hanging, hanging by a thread." Still, after what had just happened no one was ready to call Florida again. . . .

Along with the change in status of Florida from Gore to undecided, over the next few hours Bush either won or remained in the running in enough of the states to keep alive the possibility of his winning an electoral victory without carrying Florida. This possibility, greater than most had earlier expected, surged and then faded as more states were called. At one point, indeed, NBC's Tim Russert, who had abandoned high-technology graphics for makeshift calculations with a Magic Marker, sketched a highly plausible scenario under which each candidate would win 269 electoral votes, a tie that would throw the election into the House of Representatives. But by about 1 A.M., the possibility of Bush winning without capturing Florida ended, as Gore closed in on the contested states of Iowa, Minnesota, and Wisconsin. Everything finally narrowed down to just Florida. Like the classic drama, in which all of the subplots must first be resolved before turning back to the central story line, whoever now carried Florida would pass the threshold of 270 electoral votes and become the 43rd president of the United States.

In the actual vote count in Florida, George Bush now held a modest lead, although commentators noted that some of the Democratic-leaning areas in large southern Florida counties had not yet reported. Bush's lead began to dwindle, but so too did the number of precincts outstanding. It was a race between Bush's vote margin (his distance ahead) and the precincts remaining (the distance to the finish line). Would Bush be able to hold on? His lead, once 130,000 votes, shrank to 30,000. Then, just after 2 A.M., his lead ballooned again to 59,000, a seemingly insurmountable advantage. One network after another announced Florida for George W. Bush, making him the 43rd president of the United States. . . .

PREMATURE CONCESSION

But this drama was nowhere near being over.

Having watched the network's declaration of Bush's victory, Vice President Gore called Governor Bush and graciously offered his congratulations in what was reported as a brief, but correct and pleasant, conversation. Gore said that he would be making his way shortly from his hotel to the Legislative Plaza, where he would offer his public concession. Governor Bush began to go over his victory comments.

As Vice President Gore's motorcade made its way to the plaza, the television anchors proceeded with their soothing narrative. They were now clearly more relaxed with everything in the studio once again under control, even as they felt compelled, with a great deal of relief, to mention the turbulence earlier in the evening. As the various pundits, commentators, and anchors continued on, Bush's vote margin in Florida, displayed on the boards behind the anchor desks, began to shrink dramatically. Some took note of this fact in passing, as if it were a small curiosity. It was inconceivable that their system for calling elections could fail a second time. But suddenly, when the margin fell beneath 6,000 votes, the actual vote totals could not be ignored.

Meanwhile back in the real world, frantic calls were placed from Gore supporters in Florida to his headquarters, and then from his headquarters to the motorcade, trying to get the message through to the vice president not to go ahead with a public concession. On arriving at the plaza and learning of the closeness of the vote, a decision was made to wait. Shortly thereafter, the vice president made a second call to Governor Bush [retracting his concession]. . . .

For the second time that night, the networks now had to retract their Florida call. . . . George Bush was ahead in the counting of the ballots in Florida, and this result was—and would have to be—the most important material fact. But with a lead this narrow, nobody could have expected the vice president to forgo the automatic recount to which he

was entitled under Florida law, and no one would have expected that he should concede until that recount had taken
place. The only "real" story, then, was that no definitive result had yet occurred. The networks' call helped to set in
motion a different story, where one candidate (Gore) now
seemed to have to go further to change a "result," while the
other (Bush) was pushed into an awkward position of grov-
eling for the office that had been "awarded" to him.

At just about this point, as if to relieve momentarily the
gathering tension, another singular event, unrelated to the
main drama, intruded itself. All night long, George Bush had
been ahead in the national popular vote, even as he trailed
at times in the electoral vote. This result corresponded to a
scenario that had been widely discussed before the election:
a race that would be close enough to enable Al Gore to win
the electoral vote while losing the popular. Gore, in fact, had
been queried on this matter in a number of television interviews. Very few thought that the race could ever turn out the
other way, with Bush losing the popular vote but winning
the presidency. Yet now, with the returns from California
coming in, Al Gore for the first time pulled ahead in the national popular vote, and it was a safe bet that he would remain so. If Bush were to win the presidency, he would be the
one, strangely enough, to be the "minority" president. Commentators took note of this striking fact, important politically because the Democrats would by the next day begin to
use it to Gore's advantage. But its significance for the moment paled next to the outcome of the real drama.

Having now "unconceded," Al Gore returned to his hotel
room reportedly to go to sleep. The emotional swings of
what remained of the two crowds were on the surface a near
reversal of what had taken place a couple of hours earlier: in
Gore's camp, renewed hope and chants of "recount, recount"; in Bush's camp, frustration. Probably a fairer description of the scenes was that partisans on both sides were
more dazed than energized. There had been one twist of fortune too many. Instead of the vice president arriving to deliver his concession, it was William Daley, Gore's campaign
chairman, who appeared before the crowd. Daley made
clear that the election was not over, and that "until the results, the recount, is concluded and the results of Florida become official, our campaign continues." An hour later Donald L. Evans briefly addressed the few remaining Bush

supporters. "We hope and believe we have elected the next president of the United States."

What had begun was another phase of the 2000 race, a postelection campaign that would last five more weeks and that would be filled with as many ups and downs as the melodrama of election eve.

Victory at Last

Andrew Phillips

After thirty-five days of post-election campaigning in
U.S. courts, President George W. Bush turned immediately to his two political priorities: people and policy. Whatever doubts surrounded his election, Bush's
priority would be to reconcile the nation after year-
long campaign rancor and to facilitate a spirit of cooperation with the Democrats.

In this December 2000 article, Andrew Phillips
reports on the victory of George W. Bush in the
highly contested presidential election and discusses
how the questionable legitimacy of the presidency, a
divided Congress, and a slowing economy were the
best things President Bush had going for him. Phillips
covers Washington for Rogers Media.

Expect to hear a lot over the next few weeks about Bob Bullock, a legendary Texas Democrat who plays a key role in
the George W. Bush Official Mythology. When Bush was first
running to be governor in 1994, Bullock was the state's powerful lieutenant-governor and the key power broker in its
legislature. Bush knew he could get little done without Bullock's cooperation, so three weeks before the election he
went to the older man's home and told him: "I'm here to tell
you that I want to work with you." After Bush won, the Republican governor and the Democratic lawmaker did forge a
successful partnership—one that allowed Bush to take credit
for a string of reforms that he used to demonstrate his readiness for the White House.

The story is dear to Bush supporters, who use it as proof
that their man has what it takes to unite bitter rivals and
heal old wounds. Bush himself invoked the name of Bullock
(who died in 1999) . . . as he stood in the chamber of the
Democratic-controlled Texas House of Representatives to
address Americans for the first time as their president-elect.

Exactly an hour earlier, Vice-President Al Gore had finally bowed to the inevitable and gracefully conceded defeat. Now, Bush implicitly promised, he would do for the United States what he did for Texas—reach out to his opponents. Five weeks of recounting and recrimination would give way to reconciliation and renewal. "I was not elected to serve one party," he pledged, "but to serve one nation."

A DIVIDED NATION

Good luck. The Bullock story, like so many others in Bush's improbable rise to power, conceals as much as it reveals. Gov. Bush had to deal with a state legislature that meets only every two years for a session limited to 140 days, and a Democratic party dominated by old-style conservatives (like Bullock) who would be well to the right of Republicans in many parts of the country. President Bush will take office at noon on Jan. 20 on the steps of a Congress divided and riven by round-the-clock ideological warfare. The Democrats he will face are decidedly not the get-along, cut-a-deal types he so successfully charmed back home.

Just as bad, right-wingers in his own party may quickly become impatient if Bush does stick to the middle. The politics of personal persuasion, he may quickly find, don't go all that far in a capital better known for tear-out-the-throat attack politics. "The Democrats are going to be like sharks," warns Allan Lichtman, an expert on the presidency at American University in Washington. "They're going to be swimming silently for a while, but as soon as there's any blood from Bush in the water, there will be a feeding frenzy."

Still, soothing words about unity and cooperation were clearly what Americans wanted to hear after a year-long election campaign—plus the rancorous fight over ballots triggered by the photo finish in Florida. The back-to-back speeches by Gore and Bush capped an extraordinary six days that saw Gore's hopes momentarily revived by one Supreme Court (the one in Florida), then finally dashed by another (the one in Washington). The man who had hoped to arrive in the White House as a healing "uniter, not a divider," promising to "change the tone in Washington," instead found himself winning only after a legal donnybrook far more divisive than the lacklustre campaign.

The omens are not good, although Gore did his part to repair the breach. After taking a night to digest the Supreme

Court's confusing but ultimately devastating ruling, he made his decision. The presidency, the job for which he had been groomed from childhood by his senator father, for which he had worked all his adult life, would not be his. . . .

Gore managed to strike a tone that was both self-deprecating and dignified, a combination he never seemed to find during the campaign itself. He acknowledged Bush's right to claim the White House and promised his support despite the bitterness of losing the presidency through a decision by a Supreme Court split cleanly along ideological lines. "While I strongly disagree with the Supreme Court's decision," said Gore, "I accept it. I accept the finality of the outcome. What remains of partisan rancour must now be put aside."

A Tough Job Ahead

But nothing could hide the fact that Bush will always be "President Asterisk"—the man who won the office on a technicality, whose victory hangs on the slenderest of threads. The validity of his court-mandated victory in Florida will be questioned for years to come; he won the electoral college by a single vote more than the bare majority needed; and he lost the nationwide popular vote by 337,576 votes. Only three other men won the presidency while losing the overall vote —and historians have been quick to recall that all three served a single, troubled term in office. The first of them, John Quincy Adams in 1824, was also the only other son of a president to win the office himself.

Bush, clearly, must beat the odds—a tall order for a man who turned seriously to politics only six years ago and who must battle the perception that he is an empty suit, propped up by Republican heavyweights and his father's old lieutenants. The road to his eventual victory only made a tough job more difficult. The campaign itself, though inevitably partisan, was not particularly divisive. The candidates were uninspiring; few but the most partisan voters found much to fight about. Instead, it was the unprecedented 35-day recount circus in Florida that inflamed passions. And the final scene of the play, with the U.S. Supreme Court first intervening in dramatic style to stop another effort to count disputed ballots, and then finally crushing Gore's remaining chance at victory, left a bitter taste.

There were few hopes that the high court would allow a

recount when it met on Dec. 11 to hear 90 minutes of oral arguments in Bush v. Gore, Case No. 00-949. Two days earlier, the court had split 5 to 4, between its conservative majority and its moderate-to-liberal minority, and ordered an immediate halt to a recount authorized by the more liberal Florida Supreme Court. The complex arguments came down to an essential choice: would the federal court decide that manual recounts amounted to an illegal change in the rules of the election after the votes were cast (as the Bush team argued), or would it rule that a recount could be done to make sure that all votes were tallied (as Gore's lawyers contended)?

In the end, the court split again along its ideological fault line. Anyone who had hoped that the Supreme Court might be able to resolve an issue that had already ensnarled state courts and the Florida legislature and threatened to spill over into Congress was sure to be disappointed. The five most conservative judges—Chief Justice William Rehnquist, along with justices Antonin Scalia, Anthony Kennedy, Sandra Day O'Connor and Clarence Thomas—ruled on Dec. 12 against any further recounting of the contested Florida ballots. It came down, they said, to the fact that there was no clear standard for deciding when a voter had marked a punch card for Gore or for Bush—and that would violate the clause in the Constitution guaranteeing "equal protection" to all citizens.

Further, they ruled, prolonging the count beyond Dec. 12 would throw doubt on the validity of the presidential electors selected by Florida because of a federal law protecting electors from challenge if they are chosen by that day. As a result, the five judges wrote, "it is obvious that the count cannot be conducted in compliance with the requirement of equal protection and due process." The bottom line: no more recounts. Bush would be the victor in Florida by a margin of just 537 votes out of six million statewide.

Gore supporters were outraged—and they needed to look no further for ammunition than the series of blistering dissenting opinions issued by the four judges who found themselves in the minority. Ironically, it was the liberal minority that ended up lecturing the conservative majority for failing to respect the authority of a state court—a traditional conservative position. Justice John Paul Stevens, appointed in 1975 by President Gerald Ford, accused the five-member majority of effectively disenfranchising voters whose choices were not registered during machine counts of the ballots. And, he wrote, the court showed no confidence in the state judges who would be called on to oversee any new recount: "Although we may never know with complete certainty the identity of the winner of this year's presidential election, the identity of the loser is perfectly clear. It is the nation's confidence in the judge as an impartial guardian of the rule of law."

Justice David Souter, another liberal, appointed in 1990 by the new president-elect's father, underlined the paradox involved in the court's first halting the recount—and then ruling that it could not continue because time had run out: "If this court had allowed the state to follow the course indi-

---

Post-Election Events

The post-election campaign encompassed five weeks of battling in the state and U.S. federal courts. Election analysts James W. Ceaser and Andrew E. Busch show by date the unfolding of events that ultimately gave George W. Bush the White House victory.

- Nov. 8th: The morning after: Bush leads by 926 votes; automatic machine recount begins.
- Nov. 9th: Gore requests hand counts in Broward, Miami-Dade, Palm Beach, and Volusia counties.
- Nov. 10th: The machine recount is completed; Bush's lead slips to 327 votes.
- Nov. 12th: Palm Beach and Volusia counties begin their hand recount.
- Nov. 15th: Katherine Harris collects the final votes from all Florida counties.
- Nov. 17th: The Florida Supreme Court issues an injunction, blocking certification of a final vote tally.
- Nov. 18th: Overseas absentee ballots are counted; Bush's lead is back up to 930 votes.
- Nov. 20th: The Florida Supreme Court holds its hearing on Gore's motion to include late hand-recount totals in the official vote certification.
- Nov. 21st: The Florida Supreme Court hands down ruling, extending the certification deadline five days.
- Nov. 24th: The U.S. Supreme Court announces it will hear Bush's appeal of the Florida Supreme Court decision.
- Nov. 25th: The "Brooks Brothers Revolution" erupts, and Miami-Dade County stops its hand recount.

cated by the opinions of its own Supreme Court, it is entirely possible that there would ultimately have been no issue requiring our review, and political tension could have worked itself out in Congress."

The ruling may have shattered any illusion that the top court is above the partisan fray. Critics of the conservative majority found even more to fuel their concerns in reports that one of Scalia's sons works for the Washington law firm that argued Bush's case before the Supreme Court, while Thomas's wife is at a right-wing think-tank in the capital, helping to recruit prospective members of a new Bush administration. It all looked too convenient, though Thomas told high-school students the morning after the momentous

---

- Nov. 26th: Katherine Harris certifies the vote, giving Bush a 537-vote victory.
- Nov. 27th: Gore contests the certification.
- Nov. 30th: The Florida legislature announces a special session to debate naming Florida's electors themselves.
- Dec. 1st: The U.S. Supreme Court hears oral arguments on the Florida Supreme Court recount deadline extension decision.
- Dec. 4th: Judge N. Sanders Sauls rejects Gore's contestation of the certified results, and the U.S. Supreme Court vacates and remands the Florida Supreme Court's certification deadline extension decision.
- Dec. 8th: The Florida Supreme Court orders manual recounts of all counties with significant numbers of undervotes.
- Dec. 9th: The U.S. Supreme Court halts the manual recounts and schedules oral arguments on Bush's appeal of the Florida Supreme Court order.
- Dec. 11th: The U.S. Supreme Court holds oral arguments in *Bush v. Gore.*
- Dec. 12th: The U.S. Supreme Court rules for Bush, effectively ending the hand recounts.
- Dec. 13th: Gore concedes defeat, and Bush accepts victory.
- Dec. 18th: Individual state electors make official Bush's 271-to-266-vote victory in the Electoral College.
- Jan. 6th: A joint session of Congress opens and agrees to the electoral votes submitted by the states.
- Jan. 20th: Bush is sworn in as the president of the United States.

James W. Ceaser and Andrew E. Busch, *The Perfect Tie: The True Story of the 2000 Presidential Election.* Lanham, MD: Rowman & Littlefield, 2001.

ruling that he has never heard his fellow judges discuss partisan politics. "Don't try to apply the rules of the political world to this institution," he said. "They do not apply."

BUSH'S IMMEDIATE PRIORITIES

Whatever the doubts surrounding his election, the newly anointed president-elect had to turn immediately to two priorities: people and policy. A new administration must fill some 6,000 jobs, including several hundred senior positions that must be confirmed by the Senate. Doubts over the outcome in Florida made it awkward for Bush to publicly announce top appointments—and impossible to begin the lengthy background and security checks needed to get a new administration in place by Jan. 20 [2001]. But that changed quickly with the naming of retired general Colin Powell as secretary of state, four days after the Supreme Court decision. Condoleezza Rice, a foreign policy veteran of the previous Bush administration, . . . [was] named national security adviser. They would be the most senior African-Americans appointed to any U.S. cabinet—a move that might help Bush among black voters, who opposed him on election day by a whopping nine to one. . . .

Bush will have to decide how to best use his small stock of political capital. Right-wingers in his own party are champing at the bit. Tom DeLay, the ultraconservative Republican whip in the House of Representatives, said recently that he had been waiting his whole life to have his party control the White House as well as both houses of Congress (Republicans have a very slight edge in the House, and the tie in the Senate can be broken by the vice-president). "The things we have been dreaming about we can now do unfettered," he said.

But Bush's advisers have made clear that they know they will be anything but unfettered. Instead, Bush said . . . he will start off by proposing action on education reform and lowering prescription drug prices for seniors—areas where he may be able to find allies among Democrats. And rather than push ahead with a massive tax cut, as he proposed during the campaign, he is more likely to start with something more modest, such as doing away with the federal inheritance tax.

Expectations could hardly be lower—questionable legitimacy, a divided Congress, even a slowing economy. Of course, low expectations may be the best thing Bush has going for him. He likes to remind people that he has always been underestimated, even by his parents, who earlier put their White House hopes on his smarter, more telegenic brother, Jeb, now governor of Florida. In the best of circumstances, George W. Bush was unlikely to be a great president. Now, with so many obvious handicaps, even modest achievements may be greeted as major triumphs.

CHAPTER 4

THE WHITE HOUSE

PEOPLE
WHO MADE
HISTORY

GEORGE W. BUSH

The First Foreign Policy Test

William Schneider

Chicago Tribune writer William Schneider evaluates President Bush's handling of his first foreign policy challenge in office. In April 2001, a U.S. Navy spy plane collided with a Chinese fighter pilot over China. The U.S. plane was forced to land inside the Communist nation with twenty-four Americans on board. China demanded that the American government apologize for the incident. Schneider states that Bush's discipline and deal-making were responsible for getting the hostages returned without acquiescing to the Chinese. For ten days, Bush relied heavily on his team of experienced advisers to find the formula that would satisfy the Chinese government. The Bush administration released tapes showing the incident was the fault of the Chinese pilot and that China had a policy of harassing U.S. reconnaissance planes. Once the incident was resolved, Bush also avoided political pressure to make the Chinese pay for the incident.

As a result of the 11-day standoff between the United States and China, we learned something about President Bush and something about the American people.

We learned that President Bush is not a confrontation-seeker. He's a deal-maker. Bush was serious when he said in debating Al Gore last October: "If we're an arrogant nation, they'll resent us. If we're a humble nation but strong, they'll welcome us." Or at least, go along with us.

What we learned about the American people is the same thing. Americans, too, prefer a deal to a showdown. Like their President, the American people show no excess devotion to abstract principles. . . . The rule in this case was, "Get

William Schneider, "Bush Wins 'Let's Make a Deal,'" *National Journal,* vol. 33, April 21, 2001, p. 1194. Copyright © 2001 by National Journal Group, Inc. Reproduced by permission.

the crew." They're back. We won. Let's move on.

By that standard, Bush passed his first test in an international crisis. He demonstrated resolve by resisting pressure to do something rash that might have endangered American lives. "Our approach has been to keep this accident from becoming an international incident," the President said at the outset. The China standoff ended just in time. It was in danger of turning into a full-fledged hostage situation, with debilitating consequences for Bush. The U.S. government could have ended up being held hostage by the crisis, as the Carter Administration was during the Iranian ordeal: "America Held Hostage" became the media drumbeat.

In this case, the Bush Administration had to spend 10 days publicly searching for a formula that would satisfy the Chinese. "Sorry" wouldn't do. We had to be "very sorry" for the loss of the Chinese pilot. Were we also "very sorry" that our pilot entered their air space without permission? Not particularly. "For that, we are very sorry," Secretary of State Colin L. Powell said, "but glad he did it."

Former U.S. Ambassador James Lilley noted: "The Chinese insist upon sincerity. I notice that 'sincere regret' was put in there. That must have given them a blush of pleasure." But it certainly did not give Americans a blush of pride.

PUBLIC OPINION

A week into the crisis, the Gallup Poll asked Americans whether the U.S. should apologize to the Chinese. The answer was no, by 54 percent to 41 percent. That's a "No," but it's not a "Hell, no."

To hear "Hell, no," you had to ask men. Men opposed an apology by 64 percent to 31 percent. Being a man, apparently, means never having to say you're sorry. On the other hand, women favored an apology by 51 percent to 44 percent: "Well, maybe, yes, if it will get our crew back."

Conservatives were certainly not happy with the U.S. loss of face. The *Weekly Standard* declared: "President Bush has revealed weakness. And he has revealed fear: fear of the political, strategic, and economic consequences of meeting a Chinese challenge." For the most part, however, conservatives were willing to cut Bush some slack. Imagine what would have happened if Bill Clinton had been the President who made those concessions to China. Conservatives would be howling for his blood.

The Chinese extorted concessions from the United States. Embarrassing? Yes, but Americans put saving lives over saving face. Once the lives of the crew were saved, Bush felt some pressure to regain face. So he took a harder line: "China's decision to prevent the return of our crew for 11 days is inconsistent with the kind of relationship we have both said we wish to have."

The Administration also released information showing that the accident was the fault of the Chinese pilot and that the Chinese had a policy of deliberately harassing U.S. reconnaissance planes. Moreover, US. officials claim the crew destroyed all vital security information before surrendering to the Chinese.

THE QUESTION OF RETALIATION

Beyond those face-saving revelations, there doesn't seem to be a lot of political pressure to make the Chinese pay. Impose trade sanctions? U.S. business interests would strongly resist that. Sell advanced weapons to Taiwan? The Chinese warn that such a step could be dangerous and provocative. Keep China from hosting the 2008 Olympics? That invites an unflattering comparison to Carter's "punishment" of the Soviet Union for its 1979 invasion of Afghanistan.

Why so little pressure for retaliation? Because Americans don't care that much about foreign policy these days, as long as American lives and interests are not threatened.

Bush provided the one element necessary for diplomatic success: patience. As Condoleezza Rice, his national security adviser, acknowledged: "From time to time, he would buck us up a little bit and say, 'You know, diplomacy takes time.'"

Bush shunned confrontation with China, just as he shunned confrontation with the Senate over his budget. When the Senate slashed Bush's tax cut by a quarter, the President's response was to declare victory and move on. Both actions were perfectly consistent with the American public's mood.

Fulfilling Education Promises

Siobhan Gorman

Postponed by tax cuts and terrorist attacks in the United States, President Bush declared a new era in public education in America by signing a federal education bill into law in 2002. Expanding on the current education package, the Bush administration put statewide accountability systems in place. The new system implements rigid testing requirements, exemplifying Bush's tough-love approach to education reform. But according to Siobhan Gorman, who covers education for the *National Journal*, Bush's real impact on education will be the accountability of his administration to enforce this expanded education bill and all its requirements in the public school system. Gorman states that even with a troubled economy and continuing worries about terrorism, education remains a primary concern for the American people and Bush's presidency.

Amid a throng of cheering teenagers in the Hamilton High School gymnasium, President Bush declared victory. "Today begins a new era, a new time in public education in our country," he intoned confidently into the microphone. "As of this hour, America's schools will be on a new path of reform, and a new path of results." With that, he signed into law the bill that reflected much of his education agenda. This Ohio school was the first stop of the two day tour the president and his merry band of liberal and conservative lawmakers took in January [2002] to celebrate the president's first true bipartisan triumph.

But the party's a bit premature. To be sure, the president gets credit for forging a consensus after years of ideological and political gridlock. And the law does make some significant changes in federal education policy. Nevertheless, the reauthorized Elementary and Secondary Education Act (ESEA) hardly represents a new era. Instead, it builds on at least a decade's worth of federal reform efforts. Where the Bush administration could make its mark is in its enforcement of the law, an area in which few, if any, previous administrations have found the political will to play rough with the states.

The law calls for annual tests in reading and math for children in grades 3 through 8, plus a science test in three different grade levels by the 2007–08 school year. (States were already required to test students once in high school.) States must also establish a definition of a failing school that meets federal guidelines. Schools labeled failing for two or more years face increasingly stringent penalties, which states must impose. The law also leaves a host of issues unresolved, giving the states and the federal Department of Education plenty of wiggle room. Thus the quality of implementation may vary widely. . . .

Lawmakers in both parties hope that this time a combination of tough federal sanctions, more public reporting of student performance, and an aggressive White House will be enough to prompt change in the schoolhouse. "This bill delivers the goals and the tools to achieve them," says Congressman George Miller, D-California, one of the four top congressional negotiators on the bill. Still, he says, "The bill is not a silver bullet."

BUILDING ON PAST PROPOSALS

President Clinton kicked off the ESEA debate in May 1999, when he submitted his proposal to reauthorize the law, which was due to expire that year. But Congress continued arguing about the proposal into 2000, and it was shelved in the din of the presidential election. With the two candidates [Bush and Democrat Al Gore] running even in the polls, neither party wanted to risk passing a bill when there was a good chance that they could send a bill that was more to their guy's liking the next year. Furthermore, education would be a less potent issue on the campaign trail if Congress passed a major education reform bill.

Once elected, President Bush sent the early message that he wanted an education bill, and he wanted it to be a bipartisan one. Before his inauguration, Bush held a bipartisan education meeting in Austin, and among the hand-picked Democrats attending was Sen. Evan Bayh, D-Ind. Bayh and Sen. Joseph I. Lieberman, D-Conn., had put forth an education reform bill in early 2000 called the Three R's, aimed at bridging the partisan divide in education.

Borrowing liberally from Lieberman and Bayh's reform package, Bush said that the 54 federal elementary and secondary education programs should be consolidated into five categories reflecting federal priorities: 1) educating disadvantaged students; 2) teacher quality; 3) English fluency; 4) school choice; and 5) school safety. Bush also proposed that states begin testing children in grades 3 through 8. He wanted to allow children in schools that failed to close the achievement gap for three straight years to use federal money to attend private schools. On his second full day in office, Bush unveiled an education "blueprint" that was essentially the same as his campaign proposal. The White House immediately began negotiating with the 10 centrist Democrats cosponsoring the Lieberman-Bayh bill, which they reintroduced the day Bush unveiled his proposal, in an effort to cut a deal quickly.

VOUCHERS AND BLOCK GRANTS

However, when it became clear by the spring that Bush's tax cut would pass with the help of a few centrist Democrats, the Lieberman-Bayh group became leery of ditching their party a second time. The White House had also begun negotiating with Sen. Edward M. Kennedy, D-Mass., and the centrist Democrats feared that the White House would play the centrist and liberal Democrats against one another. For instance, the White House got Kennedy to agree to a limited voucher to pay for tutoring services. It then took that agreement to the New Democrats, who had been holding out on a voucher compromise, to try to get the New Democrats to incorporate the tutoring proposal into the deal they were negotiating separately with the White House. To avoid this, Lieberman decided that future negotiations would have to include Kennedy.

A new negotiating group formed, this time including the White House, Republicans, New Democrats, and Kennedy sympathizers. After a month of negotiations, the group reached agreement on the two most controversial issues: vouchers and block grants. They went with Kennedy's voucher compromise, which allowed students in failing schools to use federal money for private tutoring. They also agreed to a scaled-back block-grant proposal that would have allowed 7 states and 25 school districts to sign a performance contract with the federal government that would free them of most federal education regulations in exchange for a promise to improve student performance. They thought they had a bill ready to send to the Senate floor.

But at a late-night meeting in mid-April, one congressional aide announced that 80 to 90 percent of the schools in states like Texas and North Carolina, both of which had seen rising achievement scores through the 1990s, would be deemed "failing" under the bill's definition. The bill required states to set performance goals for every demographic group of students. The problem was that if a school didn't meet that goal for any one group in any grade level in any one year, it would be labeled failing.

Two weeks later, the senators settled on a complicated formula that required states to calculate an overall performance grade for a school based on several factors, including improving test scores for poor and minority children. But no longer could a school receive a failing grade solely because its poor and minority students didn't see their test scores rise. By the time this definition was devised, it was early May. The Senate began debate, but it dragged on for six weeks as the Senate juggled campaign finance reform and turned over to Democratic control.

On the House side, the bill moved more quickly. A series of bipartisan negotiations between Reps. Miller and John Boehner, R-Ohio, chairman of the House Committee on Education and the Workforce, produced a bill that was similar to the Senate's, but without the block-grant provisions. The Republican leadership and a handful of rank-and-file conservatives protested. But President Bush weighed in on Boehner and Miller's side, and the House passed the bill on May 23. The Senate passed its version a few weeks later.

SQUABBLING TOWARD COMPROMISE

Still, little was settled on the accountability front. The Senate's rejiggered formula was widely seen as too complicated for parents to understand, and the House's formula would run into the same reality-check problems that the Senate's had before it was revised. The conference committee charged with resolving differences between the House and Senate versions of the bill began meeting in late July, but the bill languished in committee as the members squabbled over details small and large.

In the meantime, fears over the shrinking surplus were beginning to dominate debate on Capitol Hill. Democrats charged that Bush's tax cut made it impossible to fund education adequately. Interest groups concerned with some of the testing and accountability requirements began circling.

"There weren't a lot of bipartisan feelings," remembers Bush education adviser Sandy Kress. "[Bush] was concerned. . . . The momentum clearly had slowed. He was aware of the mood and the difficulties when we came back from the August recess. We were supposed to be farther along."

Then September 11 intervened. When he first heard of the terrorist attacks on the World Trade Center and the Pentagon, Bush was visiting a Florida elementary school to publicly prod Congress to send him a final bill. Perversely enough, the attacks probably helped get the process back on track by ending the political bickering, congressional aides said. The negotiations were kicked up to the conference's top four members: Reps. Miller and Boehner and Sens. Kennedy and Judd Gregg, R-N.H. The thorniest issue—the definition of a failing school—was resolved by the Big Four by late September.

Under the new definition, states must design a plan to raise the children in several demographic groups—black, white, Hispanic, poor, and disabled—to a "proficient" level of achievement on state tests within 12 years. States determine what a proficient score will be and choose an initial goal for the percentage of students in each group that will attain a proficient grade that year. They must raise that bar over time, so that each state reaches 100 percent proficiency 12 years later. If a school does not meet the performance goal for one demographic group, but reduces the number of children who are not proficient by 10 percent, the school will avoid federal penalties. Schools that don't meet either goal will be labeled failing.

While congressional negotiators had agreed to this compromise in September, they didn't announce it until the final conference bill was set in order to avoid opening it up to too much criticism from interest groups and others (as had happened in August) and jeopardizing other negotiations in progress. "We kept it quiet for a long time," said one lawmaker involved in the negotiations process. "It was the most sensitive part of the bill."

THE FINAL BILL

The new testing requirement exemplifies Bush's tough love approach to education reform. "I understand taking tests aren't [sic] fun," the self-proclaimed C student at Yale University told the crowd at Hamilton High. "Too bad." One of the least debated provisions, the requirement for annual testing, is probably the biggest change in the 2002 law. Though the numbers vary depending on how you read the new law, 15 states currently meet the annual testing requirement in math, 17 in reading, and 24 have established a science test, according to the Education Commission of the States.

This is not, however, a sea change in federal policy. Annual testing builds on the efforts initiated by the Clinton administration in 1994, which in turn built on ideas put forth by President George H.W. Bush when he convened the state governors at the first National Education Summit in 1989. "It's a continuation of an era," said John F. "Jack" Jennings, director of the Center on Education Policy and a longtime Democratic aide on the House education committee.

In 1994, Congress began requiring states to establish academic standards in each grade and to create tests to assess whether children have learned the material. Those tests had to be administered to all poor children at least once in grades 3 through 5, 6 through 9, and 10 through 12. Clinton's 1999 proposal would have expanded that testing to all students. The new law mandates that all students take tests that measure their progress against state standards every year in grades 3 through 8.

The bill Bush signed also requires that the National Assessment of Educational Progress (NAEP) be given in every state every other year in math and reading, but the results cannot influence whether a school is designated as failing. Initially, Bush had proposed that NAEP be administered every year as a national barometer for the state tests. Currently, NAEP is administered in those subjects every four years in about 40 states, a number that fluctuates from test to test depending on which states decline to participate.

The 1994 legislation only suggested penalties for schools that failed to improve student test scores, but Clinton's 1999 proposal, which never made it into law, would have required that states intervene in perpetually failing schools. "The Bush administration took the Clinton administration's ideas and ran with them," said one bemused Democratic congressional aide who worked at the Department of Education under Clinton.

The new law sets out a timeline of increasingly severe sanctions to nudge recalcitrant schools along. If a school fails to meet annual state test-score goals for two years, students can transfer to another public school in the district. The failing school also receives extra money to revamp academic programs. After three years of failure, the district must use 5 percent of the money it receives for poor children under the federal Title I program's "Basic Grants" section to pay for outside tutoring services. After four failing years, a school must make significant structural changes, such as revamping the curriculum or firing staff, and may be eligible for a state takeover the following year. At no point does a state or school lose money if it continues producing poor results, although districts eventually have to divert federal money to pay for tutoring services.

Building on the work of one's predecessors can produce success stories. That's just what Bush did as governor of Texas. His reforms expanded those of former governor Ann Richards, whose reforms built on those in places like Dallas and previous statewide efforts led by, of all people, Ross Perot. Dallas, it happens, is where then–school board president Sandy Kress initiated accountability—using standardized tests to reward and sanction schools. "This is our theme," Kress said. "We may not know a lot of music in Texas, but we can sing the song we know well."

A Difficult Road Ahead

The Bush administration tried to set a new tone the night after the president signed the education bill, when Secretary of Education Rod Paige invited 30 state education chiefs to Mount Vernon to discuss the new law and his expectations for the states. After dining on pork and pumpkin mousse, Paige made his pitch: The old days of waivers and delays and closing our eyes to enforcement problems are over.

Analysts say the tough-love message is a good one, but that backing it up will be difficult. "Everybody jumps on this wagon and says we're really going to be tough," said Marshall S. Smith, the acting deputy secretary of education in the Clinton administration. "That's macho talk. That's not going to work in the real world of kids and schools."

So far, only 16 states have complied with the requirements of the 1994 law. The Bush administration's first task will be to get the other 34 states into compliance. Then, they'll have to review the new statewide plans for getting every child in every demographic group to a "proficient" level of achievement within 12 years. After the states have set their yearly performance goals, the Department of Education will have to monitor the performance of the nation's 92,000 public schools to see whether each demographic group in each grade being tested is meeting the state performance goals.

The law also leaves open a number of questions, mostly surrounding the quality of the reforms states undertake. One of the most significant ambiguities is whether states can develop an annual testing system by piecing together state and district tests given in different grade levels. Some critics worry that states will create systems where a student's results on a district test one year cannot be compared with results on a state test the next year. "There's going to be a lot of discussion about that," Kress said. "There's no easy answer right now."

Others worry that with 50 different statewide tests, the federal government will lack a meaningful tool with which to compare test scores across state lines. "What happened was you had a whole bunch of folks who wanted standards but not standardization," said Arnold Fege, president of Public Advocacy for Kids, a nonprofit public education advocacy group. "As a result, we've got 49 different states with 49 different standards and 49 different testing systems. The question is what does it all mean? You can't compare the states." (The number is only 49 because Iowa declined to create statewide academic standards per the 1994 law's requirements.)

For many of the testing quality issues, the federal government is taking a hands-off approach. "Our job will not be to pass judgment on the quality of state standards or the quality of the assessments based on those standards," said Undersecretary Eugene Hickok, the Department of Education's point person on enforcement.

ENFORCEMENT

The department's approach to enforcement is largely preventative. Hickok is setting up an implementation team in Washington that will be bolstered by staff members in the department's regional offices. The team will assemble an analysis of where states are in the reform process, and it will be updated as states make additional changes. Meanwhile, top department officials will reach out to state officials to encourage them to comply. "Our goal is to respond as quickly as possible, and not just to say yes or no, but to help them achieve it," Hickok said.

Some states and schools are likely to test how serious the administration is about enforcement. "There are going to be a lot of schools that take a wait and see attitude with compliance," said David Shreve, senior committee director for the National Conference of State Legislatures. "I think there will be a great number of states and systems that will say, 'Let's do as much as we can without breaking our backs,' knowing full well that the bill will be up for a new reauthorization before any of these really bad consequences kick in."

States are also now facing budget deficits—at least in the near term. Some liberal members of Congress, like Sens. Paul Wellstone, D-Minn., and James M. Jeffords, I-Vt., even voted against the bill because they view the funding level as insufficient to help the reforms really take hold. Jeffords called the bill "counterproductive, if not destructive." Even Miller, who advocated accountability before it was cool, worries about states being able to pay to fix the problems the test scores highlight. "It comes in a down economy, and we worry the states are going to be forced to make cuts that will challenge the success of this bill," he said. Just a month after Bush signed the education bill, with Miller and Kennedy at his side, the two Democrats held a press conference to denounce Bush's 2003 education budget, which they say falls way short of what's needed to fulfill the mandates of the new education law.

To a large degree, says Hickok, the key to enforcement will be parents. He hopes that parents of children in failing schools, armed with information about how their schools and children are doing, will force schools to offer them the options that are laid out in the federal law. Having been there and done that in Washington, Marshall Smith agrees. "The only way you're really going to get accountability—accountability at the point where politicians really feel the pressure—is bad press," he said. But, he says, the statistics the federal government is requiring schools to report offer parents no useful information about what their children do and don't know.

The first test of the Bush administration's enforcement chops will come in handling the schools that are already on the Department of Education's list of failing schools. Students in schools that have been on the list for three or more years, estimated to be at least 3,000, should now be entitled to tutoring services, and students in at least 6,500 should earn the option to transfer to another public school.

Once the statewide accountability systems are in place, enforcement will get increasingly difficult as states are required to raise the goals for student achievement no less than every three years. As more and more schools face sanctions, how will the administration handle the inevitable logistical and political quicksand? What happens if all the high-performing schools in a district are full and can't take the children who were granted public school choice because their own school failed two years in a row? "We've had a lot of discussion about it," Hickok said. "The law does not impose the Department of Education into the state to make sure they're doing public school choice the way we want to or supplemental services the way we want to." In fact, Hickok isn't even sure what the federal government can do if students in a failing school can't transfer to another public school in the district because there's no room at the better schools.

Sustaining the momentum on enforcement may be the administration's biggest challenge. "Paige is saying he won't give any waivers. Now we shall see. I hope that he can keep the pressure on," says Jack Jennings of the Center on Education Policy. "Elections come up. Is Bush going to deny [New York] Gov. [George] Pataki federal aid when he's running for reelection, if the state has not met its testing requirements?" (Money can be withheld from a state for not complying with the requirements of the law, but not for poor results.)

Even with a troubled economy and continuing worries about terrorism, education remains a high-level concern among voters. Bush's education record will no doubt play an important role in the next election. That means the person who will ultimately be held most accountable in the eyes of the public for reforming the schools is President Bush.

Resurrecting the Economy

Richard Cheney

George W. Bush and Vice President Richard Cheney
took office in the height of an economic recession. In
the following speech made in August 2002, Vice
President Cheney discusses economic revival under
the Bush administration. In spite of a terrorist attack
at home, war abroad, and economic slow down,
Cheney highlights conditions set in place by Bush to
stimulate the economy and formulate long-term
growth. Cheney states that lengthening unemployment benefits, providing tax incentives for business,
issuing $11 million in tax rebate checks, and signing
a corporate integrity bill to renew confidence in
American business practices are all tools Bush has
used to propel the nation's sluggish economy.

In the past eighteen months, the United States has gone
through a serious economic slowdown, a great national
emergency, a war abroad, and a series of scandals in corporate America. Yet there is no doubt about our nation's
strength. This is a tribute, above all, to the American worker
and entrepreneur. Worker productivity in the last four quarters has been impressive. Higher productivity leads to wage
increases, greater investment, and even more jobs down the
line. In the month of June, personal income rose at the
fastest pace in two years. Also in June, sales of new homes
reached an all-time high. The number of unemployment
claims has remained below the 400,000 mark for most of the
last nine weeks. Industrial production has been rising since
January, after 17 months of almost steady decline. Mortgage
interest rates stand at near 30-year lows. Inflation remains
firmly under control.

We have the most productive, creative, and promising eco-

Richard Cheney, "Vice President Discusses the President's Economic Security Agenda,"
www.whitehouse.gov, August 7, 2002.

nomic system the world has ever seen. In America we value freedom of movement, competition, private property rights, the rule of law, and limited government—and all these have made our country the best place to work and invest. We lead the world in technological progress, and scientific and medical breakthroughs. We have by far the most skilled and productive work force. Our companies and universities attract the greatest talent from every continent. The energy and innovativeness of American business, especially in the high-tech industries, have made the economy much more flexible and better able to absorb the kinds of shocks we've experienced in recent months.

All of these conditions create a platform for long-term growth and prosperity. . . . If we continue in the positive direction President Bush has set for the nation—with solid, pro-growth, pro-job reforms—Americans will enjoy even greater prosperity in the years ahead. We will not be satisfied until every sector of this economy—from agriculture to high-tech—is vigorous and growing. We will not rest until every person who wants to work can find a job.

The primary objective of this administration's economic policy is faster growth that leads to new jobs. Here the federal government's responsibility is plain. Outside its own limited functions, government doesn't build plants or create jobs. Our responsibility is to create an environment in which private-sector employers want to expand and hire more people. That is the way to lift wages and the standard of living across the country. That is the way for companies to innovate, and grow, and produce value that attracts investors.

A growing economy brings the added benefit of higher revenues for the government—revenues that permit us to balance the budget, meet key priorities, and protect Social Security and Medicare, without ever resorting to ruinous tax increases on the American people.

RECESSION

The President and I ran for office on a growth agenda, starting with an across-the-board rate reduction for every income taxpayer in the nation. Our goal was to ensure long-term prosperity by increasing the incentives to produce, save, and invest—and by limiting the total amount of our national wealth controlled by the federal government. Bipartisan majorities in both Houses of Congress agreed with us.

Under the 2001 tax cut we reduced the tax bills of more than a hundred million individuals, families, and sole proprietorships—the largest reduction in a generation. We made those reductions retroactive to the first of January, 2001, in order to give the economy an immediate boost.

January of 2001 was also the month that brought a change in administrations. It is now clear from the data that when President Bush and I took office, the nation had slid into a full-blown economic recession. The first sign of a slowdown had appeared around the summer of 2000. Among the contributing factors were high and unpredictable energy prices, a steadily rising tax burden, and high interest rates. By inauguration day, business investment growth had halted—and the nation had already lost nearly a third of a million manufacturing jobs in a year's time. The slide continued, with the economy contracting throughout the first, second, and third quarters of 2001.

In the third quarter, of course, we had the terrorists attacks [on September 11, or 9/11], which themselves caused a massive disruption of economic activity throughout the country. Every foreign and domestic flight was cancelled for days, some of them for weeks or even months. For a time, many hotels, shopping malls, and restaurants went practically empty. Stock trading was halted for nearly a week. Hundreds of thousands of Americans were laid off, some of them still looking for work to this day. Overall, the attacks cost the economy about 120 billion dollars in the last few months of 2001 alone.

Even so, the worst period for the economy last year was actually the second quarter, prior to the attacks. By September 11, millions of tax rebate checks had already arrived in American homes, and had begun to strengthen the economy. The Bush tax cut came just in time. Together with the great flexibility of this economy, and the extraordinary resilience of the American people, tax relief helped us to climb out of the recession, and to weather the terrible financial effects of 9/11.

The nation gained as well from the President's economic stimulus package, enacted last March. We lengthened unemployment benefits for those who lost jobs in the recession or in the aftermath of 9/11. We provided tax incentives for companies to expand by investing in plant and equipment. The stimulus also extended net operating loss rules, granted some alternative minimum tax relief, and provided more than five billion dollars in tax relief to assist in the economic recovery of lower Manhattan. Following passage of the stimulus, business investment in equipment and software went up by 2.9 percent in the second quarter, the first gain in a year and a half.

All of these steps—the rebate checks, the additional rate reductions on tax day, and the stimulus package—have helped turn three quarters of decline into three quarters of positive growth. By leaving more money in the hands that earned it, we trusted the American people—and the American people have produced this recovery.

ECONOMIC GROWTH

So far this year, the economy has grown at an annual rate of about three percent. This is significantly better than those nine months of recession in 2001. Many private sector forecasters anticipate that we'll stay at a solid three percent growth rate for the balance of the year. Just as the President's tax cuts put a floor under the recession, Federal Reserve policy has been critical to our progress. Eleven consecutive cuts in interest rates have reduced deflationary pressures and helped stabilize prices. We believe the economy is poised for sustained growth without inflation—so long as we hold to the right policies.

Going forward, our Administration will continue the work of strengthening the free enterprise system and reducing the barriers to further growth. We will keep the federal government squarely on the side of growth, business starts, and new jobs.

I am not here today to analyze the stock market. Yet we're all aware that just as the first signs of recession became visible in 2000, the equity markets began a major adjustment in the spring of that year. Some of the more recent declines are at least partly explained by a loss of confidence in the corporate sector.

The President has acted firmly on the matter of corporate integrity, because it goes to the heart of our economic system. That system rests on confidence—the basic belief that corporate officials are truthful, numbers are real, audits are thorough and independent, and investors are protected by law from fraud and deception.

All of us recognize that the vast majority of men and women in the business community are honest and above-board. They run solid companies, providing the goods and services that enhance our quality of life—and, for some of us, even save our lives. At the same time they provide jobs for their workers and real value for investors. Acts of fraud and theft are outside the norm in corporate America. But when those acts do occur—where corporate greed and malfeasance causes honest people to lose their jobs, life savings, and pensions, the people's confidence in the system is undermined—and the wrongdoers must be held to account.

We are pleased that Congress came together to pass the President's corporate integrity proposals, and last week he signed the most far-reaching reforms of American business practice since Franklin Roosevelt lived in the White House. Under this law, financial disclosures will be broader and better for the sake of shareholders and investors. Corporate officials will be held to higher standards of accountability for the statements they make and the papers they sign. For the first time ever, the accounting profession will be regulated by an independent board, which sets clear standards to uphold the integrity of public audits.

These reforms will bring out the best in the free enterprise system, answering abusive practices with stricter enforcement and higher ethical standards. When there is corporate fraud, the American people can be certain that the government will fully investigate, arrest, and prosecute those responsible.

We intend to do even more to protect the interests of the small investor and pension holder. More than 84 million Americans own stock, either as individuals or through their retirement plans. This level of participation in the market is unprecedented, and it is good for the country.

Investing in the stock market gives individuals the opportunity to build wealth over the long term—a real chance to enjoy a level of security and independence in retirement that was out of reach to earlier generations. This is precisely the kind of responsible investing we should promote in America. And one of the best ways to encourage stock ownership is to make sure that pension plans give workers better information, and treat them fairly.

Some workers today are locked into pension plans that hold stock in a single company, which is sometimes an unwise risk. Workers should be able to sell company stock and diversify into other investments after three years in their own company's plan. They should receive updates on their retirement savings every three months. And they should have access to sound investment advice. President Bush has proposed these and other reforms to protect Americans and their pensions. The House has passed this legislation. It remains only for the Senate to act, and we call on them to do so as soon as possible.

We are also asking Congress to take the next crucial step to reduce the tax burden on the nation's families and entrepreneurs.

Under present law the reductions we worked so hard to enact are scheduled to expire in 2011. The return of higher marginal tax rates, a restoration of the marriage penalty, a cut in the child credit—all these would almost certainly cause an economic reversal. Even the expectation of these events will put downward pressure on the economy's ability to grow, as families and firms prepare for an approaching tax increase. We should prevent that increase, and make the President's income tax reductions permanent. The House has already voted for permanent tax relief—and here again, we call on the Senate to do the same.

The death tax is also scheduled to return nine years from now. That would spell trouble for farmers, small business owners, and employees across America. A farm or a family business should be a legacy for your children, not a target for the tax collector.

We need to pass terrorism risk insurance. The latest figures show a decline in construction spending. The fact is that billions of dollars in projects are on hold today because the developers can't obtain coverage against the risk of terrorism. This problem also affects the transportation industry. With terrorism risk insurance, the federal government would step in and cover losses above a certain level of claim. Coverage would therefore become both accessible and affordable to employers across the country. Congress should enact this reform without delay—and without offering a windfall to trial lawyers.

BUSH'S BUDGET

We in Washington must also keep federal spending under control. A period of war and recession-induced deficits imposes the need for extra care in our spending priorities, and discipline that fits the times. The President's budget commits most new spending to national security and homeland defense, and seeks to hold the rest of government to an increase of two percent.

We will meet these and other priorities, but we must not permit spending to grow without restraint. This would divert more billions from families and entrepreneurs, limiting the economy's ability to expand in the future. President Bush is going to insist on spending discipline in Washington, and use his veto power if necessary.

Another fundamental condition of long-term growth is a reliable and affordable supply of energy. If we are to avoid regular price spikes and chronic shortages, we must continue our progress in energy efficiency and conservation, and increase energy production here at home. The Congress should pass the President's energy plan to strengthen our economy and reduce our dependence on foreign oil.

Our administration is committed to a broad agenda to promote small business. To buy or start a small business is to stake one's livelihood on the American Dream—believing that good ideas, hard work, and fair dealing will pay off in the end. Because so many have put forth that effort, smaller firms today create three out of every four new jobs, and account for half the private-sector output of the entire economy. The small business sector has become an especially promising avenue of opportunity for women. Over the last five years, the number of women-owned businesses has increased by 14 percent nationwide, twice the rate of firms overall. This economy can thrive only if our small businesses thrive—and we want to see a lot more small businesses in all parts of the country.

One way to make that occur is to continue holding the line on federal regulations, which so often cause wasted effort, lost jobs, and higher costs to the consumer. The annual cost of federal regulations now stands at some 8,000 dollars per household. I'm pleased to note that the year 2001 brought an actual decrease in the number of new regulations coming out of Washington. That's a positive trend we hope to continue.

Small business also stands at the center of America's trade policy. Fully ninety-six percent of America's exporters are firms with fewer than 500 employees. The nation's farmers and ranchers receive a quarter of their income from sales abroad, and one out of every three acres is producing goods for export. For the farms and ranches and manufacturers who trade with the world, the prospects have grown even brighter with the passage of trade promotion authority. It's been more than eight years since a president had that tool. Last week Congress, on a bipartisan basis, granted this authority to the President. Yesterday he signed it into law. He will use it to enter into favorable trade agreements wherever possible, giving people around the world many more opportunities to buy American.

GLOBAL TRADE

America strongly supports a new round of global trade negotiations. We're also working with nations in Central and South America to establish a Free Trade Area of the Americas by January of 2005. We will move quickly to build free trade relationships with individual nations such as Chile, Singapore, and Morocco. Such agreements, and others we intend to pursue, will create jobs in America and hope around the world.

Every advance for global trade is an opportunity to expand our economy, and include more of our people in the nation's prosperity. America is also the engine of economic growth for the rest of the world. Just as we stand to gain from wider trade, so do our trading partners—especially the less developed nations. For them, the stakes are even higher. Short-term grants and foreign aid can only go so far. In the long term, open trade and investment can bring their first real hope for material uplift all the more when economic reforms are joined with political freedom. And we must provide it.

Many nations on the path of democracy and open economies look to the United States as an example, and an ally. They rely on our support, our encouragement, and our leadership in the world—and we must always provide it.

Our future security, and the hopes of the civilized world, also depend upon America's continued leadership in the war on terror. Even with a very full agenda for this fall and beyond, never for a moment do the President and I forget the most important responsibility we have: To protect this nation against further attack, and win the war that began on September 11.

We still face an enemy determined to kill Americans by any means, on any scale, and on our own soil. We're dealing with a terror network that has cells in more than 60 countries. Such a group cannot be held back by deterrence nor reasoned with by diplomats. For this reason, the war against terror will not end in a treaty. There will be no summit meeting or negotiations with the terrorists. This conflict can end only in their complete and utter destruction.

In this challenge to our freedom we have already asked a great deal of the men and women who wear our country's uniform. And as a former Secretary of Defense, I've never been more proud of our military. For missions that lie ahead, we are investing in our military so we can deploy swift and agile forces—anyplace and anytime they're needed. We are building precision weapons that can spare the lives of American soldiers in combat, and innocent civilians in foreign lands. We will multiply every advantage in order to prevail over any enemy. . . .

President Bush has made very clear, the government of the United States will not look the other way as threats accumulate against us. . . . The President and I are mindful of the tremendous responsibilities that have been placed in our hands. And we are grateful to you, our fellow citizens, for giving us the opportunity to serve the greatest nation on the face of the earth.

CHAPTER 5

TERRORISM ON AMERICAN SOIL

GEORGE W. BUSH

Terrorism Changes the Bush Presidency

Robin Wright

In the following article, Los Angeles Times journalist Robin Wright analyzes President Bush's strides in worldwide diplomacy following the terrorist attacks in America on September 11, 2001. Wright credits Bush's embrace of a global solution to the war on terrorism for his increase in international respect.

According to Wright, Bush created a new coalition to move beyond retaliation for America's attacks. The new multinational agenda focused on eliminating terrorism in the name of global security.

Six weeks ago, George W. Bush was still the new kid on the global block, widely perceived by his peers as a good-old-boy Texan grappling, and sometimes fumbling, with the sophisticated nuances of foreign policy.

He was under fire for his controversial missile defense plan, resented for his go-it-alone approach and challenged for doing too little or nothing on the Middle East conflict, nuclear testing, climate change, land mines, creation of an international criminal court, chemical weapons and children's rights.

Today, presidents, prime ministers, sultans, sheiks and kings defer to him. He has redefined the global agenda. And everyone wants to see him.

The shift has been the most striking part of the Asia-Pacific Economic Cooperation. . . . Chinese President Jiang Zemin . . . hosted . . . [a] summit of 21 member economies [to] highlight his nation's leadership and transformation. . . .

But the summit decidedly was Bush's show.

In a telling episode, Japanese Prime Minister Junichiro Koizumi, whose country is one of America's closest allies and the world's second-largest economy, kept apologizing for taking up Bush's time Saturday during their one-hour bi-lateral meeting.

"I appreciate your strong leadership to fight terrorism. Your determination and patience, I appreciate," the prime minister said during a photo opportunity.

Koizumi also presented Bush with a decorative arrow used by Japanese warriors dating to the 6th century that, when shot, produces a sharp whistle signaling the onset of battle. On the wooden box containing the arrow, Koizumi personally inscribed, in calligraphy, "to defeat evil and bring peace on Earth."

A FRESH START

One of the unexpected consequences of the Sept. 11 tragedy is that it has given the new American president a fresh start on foreign policy. It's a sort of second honeymoon with the world to revive a marriage that, U.S. officials concede, wasn't going all that well.

"At earlier meetings, he either had to overcome misconceptions or face the implication that people were going to teach him something about how the world works," said a senior U.S. official who has worked with both Republican and Democratic administrations. "He came to this meeting having stood up and established himself on the issue, where he's demonstrating U.S. leadership to a world that is looking for it."

The global challenge of terrorism has helped. The United States is a relative newcomer in dealing with terrorism on its own turf, though it has been a long-standing problem for many countries.

"The issue makes it easier to empathize with our objectives. Unlike missile defense, where we appear to be doing something to protect ourselves, this is something where other countries feel a broad common interest," said James Steinberg, deputy national security advisor in the Clinton administration and now director of foreign policy studies at the Brookings Institution in Washington.

NEW RESPECT

Bush is winning new respect in large part because of his reaction, which was to not go it alone. At least on terrorism, his approach has embraced the era and ideas of globalization.

"The people in this administration have gone from being

serious unilateralists to being active multilateralists," said Moises Naim, editor of Foreign Policy magazine. "Everyone sees that both Bush and [Secretary of State Colin L.] Powell are on the phone constantly, consulting with other countries that are playing important roles in the new coalition."

The fact that one of the first things the Bush administration did after the Sept. 11 attacks was to make a long-delayed payment of dues to the United Nations helped prove its intent, Steinberg added.

Substantively, Bush also has scored points by not acting precipitously and devising a deliberate longer-term strategy to deal with terrorism, U.S. analysts and officials agree.

"The initial concept of response was that we were going to do what we did in the past—blow some holes in something and maybe get some U.N. resolutions that these criminals had to be brought to justice," said a senior State De-

---

DEFINING MOMENT

John Hughes describes how Americans rallied behind Bush following the September 11, 2001, terrorist attacks and discusses two defining moments where Bush showed his capabilities as a world leader.

In two defining moments during the crisis over terrorism, George W. Bush crossed the dramatic threshold from amiable domestic politician to confident world leader.

The first moment was in the early minutes after the attack on New York. Air Force One, with President Bush on board, was soaring away from Florida at 40,000 feet, shepherded by an escort of F-16s. Vice President Cheney, secure in a bomb-proof shelter in the White House basement, warned the airborne president that the threat to Washington by additional hijacked jets was real. In the seconds available for decision, Mr. Bush had to issue one of the most chilling instructions a president could make. It was to shoot down any airliner that imperiled Washington, even though it might be crowded with captive passengers.

The second moment came during Bush's speech to a joint session of Congress and the nation. Tight-jawed, with an expression of righteous menace, he seemed to look through the camera lens, and over the jagged mountains of Afghanistan into the very eyes of Osama bin Laden, to promise: "Whether we bring our enemies to justice, or bring justice to our enemies, justice will be done."

partment official who asked to remain anonymous.

"But Bush said those things may have stopped a particular type of terrorism or changed the behavior of certain countries, but they didn't stop terrorism or make us any safer," the official added. "So he said we have to take this to the next level—to move beyond retaliation to a long-term struggle to eliminate terrorism. And that meant getting everybody to do something, like choke off safe havens or close down financial networks, not just military actions."

For a man sometimes perceived as insensitive to other nations' concerns, Bush also publicly demonstrated sensitivity to an array of background issues, Steinberg said.

After initially bumbling by referring to the global effort against Islamic extremists as a "crusade," he subsequently stressed that the U.S. is not at war with Islam. He went to the Islamic Center of Washington on Sept. 17 to meet with Mus

Thus was completed Bush's presidential coming of age, suddenly burdened with the most awesome responsibilities of that office, but at ease with deploying the weapons of diplomacy and military power he can project around the world.

A couple of years ago on the campaign trail, a mischievous reported sand-bagged Bush because the presidential candidate wasn't entirely sure who was the new leader of Pakistan. Today, Bush has co-opted a now-familiar Pakistani president (Gen. Pervez Musharraf) in the campaign against terrorism, engaged in near-daily conversations with President Putin as he ensures Russia's cooperation, rekindled the Anglo-American alliance, and and established a Rolodex of world leaders whom he has persuaded to stand on his side of the line he has drawn in the sand. . . .

Americans seem rallied behind their president, ready to pay the price for defending these freedoms. They give blood to the Red Cross. They volunteer. They donate money in the millions for disaster relief and to aid the families of those killed. They're putting up good-naturedly with cumbersome new security restrictions. . . .

Some Americans may know as little about geopolitics and the president of Pakistan as George Bush did a couple of years ago.

But they sure can identify with their president when he tells them: "Freedom and fear, justice and cruelty, have always been at war, and we know that God is not neutral between them."

John Hughes, "Bush's Coming of Age," *Christian Science Monitor,* September 26, 2001.

lim leaders. And he included Muslims in official remembrances, speeches and public events.

To avoid the kind of political fallout that accompanied the Persian Gulf War against Iraq, the administration also began dropping bombs and food in Afghanistan at the same time, Steinberg noted.

MAINTAINING INTERNATIONAL SUPPORT

Honeymoons always end, however, and the international support Bush is receiving is unlikely to be as cohesive or widespread indefinitely.

"It won't easily be sustained unless our strategy takes others' interests into account," said Les Gelb, president of the Council on Foreign Relations in New York.

Most of the world is generally in sync about the Sept. 11 attacks, which offers the U.S. cover for the first phase of its war against Osama bin Laden, his al Qaeda terrorism network and their Afghan hosts. But cooperation within the loosely knit coalition and support for the war on terrorism could face hurdles if or when the U.S. moves beyond Afghanistan.

"That's when we face a real hard trade-off between what we need to do to get their support for our [war on] terrorism and our values regarding other countries' treatment of political opposition," Gelb said.

Many countries have signed on to the coalition partly because of their own domestic problems. Russia's most serious security challenge is from Muslim guerrillas in its republic of Chechnya, while China faces Uighur Muslim militants in the western province of Xinjiang. Though Washington concedes that some Chechens and Uighurs have engaged in terrorism, the U.S. also has traditionally viewed both problems as political issues that grew out of repression of minorities and human rights violations.

Bush's legacy almost certainly will be determined by how his war turns out, analysts predict. But the verdict may not be in until long after he leaves office.

Terrorism Gives Bush a New Image

Jeffrey H. Birnbaum

The mission of a war on terrorism in the aftermath of September 11, 2001, helped George W. Bush find his identity as president of the United States. As commander in chief during this crisis, his approval ratings soared. He coordinated police actions around the world to round up terrorists, assembled a coalition of nations to fight terrorism, froze millions in financial assets owned by terrorist groups, and organized a successful military campaign in Afghanistan.

In this 2001 article, Jeffrey H. Birnbaum examines how the leadership role of Bush grew under the pressure of the terrorist crisis. According to Birnbaum, Bush's ability to command under pressure and to stir the American people with his words were two traits of the new president that were unseen before the terrorists attacks in New York and Washington, D.C. His newfound presidential image has also helped Bush press his domestic policies, and it is on these issues that the success of Bush's presidency may ultimately rest.

Birnbaum is the Washington bureau chief of *Fortune* magazine and a contributor to the Fox News Channel.

Seven months into the new administration in Washington, D.C., George W. Bush was still an enigma. Everyone wanted to know: Was he a conservative ideologue or the compromiser-in-chief? One minute he was eager to drill in the fragile Alaskan wilderness, the next he was cutting deals with [renown Democrat] Ted Kennedy to spend more money on education. Europeans didn't like him much and Americans were split. Nobody knew what to make of the United States' new president.

Jeffrey H. Birnbaum, "Bush's Growth Spurt: George W. Has Found His Presidential Authority and Voice Since September 11th," *The International Economy*, November/December 2001. Copyright © 2001 by *The International Economy*. Reproduced by permission.

Then tragedy struck. The September 11th attacks gave Bush, indeed his entire Baby Boom generation, its mission and, as Bush told us, its "moment." It is said that great presidents can emerge only at times of great struggle. Well, Bush now faces such a crisis. The question is: Is he up to the task? . . . He clearly seemed to be. He was moving methodically, effectively, and, yes, impressively against an intractable foe. He had assembled an expansive coalition of nations willing to help militarily and otherwise to defeat the terrorism of al-Qaeda, the Taliban, and Osama bin Laden. Coordinated police actions throughout the world had rounded up hundreds of suspected terrorists. Millions of dollars in assets tied to the plotters had been frozen. Military strikes were underway and hitting their targets in Afghanistan.

By all accounts, Bush, with his astronomically high job-approval ratings in the polls, had gone from goat to hero in Americans' minds, and in the minds of civilized people around the world. But as any student of management will attest, that's a superficial and probably fleeting assessment. The war won't last forever, at least not at its initial, fevered pitch. So qualities beyond that extraordinary circumstance will be the ultimate measure of the man. This article takes that broader view.

NOT MERELY A FIGUREHEAD

Bush's ability to command under pressure and to stir the American people with his words were two traits not apparent prior to the attacks on New York and Washington. But clearly he possesses both. We also now know that he is willing, actually, eager, to delegate as long as he has competent appointees. And his appointees have turned out to be first rate.

Bush all but turned over centralized control of the emergency on September 11th to his chief lieutenant, Vice President Dick Cheney. It was Cheney who ordered the evacuation of congressional leaders as well as the hopscotch trek across the country of the President himself aboard Air Force One on that fateful day. In addition, the able team of Secretary of State Colin Powell and Defense Secretary Donald Rumsfeld pieced together the international coalition.

Bush has taken this delegation of authority so far that we can now say that for the first time in decades, true Cabinet government has been restored. For years, the White House staff had been preeminent in policy matters, and the cabinet was mostly a mouthpiece. No longer. Cabinet members are true players, not public relations purveyors, in Washington. At the same time, Bush makes the final decisions on strategic matters. He isn't a figurehead CEO.

DETERMINATION

Bush is also as determined as any president in memory to get what he wants on the domestic front, even when facing war abroad. His behavior on domestic issues, in fact, can shed some insight into his overall presidential style. To wit: Bush swaggers and promises a lot, never expecting to get everything. And in that way he accomplishes more of what he wishes than anyone might have anticipated.

This cowboy demeanor is partly a Texas tendency, one that annoys many Europeans. But it is also a calculated strategy. Bush likes to promise the moon, as he did when he pledged to eradicate global terrorism. But that is mostly an expression of resolve, meant both to inspire and provoke. He will always accept less, when he has to.

There are many examples of this. When Nick Calio, the President's top congressional lobbyist, first visited the then-President-elect in Texas in January, Bush told him, "We're not going to negotiate with ourselves." The modus operandi of his White House, Bush explained, will be to talk tough for as long as possible, but mostly as a bargaining tool. Referring specifically to tax cuts, a top priority at the time, Bush described the strategy this way: "We're not going to negotiate with ourselves on taxes. We'll say, '$1.6 trillion over ten years,' and they'll move toward us. We won't get everything we want but we'll get a tax bill." In other words, Bush never expects to win what he wants. But he intends to state loudly and clearly his fondest wish for as long as he can as a way to make the other side compromise more. A similar tack was used against the Taliban when Bush announced jauntily that he wanted bin Laden "dead or alive."

The danger is that Bush often overpromises, as Calio soon found out. The grousing on Capitol Hill about the size of the tax reduction rapidly grew shrill in early 2001. And when Calio went to Bush to seek guidance, Bush wouldn't bend. He reminded Calio of the game plan. "Don't wobble," Bush urged. Calio did what he was told. And lo and behold, the stubbornness paid off. In May, Bush managed to get most of what he desired. Congress passed and he signed into law

$1.35 trillion in tax relief over eleven years. The wisdom of his tactic became manifest. And a pattern of his presidency became clear.

Here's what you need to know: Bush can't be seen in a snap shot. He's a moving target. He begins with a firm position, almost always on the political right, and moves leftward only when he has to. He will issue veto threats, as he did once with the so-called Patients' Bill of Rights (health care reform), and he will swear support for proposals, such as education vouchers, that he knows have no chance. He will strut and bluster (to the pleasure of Republican stalwarts) until he gets as much as he can. Then he'll relent, declare victory, and move on. And that's the key. "The goal," Calio says, "is to get things done." Bush believes he'll be judged by results, not process. His administration's daily press briefings detailing progress on the war front (bombings, numbers of people arrested, etc.) all fit with the philosophy.

TOO MUCH SWAGGER?

This tactic may work in the long run, but in the short run it is exceedingly messy. On domestic issues, middle-of-the-road and left-of-center American voters, as well as plenty of foreigners, will see him as too conservative. Indeed, to watch the President at the beginning of any debate, you'd never know that he won the White House after losing the popular vote. He operates with the confidence of a landslide victor. He acts as if he has a mandate from the electorate to govern as far to the political right as he can reach.

In fact, he has no such mandate. So by pushing so hard for so long to the right, he not only angers the left but also gives false hope to his conservative loyalists. When he's through with a legislative debate, and he compromises leftward as he almost always must, his credibility with congressional allies (read: conservatives and Republicans) will often be in shambles. They will see him as too liberal and too willing to accommodate. Over time, he will be stranded alone, with little more than his swagger. His fellow Republicans will be especially disappointed.

Before Bush got his tax cut, for instance, his aides had to meet somber-faced Republican leaders in a Capitol hideaway to implore them to accept more tax breaks for low-income parents than they had planned. The lawmakers shook their heads but acceded. Prior to that, angry Republicans, including House Majority Leader Dick Armey and House Whip Tom DeLay, had to be brought to an Oval Office showdown with the President before they accepted a hugely expensive education bill. This will also be part of the Bush pattern: carnage on the political right after lengthy despair on the left.

Much of this division has been hidden for the sake of the war effort. Bush is slightly more willing to compromise with the Democrats to display unity as far as is possible. His tough posture, however, carries risks. If he presses Arab allies too hard, he could ignite dissension that could topple their regimes. Bin Laden could become more of an icon than he already is. Bush also might prove unable to topple terrorism, and this could create a backlash that would undermine his standing both at home and abroad.

One bulwark against such calamities is the fact that his White House is exceptionally well run. George W., a Harvard MBA, insists on complete loyalty and organizational discipline among his underlings. The Bush I [George H.W. Bush] White House wasn't nearly as collegial; its aides always feuded, and George W. saw that and hated the situation. Bush II staffers, by contrast, get along well, perhaps because they have to. War will do that.

Nevertheless an inevitable question remains: How long will Bush's own party continue to back him if he keeps tugging it to the center? The answer is: probably forever. "The right is as house broken as the President's dog," says Marshall Wittmann, a Republican analyst at the Hudson Institute. The reason: Republicans prefer having their own guy in the White House and they realize that the best way to keep him there is to hold their nose and vote for watered-down legislation. More important, war requires more solidarity than is usual, and Bush will certainly get it from Republicans and Democrats.

STANDING FIRM

Bush also benefits from being underestimated. For example, Republican insiders worried prior to his speech on federal stem cell research over the summer [of 2001] that Bush had chosen an obscure, no-win topic for his first nationally televised address. But Bush knew better. He understood that bioethics is a political frontier that Presidents will have to cross in the new century. He also was willing to risk a display of courage. Sometimes that backfires. But not this time. Bush came out a winner. He delivered a thoughtful and eloquent explanation for his preference for allowing limited research by the federal government. He worked hard at showing how thoroughly he had studied the complex issues. . . . And in so doing, he effectively undercut the raps against him that he is camera shy and slow-witted. In truth, he is neither and his enemies merely fall into his trap if they try to sell the story, so popular in Europe, that he is a buffoon or a naif.

He is, in fact, a fellow amply clever enough to change his mind if he is forced to. And also to express unflinching determination when he must. His top White House counselor, Karl Rove, who is considered the reigning political genius of the Republican Party these days, aids him when he needs to know when to do which. A better helpmate would be hard to find.

Before the terror events, Bush was flexible to a fault. Every time you looked up, you saw a new George W. Whether he was endorsing a form of energy-price controls after decrying them, stumping against global warming after downplaying it, or ending bombing on Vieques Island, Puerto Rico, after permitting it, the President was forever changing course. Such flips have happened so frequently that the White House devised a euphemism to describe them: mid-course corrections. In truth, they were reversals made in response to international pressure or voter opinion, making Bush, early on, the U-turn President.

Yet when war came, he showed that he could stand firm as well. He refused to negotiate with the Taliban, for instance. He also remained nimble enough not to press the coalition into doing things that could cause strife within the partners' own borders. When Saudi Arabia and Egypt expressed concern that public support might undermine their own power to control the mob, Bush reportedly accepted private assurances and deals under-the-table, the details of which we aren't likely to know for years. In addition, Bush balanced our guns with butter by delivering humanitarian aid packages along with military salvos to the people of Afghanistan. Unlike his predecessor Bill Clinton, Bush doesn't pander at the drop of a poll. He isn't oblivious to his popularity, but he also doesn't make a fetish of finding his policy positions at a focus group. Bush can't be counted on to do things just because they gain him votes. At the same time, a more complete picture of Bush must include the following:

Bush understands that, at times, he will have to adapt to forces beyond his control, such as a diverse international partnership against terrorism and a U.S. Senate controlled by the opposition party.

Take the situation at home. After Democrats took control of the Senate in June [2001], the Patients' Bill of Rights and an increase in the minimum wage moved to the top of the legislative calendar. Both are popular with voters but weren't what Bush wanted to tackle right away. Yet Bush embraced both and has tried to put his stamp on each. He also wanted to wait on the next Democratic agenda item, a new prescription-drug benefit for Medicare. But here, too, he will accept the inevitable, probably next year, and try to mold the finished product.

Over the long haul, reviving the economy will be as large a challenge for Bush as winning his war against terrorism. The attacks pushed the U.S. economy into a recession. As a result, there simply isn't as much money to pay for the many items that once topped his wish list, such as energy tax credits. Other propositions, like his multibillion-dollar missile defense, seem like unnecessary and anachronistic extravagances. In addition, his plan to invest in the stock market some payroll taxes that now go exclusively into the so-called Social Security Trust Fund has faded with the Dow Jones Industrial Average.

But don't count on Bush's presidency sinking with the GDP [Gross Domestic Product]. What had looked like the Bush Recession prior to September 11th is now and forever the bin Laden Recession. Besides, voters don't seem to give as much credit or blame to politicians as they once did for the state of the economy. And that can only help Bush.

A Higher Calling

Tony Carnes

The devastation from the terrorist attacks on September 11, 2001, would challenge the nation to cope with its grief and outrage. President Bush's spiritual and moral convictions helped him emerge as a strong political leader in that time of crisis. Tony Carnes, a writer for *Christian Reader*, describes President Bush's example of coping as a powerful tonic to the national mood. By calling the nation to prayer and establishing a national day of remembrance, Bush's example of faith and trust in God sustained the country during one of its darkest times in history. Bush felt he was not only a political leader with a high profile, but a servant of God called to help lead America during this time.

President Bush, from the day of the attacks on the World Trade Center (WTC) last September [2001], has led the nation with a deft spiritual presence that radiates solidarity with people of all faiths. "Bush's stature as a leader rose right before your very eyes," says Richard Cizik, vice president of the National Association of Evangelicals. The nation seemed to agree. A *Newsweek* poll taken a week after the WTC catastrophe found that 83 percent of Americans thought that the President appeared to be a strong leader. Bush administration aide Timothy Goeglein said he agrees with the widespread view that the terrorist catastrophe is "absolutely a spiritually defining moment for the country and its leader."

After the September 11, 2001, attack, Bush displayed great skill at expressing his spiritual and moral convictions. His development as a political leader took enormous strides forward as he spoke at the National Cathedral, at Ground Zero of the collapsed World Trade Center, at the White House, at a joint session of Congress, and on national television.

Tony Carnes, "Bush's Defining Moment," *Christian Reader*, vol. 40, March 2002, p. 29. Copyright © 2002 by Tony Carnes. Reproduced by permission.

BUSH'S MISSION FOR RELIGIOUS LEADERS

A few hours before his address to Congress on September 20, President Bush met at the White House with a broad spectrum of religion leaders. Twenty-seven leaders, including 13 evangelicals, attended. The group included evangelists Luis Palau and Franklin Graham, pastors Max Lucado, Bill Hybels, T.D. Jakes, and Charles Blake, and Edward Cardinal Egan of New York. Buddhist, Hindu, Sikh, and Mormon leaders also attended the meeting.

In the Roosevelt Room, the President got to the point. "I am not Pollyannish, imagining things are great," he declared. "I feel at peace, but a lot of that is due to the prayers of the American people. This is a major wake-up call for America. . . . Now, I need your help as spiritual leaders to be truthful with the American people without creating panic."

Bush then outlined what his speech to Congress and the nation would cover. He told the group that only religious leaders could give the comfort and handle the spiritual questions.

"Government will do some things, but you need to be praying and be prepared for questions," Bush told them.

Palau, who took notes at the meeting, said Bush drew a comparison between himself and the country. Bush told the gathering, "I was a sinner in need of redemption and I found it." The President was referring to the difficult time earlier in life when he was a heavy drinker and lacked a sense of purpose. But the gospel became clear to him through a conversation with evangelist Billy Graham.

Bush told the group that the nation was staggering and needed to get back on its feet. He said the devastation in New York challenged the nation to look deep into its heart. "I think this is part of a spiritual awakening in America," the President said.

Others who have talked with Bush said the President's disciplines of Bible reading and prayer sustain him.

Bush's faith is a vital part of his politics. "I don't think the President would consider himself an evangelical leader," says a prominent evangelical who knows Bush well. "He sees himself as a political leader and a man of faith."

HIGH PROFILE, HIGHER CALLING

At the White House prayer session, Bush referred to his Christian faith indirectly. It was "a candid, natural way of talking about the Lord and his faith," one participant said.

"He was very cautious and respectful in talking with the Muslims present, and he let them talk."

One purpose of the September 20 meeting was to "get Christian leaders around non-Christians ones so that [non-Christians] would feel welcomed," says Pastor Tim Keller of Redeemer Presbyterian Church in New York City.

The embrace was welcomed. Bush managed to be true to his personal evangelical testimony, while also creating a tolerant and inclusive meeting.

Gerald Kieschnick, president of the Lutheran Church-Missouri Synod, read aloud from Romans 13 and told Bush that he has a divine calling in this crisis: "Mr. President, I have just come from the World Trade Center site in Lower Manhattan, I stood where you stood. I saw what you saw. And I smelled what you smelled," Kieschnick said. "You not only have a civil calling, but a divine calling. . . . You are not just a civil servant; you are a servant of God called for such a time like this."

"I accept the responsibility," Bush said, nodding.

The President came close to tears only when he described his first thoughts after hearing that the fourth hijacked airliner may have been headed for the White House. "The White House is an old building made of plaster and brick," Bush said. "If it had been struck, it would have collapsed and many people would have been killed, including my wife."

The President paused for a long moment, squinching the side of his face as he does when he wants to hold back his emotions. "Those fellows who gave their lives—they gave their lives for freedom," Bush said. After squinching a bit more, the President said, "We need to keep people praying."

Franklin Graham and four other religious leaders were invited into the Oval Office to pray with the President. Bush pointed out a portrait of Abraham Lincoln and said it was a reminder of his own calling to extend freedom and bring the nation together.

The fusion of personal piety and civic responsibility comes from Bush's deep sense of vocation. Bush says he sensed a higher call during his second inauguration as governor of Texas. He called a friend in Fort Worth, telling him, "I believe God wants me to run for President." The President now tells friends he understands God's call with greater clarity.

"Bush believes that the Lord prepares you for whatever he

gives us," says one friend who visits the White House regularly. "The President really feels that this is his mission."

WITH GOD AT HIS SIDE

Since the terrorist attacks and the subsequent military action, the change in national mood was unmistakable. Praying and going to a religious service seemed a natural, normal thing to do. As *Wall Street Journal* columnist Peggy Noonan, put it, "God is back."

Bush's example of coping has been a powerful tonic to the national mood. Political observers say the President seems genuine, not calculated or manipulative. Ari Fleisher, press spokesman for Bush, watched the President interact with grieving families of the missing New York firefighters and police officers three days after the attack.

"He spent time listening and talking with everybody, just one on one, hearing their individual stories of their family members. It was gut-wrenching," Fleisher says. "Watching the President throughout all of this, there was a real transformation."

At the National Cathedral service, the President revealed how carefully he selected his words to fit the nation's mood. "We are here in the middle hour of our grief," he began. "We come before God to pray for the missing and the dead, and for those who loved them."

Bush said the providence of God may not be what we expect, but we can count on the grace of God. "God's signs are not always the one we look for," he told the congregation. "We learn in tragedy that His purposes are not always our own."

Since September 11, Bush's speeches have married his informal, choppy syntax with his newly forceful vision for the country. Michael Gerson, Bush's chief speechwriter and a graduate of Wheaton College, shares similar religious convictions with Bush. Gerson crafted this elegant sentence in Bush's September 20 national address: "Freedom and fear, justice and cruelty, have always been at war, and we know that God is not neutral between them."

The Bush speech was widely praised. One political columnist wrote a favorable comparison of Bush and President Lincoln. "The yardstick on how to judge a President will always be Lincoln," says Allen Guelzo, Lincoln scholar at Eastern College near Philadelphia.

Bush has "projected an image as a determined, farsighted

leader," Guelzo says, but his pieties "are still bland and conventional" compared to those of Lincoln, who was tried by the fires of the American Civil War. "Whether Bush's growth and impact lasts will depend on his resolve" as he meets further tragedies.

During White House meetings, Bush frequently shows visitors a painting inspired by the hymn "A Charge to Keep." His autobiography, released during the 2000 campaign, bears the same title as the hymn. "I still have a charge to keep," Bush tells his visitors.

Indeed, a verse from the hymn seems to fit Bush's convictions: "To serve the present age, my calling to fulfill/Oh may it all my powers engage, to do my Master's will."

CHAPTER 6

AMERICA AT WAR

PEOPLE
WHO MADE
HISTORY

GEORGE W. BUSH

The Decision to Go to War

Kenneth T. Walsh

Minutes after hearing a second plane had hit the World Trade Center, Bush told his traveling staff the United States was at war. Bush ordered his senior advisers to develop a "grand strategy" to bring down terrorist networks around the world. The radical al-Qaeda group was immediately identified as a prime suspect in the attacks. Bush and the joint chiefs of staff held meetings to set the course for military operations, vowing justice would be done.

Condemning Iraq, North Korea, and Iran as countries that encourage and harbor terrorists, Bush declared them an "axis of evil" and structured the war on terrorism to include them as well as al-Qaeda. He stated America would strike hard to destroy terrorist activity and even fight to change the political regimes of those nations that sheltered or supported terrorists.

In the following article, Kenneth T. Walsh examines Bush's actions following the September 11, 2001, terrorist attacks against the United States and the subsequent formation of his philosophies on terrorism. Walsh is the chief White House correspondent for *U.S. News & World Report;* he has taught courses on media and history at the American University and has authored several books on politics and the media.

As commander in chief, George W. Bush lives by a simple code. The military needs hardware? Send it to them. U.S. allies are hesitant to engage? Go it alone. Iraq, Iran, and North Korea are rogue nations encouraging terrorism? Condemn them as an "axis of evil." "He sees the world almost in theological terms," says Rutgers political scientist Ross Baker. "He is making a very stark distinction between the benevolent forces in the world and the forces that want to do people harm. . . . His willingness to simplify, at the risk of oversimplification, has given him a remarkable ability to be in touch with the American people. They feel that way, too."

In fact, Bush's good-vs.-evil construct is the principle on which all of his wartime decisions have been based. Most important, it is the core of an emerging "Bush Doctrine" that was cobbled together by the president and his senior advisers in the minutes and days following the September 11 attacks. That doctrine, which holds that the United States needs to exert itself more forcefully in the world, could turn out to be the most sweeping change in foreign policy since Ronald Reagan declared the Soviet Union an "evil empire."

From now on, Bush says, America will search out and destroy terrorist networks, strike equally hard at nations that harbor terrorists, and act pre-emptively if necessary to change "evil" regimes in Iran, Iraq, and North Korea if they continue to back terrorists or develop weapons of mass destruction. So far, his approach is working, which is not surprising to scholars such as Baker. They say that one of the most important attributes of any commander in chief is clarity of purpose, and Bush has demonstrated more of it than perhaps any wartime president since Franklin Roosevelt.

Even his former critics are impressed with his leadership. "No. 1," says Sandy Berger, national security adviser to President Clinton, "the president has to create the right environment for his team. He sets the tone. And the tone is either agitation and frenzy—or the tone is steadiness and calm." Berger also praises Bush for patiently waiting several weeks before launching military strikes. This gave the Pentagon enough time to properly prepare for the war in Afghanistan.

QUICK RESPONSE

Bush's moral absolutism was clear almost from the first moments of the crisis. News of the first attack came shortly before 9 A.M., when White House Counselor Karl Rove took Bush aside in the corridor of a Florida elementary school, where he was about to speak. A plane had crashed into the World Trade Center in New York, Rove said, and the cause was unclear. "What a horrible accident!" Bush replied, and he wondered if the pilot had suffered a heart attack.

A few minutes later, White House Chief of Staff Andrew Card whispered in the president's ear as he was about to address the schoolchildren, all in full view of television cameras. "A second plane hit the second tower," Card said. "America is under attack." Bush blanched and grimly pressed his lips into a thin line. He announced he would have more to say later and left the room.

He immediately got on the phone with Condoleezza Rice, his national security adviser, and others in Washington. A few minutes later, he told his traveling staff, "We're at war."

"When he went into that classroom," Card told *U.S. News,* "he was the president of the United States, talking domestic issues. He walked out of that room as the commander in chief, where he had the absolute authority to make something happen." En route from Florida to Barksdale Air Force Base in Louisiana, a secure location where Bush could consider his next moves and where Air Force One could refuel, Bush and his shocked staff watched television footage of the planes crashing into the World Trade towers. At one point,

---

AMERICA'S MILITARY

In this excerpt from his autobiography, George W. Bush discusses his belief that the nation should maintain a well-trained, well-equipped military. Arguing that America should always be prepared for conflict, he also notes that the country should only send troops into battle when all other diplomatic options have failed.

My time in the [National] Guard taught me the importance of a well-trained and well-equipped military. It gave me respect for the chain of command. It showed me, firsthand, that given proper training and adequate personnel, the military can accomplish its mission. After all, the military took a novice like me and trained me to be a skilled pilot of high-performance jets. I also learned the lesson of Vietnam. Our nation should be slow to engage troops. But when we do so, we must do so with ferocity. We must not go into a conflict unless we go in committed to win. We can never again ask the military to fight a political war. If America's strategic interests are at stake, if diplomacy fails, if no other option will accomplish the objective, the Commander in Chief must define the mission and allow the military to achieve it.

George W. Bush, *A Charge to Keep.* New York: William Morrow, 1999.

Bush calmly told Vice President Dick Cheney by secure phone that he approved of shooting down civilian aircraft if they posed another imminent threat. "You have my full authorization," Bush said.

THE GRAND STRATEGY

Since taking office, Bush had been extensively briefed by the CIA and others on "asymmetrical threats" including the al Qaeda terrorist network, and took them all seriously. In the spring of 2001, he told his senior advisers he would no longer tolerate small measures. "I'm really tired of swatting flies," he said. Bush ordered them to develop a grand strategy for "bringing down" the terrorist networks around the world, but the plan was still under development at the time of the September 11 attacks. Still, he immediately identified members of al Qaeda as the prime suspects.

Cheney told *U.S. News:* "Lots of time you don't have all the information you'd like, but that's life and you've still got to make a decision and get on with it and not agonize over it. He doesn't look back and lay awake at night, I don't think, in terms of worrying about whether or not he got it right." For his part, Bush tells friends he has not regretted a single decision he has made since September 11.

At key meetings with his war council at Camp David and at the White House over that first weekend after the attacks, he set a bold course. He chose the most extensive list of military options presented to him by the CIA and the Joint Chiefs of Staff. And he wanted his speech to a joint session of Congress that week to flesh it all out. A battery of advisers weighed in, but Bush knew just what he wanted to say. As the hour of the speech approached, aides Karen Hughes, Michael Gerson, and Dan Bartlett were working on the text in the West Wing and wondered if the Bush-approved final draft leaned too heavily toward reassuring the country. Perhaps, they told themselves, there should be more explicit warnings about the dangers ahead. Bartlett went to the East Wing to consult one last time with the president, who greeted him as he was buttoning up his dress shirt. "What do you want?" Bush said curtly. Bartlett dutifully raised the question about the speech's main theme, but Bush cut him off. "I already made that decision. Final!" the president said, and walked off. He told Congress that America's mission would be accomplished no matter what. "Whether we bring our enemies to justice or bring justice to our enemies," he said, "justice will be done."

Card says that since Bush believed there were no shades of gray, it was only natural that he devised "a doctrine that you are either with us or against us. If you harbor, protect, defend, feed, comfort, house—you're them." In his State of the Union address January 29, he condemned Iran, Iraq, and North Korea as an axis of evil because they were potentially helping the terrorists or developing weapons of mass destruction, even though some State Department experts cringed at the characterization as extreme.

When an aide recently asked Bush whether the crisis had changed him, the president said absolutely not. "Presidents either come to the Oval Office equipped and ready to deal with crises or they don't," he replied, adding: "If you're strong and firm, people follow." Rice told *U.S. News:* "He wasn't born somebody else on September 11." The question is whether his bipolar view of the world—so valuable in wartime—will provide the nuanced long-term strategy that may be needed to secure the peace.

Bush's Battle Cry: Drawing on Prayer and a Sense of Personal Mission, W Becomes a War President

T. Trent Gegax

As the death toll mounted and the economic damage became evident from the terrorist attacks in New York and Washington on September 11, 2001, President Bush called the world to war. With a military mission focused at ending terror, leaders from around the world were compelled to pledge allegiance to America's new cause. The American people seemed determined to meet the new challenges facing the nation by embracing both Bush's leadership and mission.

T. Trent Gegax spent seventeen months covering George W. Bush's 2000 presidential campaign. As a writer covering Washington for *Newsweek* magazine, Gegax outlines in this October 1, 2001, article how after the World Trade Center and Pentagon attacks, Bush drew on prayer and a sense of personal mission to become a war president.

Before he spoke his words of war for the world to hear, George W. Bush wanted to pray in private with the ordained of all faiths. It was hours before the most fateful speech of his life. Twenty-seven clergymen had been invited to meet with him. The chairs in the Roosevelt Room of the White House were arranged in a circle, prayer-meeting style. But when he walked into the room and took a seat, no one dared sit beside him for fear of seeming presumptuous. "Move in here next to me," said Bush, motioning to empty chairs on either side of him. "I feel lonely." Two men complied—Cardinal Bernard Law of Boston and Archbishop Demetrios Trakatellis of New York. For the next half hour, as he steeled himself to launch the country on a lengthy, perilous mission to purge terrorism from the world, Bush shared his burdens and hopes.

"You understand what I am facing," he said. "I have to alert the American people to the ongoing dangers without creating alarm and irrational fear. How do I walk that line?" Worry was justified. "Another crisis could hit us, more terrible than this one," he said, according to notes and recollections of several clergy. "It could be more terrible—biological, chemical or plutonium. I don't have direct evidence," he said, "but I have enough evidence." (A White House spokesman later said that Bush was speaking in general of possible threats.)

Bush said he could identify all too well with the public's fears: the White House itself had been an intended target. "It's a very old structure of plaster and brick," he said. "A lot of people could have been killed . . . including my wife." The answer, Bush had concluded, was to fight for peace and justice—and to pray. "Pray for patience, pray it will not happen again," he said. As for him, he was healthy and rested, focused and feeling "confident without being Pollyannaish." But he needed divine help, too. "Pray for wisdom, strength, clear thinking," he said, and joined hands with the circle as they did so.

In the new world of war, God matters—to both sides. Unblinkingly resolute before a cheering Congress, George Bush defiantly vowed in God's name to lead an anxious nation and the civilized world in a decisive campaign against the forces of terror. The fight would focus initially, he said, on Islamic extremist Osama bin Laden and his al-Qaeda network in the mountains of Afghanistan. As the president spoke, American warplanes, ships and troops were speeding bin Laden's way—and the dictatorial clerics who rule the country prepared for what they later called a "showdown of might" in an Islamic "holy war."

As dangerous as that conflict may be, Bush portrayed it as just the start of a decades-long struggle—a choosing of sides based not on territorial claims or clashing theories of government, but on the goal of ending terror as an instrument of human affairs. "Every nation in every region now has a decision to make," he declared. "From this day forward, any nation that continues to harbor or support terrorism will be regarded by the United States as a hostile regime." Besides allies, Bush said, America would need—and receive—assistance from Above. "Freedom and fear, justice and cruelty, have always been at war," he said, "and we know that God is not neutral between them."

Flawlessly delivering a speech that he and his aides had labored on all week, Bush appeared in the well of the House at a time of peril as severe as any since Pearl Harbor. Around the world, leaders pledged allegiance to America's new cause. But except for Britain's Tony Blair (who flew to Washington for briefings and to sit in the Gallery beside Laura Bush), it wasn't clear which countries would answer an American call for men, materiel and diplomatic muscle. Saudi Arabia, the economic and religious linchpin of the region, is allowing the use of its military bases. But it and other moderate Islamic states, facing their own threats from militants, were wary of aiding the United States too openly.

At home, the shock of the plane-bomb attacks on the World Trade Center and the Pentagon gave way to a mounting toll of death, economic damage and anxiety about the long-term impact on psyches and civil liberties. As the estimates for the missing grew to some 6,000, New York Mayor Rudolph Giuliani cautioned that the numbers could go down as various reports were coordinated. But the region was still forced to endure a procession of funerals and camera-toting visitors flocking to the jagged ruins of ground zero.

The full dimension of economic devastation was becoming apparent. The stock markets reopened but reeled, losing $1.4 trillion in book value as shares plummeted faster than they had since the depths of the Depression. The airline industry was crippled, suffering a staggering 80,000 layoffs and facing numerous bankruptcies—a crisis that prompted Bush and Congress to enact a $15 billion bailout. Federal Reserve chairman Alan Greenspan told congressional leaders in a somber private meeting that the $10 trillion-a-year economy would recover—but not any time soon. "The outlook is uncertain at best," one leader quoted him as saying.

The threat to the country's social fabric was less quantifiable but no less real, as officials and average citizens sought to find a new balance between security and privacy, antiterrorism measures and open-mindedness. A package of tough new law-enforcement measures, put forward by Attorney General John Ashcroft, sparked debate in Congress and brought assurances of compromise from the White House. Bush announced a new Office of Homeland Security to oversee border patrols, immigration, public-health threats and water supplies, and named Pennsylvania Gov. Tom Ridge to head it. Responding to scattered incidents of violence and widespread concern, the president pleaded for tolerance, especially for the nation's 6 million Muslim citizens. "We are in a fight for our principles," he declared to Congress, "and our first responsibility is to live by them."

The challenges were daunting, but the country seemed determined to meet them—and eager to embrace the disciplined and confident leadership Bush displayed in his 36-minute address. Americans share a faith of the Founders: that democratic destiny will furnish leaders the times require. Thus far, Bush has more than met the challenge of that belief. In the *Newsweek* Poll, conducted before and after the speech, voters, by an 86-10 percent margin, approved of the way he was handling his job. Asked specifically about his stewardship in the aftermath of the terrorist attacks, voters approved by an 87-7 percent margin before the speech, by a 90-7 percent margin afterward.

The president was a man on a mission—aware, aides said, that his every move was freighted with significance for the country and the free world. The Bush watchword was "focus." The battle against terrorism, at home and abroad, now would "be the focus of our administration," he told the cabinet (and probably, one top adviser said later, "of administrations to come"). "I've never seem him so focused," said another adviser. After Jacques Chirac met with Bush, the French president privately expressed astonishment to aides at the American's sure grasp of the nuances of the situation. At a staff meeting last Friday, Bush moved swiftly through a long agenda of complex items, practically barking out orders as he went. To some he seemed a bit lonely. "He's in the loneliest job in the world," observed Karl Rove, his old friend and top political adviser. Yet the president seemed comfortable with his fate. "Things have a way of being the way they are supposed to be," he told Rove with a shrug. "This is my responsibility."

To meet his responsibilities, Bush has always demanded game plans—or at least the outlines of them. The one he announced last week was devised in momentous day-long meetings a week ago Saturday at Camp David. Bush and his circle of commanders agreed on a two-pronged approach, at once sweeping (to give them latitude and time) and specific (to provide "focus" and at least one clear goal). The administration would call on all nations to join in the antiterrorism campaign, or risk becoming a foe—the Bush doctrine. Meanwhile, they would marshal military, diplomatic and economic force for the tough but unavoidable goal of destroying bin Laden and, perhaps, the Taliban.

As usual, Bush delegated the implementation. Vice President Dick Cheney, in effect, was appointed war minister—the Mr. Inside who would stay largely out of sight and oversee the campaign. Ridge, whom Bush has known since 1980, would take control of the new homeland effort. Josh Bolten, a former investment banker and White House aide known for his policy mastery and meticulous sense of organization, would chair the Domestic Consequences Group—a blandly worded euphemism for the economic-crisis-management team.

That left the president with one enormous and indispensable job: to explain the mission. His vehicle would be a meticulously crafted, carefully worded speech. There would be no freelancing of the kind that had led him to describe the task at hand as a "crusade"—a word with an unfortunately specific historical and theological meaning that had outraged Muslims when he used it. On the Sunday Bush offhandedly uttered the term, there had been no morning "message meeting." Thereafter, no day would be complete without one—and national-security adviser Condoleezza Rice would always be in them.

Bush began planning for the speech last Monday morning, days before aides would ask Hill leaders to invite the president to speak to a joint session of Congress. Bush didn't want to commit to the momentous venue unless he had a speech to match it. He asked for a draft by close of business that day. "Mr. President, I think that will be difficult, if not impossible," counselor Karen Hughes told him. His reply: "By 7." A team of speechwriters worked on the document, aiming for the blunt simplicity and muted expressions of faith he favors.

There were 19 drafts, many pencil-edited by Bush, and repeated practices before the Teleprompter in the family theater. Bush rejected suggestions for an extended discussion of the economy; he wanted the text streamlined—and didn't want to pre-empt congressional leaders, who would have their own ideas about "stimulus" measures. Bush agreed with Hughes that he should take time for plain explanation: Who was bin Laden? What was the Taliban?

But the president, who views the world in personal terms, wanted to conclude with his own witness, his own declaration of purpose. Hughes suggested that he dramatize it by showing the world the brass badge given to him by the grieving mother of a cop who had died at the World Trade Center. Bush agreed. "This is my reminder of lives that ended," he said, holding the badge aloft at a pivot point of history, "and a task that does not end."

In the Oval Office the next morning, he reminded his aides of his message. "We have to be patient," he told one. "This is going to take a long time." The atmosphere in the White House had changed since Black Tuesday—aides learned about evacuation plans, sought counseling, surfed antiterror Web sites. But the president himself was determined to return to a life that was, as he said in his speech, "almost normal." He was jogging outside again. As usual, he talked to his dad. The president asked one of his oldest friends, Commerce Secretary Donald Evans, to join him at Camp David for the weekend. They could talk about the economy. Then again, it was Evans who, long ago in west Texas, introduced Bush to Bible study. There might be time for that, too.

Bush Commits to the Middle East

Michael Duffy

Although President Bush tried to separate his administration from conflict in the Middle East, continued fighting between Israel and Palestinians was something that the United States could not ignore. In April 2002, Israeli troops invaded the West Bank region of Palestine, anti-American demonstrations were taking place all over the Middle East, oil prices soared, and the U.S. stock market plunged. Violence in the Middle East was seemingly out of control. After meeting for several days with top advisers, President Bush endorsed Palestinian statehood, but asked leader Yasser Arafat to stop terrorism and make peace with Israel. Bush also pressed Israeli prime minister Ariel Sharon to withdraw troops from the West Bank region and treat the Palestinians with compassion rather than with military force. The absolutes between good and evil that Bush had declared in the war on terrorism were now being compromised to help reshape the shakey Middle East, where terror was a weapon used by both sides.

Michael Duffy examines the factors that brought the Bush administration into the diplomatic process and some of the dangers this decision brings with it. Duffy covers Washington for *Time* magazine.

Consider the situation in the White House Situation Room last Thursday morning: Israeli troops and armor had invaded almost every city in the West Bank and surrounded about 200 Palestinian fighters barricaded inside Bethlehem's sacred Church of the Nativity. Anti-American demonstrations in Cairo, Beirut, Amman and other Middle Eastern capitals were making it impossible for Washington's Arab allies to

Michael Duffy, "After Several False Starts, George W. Bush Commits Himself Fully to Ending the Bloodshed in the Middle East. The Inside Story of His About-Face, and the Risks He Confronts," *Time*, April 15, 2002, pp. 26–31. Copyright © 2002 by Time Inc. Reproduced by permission.

stay on the fence. Egypt cut some ties with Israel and warned the White House that the rest could be in jeopardy. Oil prices spiked to $28 a barrel, and the stock market plunged. Anti-Semites vandalized synagogues in France and Belgium. American embassies cabled Washington that they might be the next targets. And White House officials were poring over satellite pictures from the region: Syria was moving its troops in the Bekaa Valley of Lebanon in anticipation of Israeli strikes across the border. The situation, a senior White House official concedes, was "getting out of control."

Talk about grabbing George W. Bush's attention: the President finally saw that he had gone down the wrong road, and he pulled a quick U-turn. When he stepped up to the Rose Garden podium Thursday morning, Bush ended more than a year of stubborn disengagement from the Middle East peace process, sending Secretary of State Colin Powell to the region to seek a solution to the Israeli-Palestinian conflict. Bush's speech was tough and elegant. "The storms of violence cannot go on," he said. "Enough is enough."

The meetings that produced the speech were even more extraordinary. For several days, the most powerful people in the Administration had served as speechwriters. Bush, Powell, Vice President Dick Cheney, Defense Secretary Donald Rumsfeld, National Security Adviser Condoleezza Rice and CIA Director George Tenet had all called or crowded into the Situation Room and worked on the speech line by line—a measure of how troubled and critical this moment really was. The team added a great deal of moral embroidery and made sure that the speech demanded something from everyone. In the Rose Garden, Bush reached out to Yasser Arafat, endorsing Palestinian statehood and giving the leader another chance to stop the terrorists and make peace—but making it clear this chance would be his last. Bush pressed Israeli Prime Minister Ariel Sharon to pull his troops and tanks from the West Bank cities and insisted that Israel begin treating the Palestinians with "compassion." Bush called on moderate Arab countries to stop wringing their hands and start helping the Palestinians build their new nation—but also warned Iraq, Iran and Syria not to undo the deal by supporting terror. During the speechwriting sessions, Administration sources told *Time*, the dependably hard-line Rumsfeld had pushed most fiercely to include tough language aimed at any nation that might try to "fish in troubled waters," as one aide put it. And these sources noticed during the several days of drafting that Cheney was particularly active, more willing than before to wager American prestige in a game with so many risks—and keen to sharpen language that warned rogue nations to stay out of the fight.

This is how a crucial policy is reborn in the Bush White House. In a single day, George W. Bush moved from keeping his distance from a region in flames to all but staking his presidency on its peace and security. He also went a long way toward diluting the simple moral code embedded in the recently hatched Bush Doctrine—the doctrine that divides the world neatly into two camps, one good and one evil. Since last September, Bush has said over and over that the nations of the world have a choice: "You're either with us, or you're with the terrorists." But by taking a chance for peace that depends on Arafat, the President is acknowledging that the moral absolutism that has worked so well in the war against terror doesn't apply to every feud. The inside story of how Bush decided to wade waist-deep into the Middle East quicksand is the story of a President who is learning that there are few simple choices in foreign policy. So it is with Arafat. "He is a liar and completely untrustworthy," says an Administration official, "but for the moment, he is the man."

POWELL WINS THE ROUND

For the past 11 or so presidents, it has been a truism that American leaders ignore the Middle East at their peril. So why did Bush think he could get away with paying so little attention to the place? As with so many questions about the Middle East, there is an answer to fit every neighborhood. Many Democrats and Republicans believe that Bush checked out of the story early in his presidency in part because he came to Washington with a reflexive desire to do the opposite of whatever his predecessor did. It is true that Bill Clinton had his hands deep in the Middle East mess from his first year in office until the final days of his presidency in a way that the Bush team found inappropriate and even dangerous, given that a taste for high-stakes summitry, in its view, led to dashed hopes and renewed violence. "It wasn't all that long ago where a summit was called and nothing happened," Bush told a television interviewer Friday in a not-so-veiled criticism of Clinton, "and as a result we had significant *intifadeh* in the area."

Bush has been unlucky in his potential partners. Last year

Israeli voters replaced Ehud Barak, who wanted peace, with Sharon, who doesn't want it very badly. Bush may have figured early on that neither Arafat nor Sharon was likely to step into the role of peacemaker anytime soon, so why bother trying to convert either? And so Bush spent the first two-thirds of 2001 worrying less about foreign policy than domestic matters. When he did look overseas, first it was Russia and China that tested him. Then it was Osama bin Laden.

But the central obstacle to engagement in the region has been Bush's senior foreign-policy advisers, led by Cheney and Rumsfeld. They are staunchly pro-Israel and have shown little regard for the peace process in the past. Concentrated at the Pentagon but salted all around the White House, the hardliners have regular access to Bush. They take a dim view of the land-for-peace swap on which every peace proposal has been based for more than a decade. Every time the Administration's moderates, led by Powell, pushed Bush for a serious peace initiative in 2001, Cheney and Rumsfeld fought them to a standstill. After a while, Powell stopped pushing. Following two trips to the region last year to try to quell the rising violence between Palestinians and Israelis, he gave up. "Colin got tired," says a veteran diplomat who knows all the players, "of going over there with nothing in his briefcase."

At the center of the hard-line ethic is a strong belief that all conflicts can fit neatly into the war between Us and Them, freedom and tyranny, good and evil. The hard-liners believe that U.S. foreign policy proceeds from straightforward choices between absolutes: trust the nations that work with you; treat everyone else as a potential adversary. The hard-liners' hero is Ronald Reagan, who labeled the former Soviet Union the "evil empire." Reagan, however, rarely let his rhetoric get in the way of pragmatic foreign policy. And Bush is now showing signs of similar flexibility.

In 1989 the first President Bush carefully weeded many of the Reagan holdovers and foreign-policy hard-liners from his Administration. Last year the second President Bush invited them back and allowed them to flourish. In this Bush Administration, it is moderates like Powell who have struggled for influence and who sometimes win only when the hard-line position fails. The two rival teams put their differences aside after Sept. 11. The Pentagon had a strange new war on its hands, and Powell had a multinational coalition against al-Qaeda to plant and nurture. But as the ground war cooled, the hard-liners got busy again. They turned their attention to Iraq, and the back-room tug-of-war began all over again. In January, while Powell was out of the country on a diplomatic mission, Cheney and Rumsfeld teamed up to persuade Bush to cut all ties with Arafat.

SADDAM ON THE BACK BURNER

That gambit fizzled when Powell found out about it, but the hawks moved again a month later, pressing Bush for a broad military action against Iraq's Saddam Hussein, America's latest target of "evil" in the region. They believed Bush should seize his chance while his postwar popularity was high. Powell and the moderates disputed the timing and tactics, if not the goal itself. But Bush agreed to send Cheney to the region last month to drum up Arab support, or at least acquiescence, for an eventual military operation against Baghdad.

Some allies didn't wait to be asked. In an effort to head off Cheney, Egyptian President Hosni Mubarak flew to Washington in early March to tell the President himself that this was no time to make war in the region. Mubarak had been a staunch supporter of Bush's father's war 11 years ago, but he drew the line now that Israel and the Palestinians were skirmishing daily. Mubarak repeated his warning to a small group of private citizens at Blair House in Washington on March 6. As long as the Middle East is in turmoil, he told his guests, there is "no support" in the region for a war on Iraq.

If all that weren't tricky enough, Sharon made things worse by invading Palestinian towns in the West Bank on the eve of Cheney's departure. The U.S. rushed its peace envoy, retired Marine General Anthony Zinni, back to the region to provide cover for Cheney's trip. And instead of talking about Iraq, Cheney had to spend 10 days hopscotching around the Middle East and listening to leaders say the road to Baghdad runs through Jerusalem. One head of state warned that if Bush proceeded with the campaign against Iraq, he would find every Muslim nation allied against him. Almost overnight the air went out of a quick campaign against Saddam; when it will reinflate is anybody's guess. Cheney returned from the trip in late March, says a U.S. official, in an altered state. The man who had dismissed the step-by-step peace process only weeks before was now offering himself up as a go-between with Arafat.

SWITCHING SIGNALS ON ARAFAT

Bush was aching to get out of Washington for Easter. He hadn't visited his ranch in three months, the longest time he has been away from Texas since becoming President. So he went to Crawford, but as the deadly suicide bombings continued, he stayed out of sight, saying nothing for the first 48 hours. His silence amounted to a green light to Israel to counterattack—which in turn triggered more suicide bombings. One reason for Bush's silence was that his aides were again fighting about what to say. The President said he didn't want to "show-boat," appearing for the cameras but not offering much. Powell argued, sources tell *Time*, that it was the moment to intervene and take a more evenhanded approach. But Rumsfeld and the hard-liners balked, arguing that terror was terror, no matter who was behind it. Other advisers wondered what Bush could conceivably do about the Holy Land's widening gyre. British Prime Minister Tony Blair weighed in, contending that making peace requires negotiating with the parties as you find them. And so, little by little, the Administration began to split the difference. On Saturday morning the U.S. voted with a near unanimous majority in the U.N. for a resolution calling on Israel to pull out of the Palestinian cities.

But that afternoon, when he finally made a statement, Bush seemed unaware of what his Administration had been up to. And he was working without a net: none of his top aides had followed him to Texas. "Everyone was on vacation," says a chagrined White House official, "and they pretty much stayed on vacation." Staffing the President was a junior press aide normally assigned to Homeland Security chief Tom Ridge, and it showed. "I can understand why the Israeli government takes the actions they take," Bush said. "Their country is under attack." Given the U.N. vote that very morning, the message was incoherent. And the imagery and atmospherics were all wrong: wearing an open-collar shirt and rocking back and forth in his chair, Bush looked like his pre–Sept. 11 self, a little bit scared and a little bit scary. A top official said later, "It was a mistake."

By the time Bush returned to Washington on Sunday, the White House knew it had a problem. Senators from both parties were calling for Bush to get more involved. Presidential counselor Karen Hughes' morning communications meeting began with an aide who complained, "We're getting killed in the media!" Hughes and Rice joined forces and went to Bush to propose that he make a clarifying statement about the region sometime during the week. This time, to the moderates' surprise, the idea had the support of Cheney, who told Bush it was time to change gears and move toward more active intervention. "He was very realistic this week," says an official in the moderate camp. "Cheney was clearly influenced by his trip." Bush agreed on Monday night but told his aides about his decision Tuesday morning.

When Bush threw himself into the Middle East peace blender, his aides knew his neat and simple foreign-policy doctrine was going to be pureed. That meant Bush's right wing would feel betrayed. Early in the week the neoconservative opinion makers William Bennett and William Kristol tell Bush to stick to his guns and show Arafat no quarter. Bennett and Kristol seemed to have an ally in Rumsfeld, who took an almost strident antiterrorist line in public one week, even as White House officials spread the word quietly that everyone actually agreed in private. Rumsfeld's remarks may have been just for show, designed to modify those Bush was about to throw over the side. If so, it worked: Kristol's criticism of Bush in the *Weekly Standard* magazine on Friday was surprisingly mild.

THE DANGERS AHEAD

Bush's opening statement wasn't exactly a beacon of clarity, since he had to carefully and judiciously slap just about everyone in the Middle East. But it may have been the beginning of a realistic policy. The main problem now is that no one knows what happens next. Arafat quickly accepted the President's proposal "without condition" as his spokesman said, but few believe he can control all the suicide bombers. Sharon pledged to withdraw from the Palestinian cities, but he seemed in a bigger hurry to mop up every potential terrorist and perhaps dismantle what was left of the civilian Palestinian Authority in the West Bank. The death toll for the week rose to more than 100, with Israeli soldiers tightening their grip around Manger Square, where Palestinian gunmen and a huddle of civilians and priests were besieged in the Church of the Nativity complex. Israeli warplanes and artillery struck targets in southern Lebanon on Saturday after Israeli posts in Israel proper and the Golan Heights were shelled by Hizballah, raising familiar fears that a widening conflict could squelch yet another peace mission before it has a chance to take root. And Bush toughened his message to Sharon and called on Israel to pull back from the West Bank cities "without delay." On Saturday, in a telephone conversation with Bush, Sharon said he would expedite the campaign.

Bush officials expect both Israeli and Palestinian positions to harden before they crack. That may explain why so many experts now believe the U.S. should come up with an ultimatum—a solution imposed from on high with new rules, sweeteners for every camp and unbearable penalties if they balk. It's an approach favored in one form or another by such old hands as Zbigniew Brzezinski, National Security Adviser in the Carter Administration, and Robert Malley, a former Clinton peace negotiator. Israeli Foreign Minister Shimon Peres thinks the U.S. should at least impose terms for a cease-fire, because "the alternative is another bazaar that will waste time and opportunities." Says Brzezinski: "The U.S. has to face the fact that the parties to the conflict are incapable of reaching a comprehensive peace on their own." But Dennis Ross, a former Bush and Clinton Middle East expert, says an ultimatum won't work. "You're not going to get them to compromise on Jerusalem now, you're not going to get them to compromise on refugees now, and you're not even going to get them to compromise on borders now," he says. "What you will produce is both sides focusing on the issues that give them the hardest line." Watching events unfold from the West Wing last week, one U.S. official sighed and said, "Better late than never." When it comes to the Middle East, that qualifies as optimism.

The Invasion of Iraq

Kenneth T. Walsh

Although it was the second U.S. invasion in twelve years, Bush's orders to begin war with Iraq in March 2003 was a historical first for the United States. After months of political negotiations through the United Nations, Bush gave Iraq's Saddam Hussein forty-eight hours to leave Baghdad or be forced out. Hours before the deadline, Bush met with advisers who had received information regarding where Hussein could be found. After a four-hour meeting with top advisers, Bush gave the word that launched the historical, preemptive attack. Despite Bush's confidence of the win, occupation and reconstruction of Iraq could take years and the war had damaged U.S. relationships with France, Germany, Russia, and other nations that opposed the rogue use of force. According to Kenneth T. Walsh, the plan was for Bush to use the success of the war with Iraq to heighten his political clout and push his domestic policies forward.

Walsh is the chief White House correspondent for *U.S. News & World Report.* He has taught courses on media and history at the American University and has authored several books on politics.

American presidents often try to remake the world. In 1823, James Monroe declared the Western Hemisphere off limits to European intervention in what became known as the Monroe Doctrine. In the 1940s, Harry Truman poured money into a shattered Europe to forestall communist takeovers after World War II as the centerpiece of the Truman Doctrine. In the 1980s, Ronald Reagan established the doctrine of rolling back, not just containing, communism. Twelve years ago, George H.W. Bush tried, with limited success, to organize a "New World Order" based on the allied victory in the first Persian Gulf War.

Kenneth T. Walsh, "Command Presence," *U.S. News & World Report,* vol. 134, March 31, 2003, pp. 30–32. Copyright © 2003 by *U.S. News & World Report.* Reproduced by permission.

Today, George W. Bush is thinking in bigger terms than most of his predecessors. His doctrine of pre-emptive war is one of the most far-reaching White House initiatives in U.S. history. "It's not a war about the past," says historian Robert Dallek. "It's a war about the future. If it goes quickly, smoothly, and comfortably, there will be more inducement for these preventive wars from now on." Iran and, conceivably, even nuclear-armed North Korea could be next, with potentially dangerous consequences: Pre-emptive war could become a model for other nations.

Bush's Certainty

Not that such perils have caused any second-guessing by the commander in chief. George W. Bush seems to reside in more of a doubt-free zone than ever. This was certainly true on the Monday [March 17, 2003] he began the final run-up to war by ending diplomatic efforts and giving Saddam Hussein 48 hours to leave Iraq. White House aides, borrowing a phrase from gunslinger folklore, called it the "get out of Dodge" speech. Bush's patience, clearly, had run out.

Then there was a bit of serendipity. Just hours before the 48-hour deadline was scheduled to elapse, U.S. officials received a tip that Saddam and his senior advisers were gathered in a fortified bunker in southern Baghdad. Bush spent nearly four hours discussing his options in the Oval Office with George Tenet, director of central intelligence, Vice President Dick Cheney, Defense Secretary Donald Rumsfeld, National Security Adviser Condoleezza Rice, White House Chief of Staff Andrew Card, and other senior U.S. officials. They became the "action officers," sifting through the intelligence, weighing the use of different weapons, and assessing whether a " decapitation" strike would change the intricately detailed war plans. Several times, *U.S. News* has learned, Bush's advisers called military commanders in the field— and possibly had others contact the source of the original tip—to get more information.

A Two-Edged Sword

At 7:12 P.M. [March 20], Bush gave the order to strike. "Let's go," he said with typical brevity. Bush also accepted his advisers' recommendation that Tomahawk cruise missiles wouldn't be enough to destroy a deeply buried bunker and that F-117 Stealth aircraft should also drop 2,000-pound "bunkerbuster" bombs on the site. Despite all of that, U.S. officials weren't sure if Saddam had been killed or wounded, or if he had escaped unharmed.

By Thursday, the day after he ordered the invasion, Bush's determination was clear at his cabinet meeting. "It was the absolute right decision to commit troops," he said. "It was the correct decision for peace and security. We tried everything possible to solve this through peace."

But Bush's certainty about the need for muscular American leadership may be a two-edged sword, some experts say. "What you have," says historian Dallek, "is sort of secular evangelism: 'I know I'm right. I know what to do.' It's very comforting when you are putting lives on the line and you are putting your administration at risk, and the public doesn't want someone that's Hamlet-like." On the other hand, Bush's certainty has alienated much of the world, evidenced by the massive antiwar demonstrations . . . in Athens, Paris, Tokyo, Great Britain, much of the Arab world, and across the United States. "There's a biblical certainty to the way he expresses himself," says Rutgers political scientist Ross K. Baker. "His self-assertiveness gets under the skin of Europeans. Rather than confident, he appears to them to be dogmatic. Rather than fortitude, he appears to be showing obduracy." Adds Baker: "The doctrine is, in effect, 'We are the world's policeman.' It may seem swaggering, or it may be the reality of the world. But when the drunken cowpokes are tearing up the saloon, who's going to settle things down? Who else is going to come through the swinging doors and put these guys in the hoosegow?"

Senior U.S. officials argue that the terrorist attacks of September 11 radicalized the president's ideas about national security. During the 2000 campaign, he criticized the Clinton administration for "nation building" and stretching the American military too thin. Now the threat of terrorism has made him more willing to take military action around the world, even unilaterally, to protect Americans from another attack. Strikes by America's enemies have become so potentially devastating in an era of weapons of mass destruction, the president believes, that the nation simply cannot afford to await the first blow.

Despite his confidence, Bush's immediate future is filled with risk. Not only does the war have to be won, but there's also the matter of the occupation and reconstruction of Iraq,

MESSAGE TO THE IRAQI PEOPLE

Shortly after America launched its invasion of Iraq, President Bush delivered the following message in a radio address to inform the Iraqi people of the intentions of U.S. military presence.

This is George W. Bush, the President of the United States. At this moment, the regime of Saddam Hussein is being removed from power, and a long era of fear and cruelty is ending. American and coalition forces are now operating inside Baghdad—and we will not stop until Saddam's corrupt gang is gone. The government of Iraq, and the future of your country, will soon belong to you.

The goals of our coalition are clear and limited. We will end a brutal regime, whose aggression and weapons of mass destruction make it a unique threat to the world. Coalition forces will help maintain law and order, so that Iraqis can live in security. We will respect your great religious traditions, whose principles of equality and compassion are essential to Iraq's future. We will help you build a peaceful and representative government that protects the rights of all citizens. And then our military forces will leave. Iraq will go forward as a unified, independent and sovereign nation that has regained a respected place in the world.

The United States and its coalition partners respect the people of Iraq. We are taking unprecedented measures to spare the lives of innocent Iraqi citizens, and are beginning to deliver food, water and medicine to those in need. Our only enemy is Saddam's brutal regime—and that regime is your enemy as well.

In the new era that is coming to Iraq, your country will no longer be held captive to the will of a cruel dictator. You will be free to build a better life, instead of building more palaces for Saddam and his sons, free to pursue economic prosperity without the hardship of economic sanctions, free to travel and speak your mind, free to join in the political affairs of Iraq. And all the people who make up your country—Kurds, Shi'a, Turkomans, Sunnis, and others—will be free of the terrible persecution that so many have endured.

The nightmare that Saddam Hussein has brought to your nation will soon be over. You are a good and gifted people— the heirs of a great civilisation that contributes to all humanity. You deserve better than tyranny and corruption and torture chambers. You deserve to live as free people. And I assure every citizen of Iraq: your nation will soon be free.

George W. Bush, President's Message to the Iraqi People, April 10, 2003.

rebuilding relationships with France, Germany, and Russia, and a host of other concerns. Says a former senior adviser to Ronald Reagan: "The next three months will be the most perilous time for the Bush presidency. We'll see if he's up to the job. And it's not just the war and its aftermath. It's the economy; it's terrorism. It's his leadership in Congress. It's North Korea. It's the price of oil and gasoline."

Administration officials are confident. Some are already discussing ways to build on what they predict will be a quick and decisive victory and say privately that Bush's popularity is sure to rise while the economy picks up steam and the stock markets begin reclaiming past losses. Newly discovered evidence of Saddam Hussein's monstrosity, these aides predict, will melt the opposition to Bush's war. After Saddam's removal, a senior White House aide says, "Iraqis will be dancing in the streets."

Bush discussed the war's aftermath in detail during a phone conversation with British Prime Minister Tony Blair last week. Among the topics: the United Nations' role in reconstructing Iraq; future efforts to "take on" weapons of mass destruction, and ways to neutralize other "rogue nations."

Just as important, Bush is intent on avoiding his father's mistake of seeming obsessed by foreign policy to the exclusion of domestic issues. At last week's cabinet meeting, he urged his senior advisers to keep working on important domestic issues, and he reiterated his support for tax cuts and other home-front priorities like Medicare reform.

If the war goes well, White House aides say, Bush will use his renewed political capital to push for a new round of tax cuts, spending reductions, and expanded prescription drug coverage for retirees.

GOOD VS. EVIL

Yet his views clearly parallel his father's in fundamental ways. Consider a poignant letter that the elder Bush wrote to his five children, including George W. Bush, on Dec. 31, 1990, just weeks before the fighting began. After explaining his concern about the deaths his decisions might cause, the elder Bush wrote: "My mind goes back to history: How many lives might have been saved if appeasement had given way to force earlier on in the late '30s or earliest '40s? How many Jews might have been spared the gas chambers, or how many Polish patriots might be alive today? I look at today's crisis as 'good' vs. 'evil'—Yes, it is that clear." He added: "Sometimes in life you have to act as you think best—you can't compromise, you can't give in—even if your critics are loud and numerous."

The younger Bush fully endorses those sentiments. In fact, his certitude has unsettled critics who see a return of the swaggering cowboy who took office in January 2001. He is so confident in the military that he feels no need to keep track of war coverage on television. Aside from watching scenes of the massive U.S. air campaign that were shown on American television Friday afternoon, aides say, he rarely turned on the TV news during the day. One aspect of the war that he *does* follow, however, is the weather, which can often limit U.S. operations. When he is relaxing in the White House residence, he sometimes tunes in the Weather Channel to check out forecasts for the Mideast, and for his beloved ranch in Crawford, Texas.

Bush's can-do attitude and willingness to take risks were illustrated during his recent meeting in the Oval Office with Italian Prime Minister Silvio Berlusconi. "It's important for a leader to lead," he said. "If you believe in something, then stand for it, and the people will follow." This is the philosophy that led George W. Bush to invade Iraq and that will guide him in the challenging days ahead.

APPENDIX OF DOCUMENTS

DOCUMENT 1: THE SPIRIT OF COOPERATION

George W. Bush addressed the nation from the Texas House of Representatives following a thirty-five-day election battle that ended with a ruling from the U.S. Supreme Court. President Bush's first speech on December 13, 2000, outlined his optimism to unite and inspire the American people after the unprecedented and divisive presidential contest.

I have a lot to be thankful for tonight. I'm thankful for America and thankful that we were able to resolve our electoral differences in a peaceful way.

I'm thankful to the American people for the great privilege of being able to serve as your next president. . . .

Tonight I chose to speak from the chamber of the Texas House of Representatives because it has been a home to bipartisan cooperation. Here in a place where Democrats have the majority, Republicans and Democrats have worked together to do what is right for the people we represent.

We've had spirited disagreements. And in the end, we found constructive consensus. It is an experience I will always carry with me, an example I will always follow. . . .

The spirit of cooperation I have seen in this hall is what is needed in Washington, D.C. It is the challenge of our moment. After a difficult election, we must put politics behind us and work together to make the promise of America available for every one of our citizens.

I am optimistic that we can change the tone in Washington, D.C.

I believe things happen for a reason, and I hope the long wait of the last five weeks will heighten a desire to move beyond the bitterness and partisanship of the recent past.

Our nation must rise above a house divided. Americans share hopes and goals and values far more important than any political disagreements.

Republicans want the best for our nation, and so do Democrats. Our votes may differ, but not our hopes.

I know America wants reconciliation and unity. I know Americans want progress. And we must seize this moment and deliver.

Together, guided by a spirit of common sense, common courtesy and common goals, we can unite and inspire the American citizens. . . .

Together we will address some of society's deepest problems one person at a time, by encouraging and empowering the good hearts and good works of the American people.

This is the essence of compassionate conservatism and it will be a foundation of my administration.

These priorities are not merely Republican concerns or Democratic concerns; they are American responsibilities.

During the fall campaign, we differed about the details of these proposals, but there was remarkable consensus about the important issues before us: excellent schools, retirement and health security, tax relief, a strong military, a more civil society.

We have discussed our differences. Now it is time to find common ground and build consensus to make America a beacon of opportunity in the 21st century. . . .

I have faith that with God's help we as a nation will move forward together as one nation, indivisible. And together we will create an America that is open, so every citizen has access to the American dream; an America that is educated, so every child has the keys to realize that dream; and an America that is united in our diversity and our shared American values that are larger than race or party.

I was not elected to serve one party, but to serve one nation.

The president of the United States is the president of every single American, of every race and every background.

Whether you voted for me or not, I will do my best to serve your interests and I will work to earn your respect. . . .

The presidency is more than an honor. It is more than an office. It is a charge to keep, and I will give it my all.

Thank you very much and God bless America.

George W. Bush, Presidential Acceptance Speech, December 13, 2000.

DOCUMENT 2: CIVIC DUTY

In his January 2001 inauguration address, George W. Bush urged citizenship over spectatorship and a sense of unity after years of poison-pen politics. Bush asked citizens to serve their nation beginning with their own neighborhoods.

I am honored and humbled to stand here, where so many of America's leaders have come before me, and so many will follow.

We have a place, all of us, in a long story—a story we continue, but whose end we will not see. It is the story of a new world that became a friend and liberator of the old, a story of a slave-holding society that became a servant of freedom, the story of a power that went into the world to protect but not possess, to defend but not to conquer.

It is the American story—a story of flawed and fallible people, united across the generations by grand and enduring ideals.

The grandest of these ideals is an unfolding American promise that everyone belongs, that everyone deserves a chance, that no insignificant person was ever born.

Americans are called to enact this promise in our lives and in our laws. And though our nation has sometimes halted, and sometimes delayed, we must follow no other course.

Through much of the last century, America's faith in freedom and democracy was a rock in a raging sea. Now it is a seed upon the wind, taking root in many nations.

Our democratic faith is more than the creed of our country, it is the inborn hope of our humanity, an ideal we carry but do not own, a trust we bear and pass along. And even after nearly 225 years, we have a long way yet to travel.

While many of our citizens prosper, others doubt the promise, even the justice, of our own country. The ambitions of some Americans are limited by failing schools and hidden prejudice and the circumstances of their birth. And sometimes our differences run so deep, it seems we share a continent, but not a country.

We do not accept this, and we will not allow it. Our unity, our union, is the serious work of leaders and citizens in every generation. And this is my solemn pledge: I will work to build a single nation of justice and opportunity.

I know this is in our reach because we are guided by a power larger than ourselves who creates us equal in His image.

And we are confident in principles that unite and lead us onward.

America has never been united by blood or birth or soil. We are bound by ideals that move us beyond our backgrounds, lift us above our interests and teach us what it means to be citizens. Every child must be taught these principles. Every citizen must uphold them. And every immigrant, by embracing these ideals, makes our country more, not less, American.

Today, we affirm a new commitment to live out our nation's promise through civility, courage, compassion and character.

America, at its best, matches a commitment to principle with a concern for civility. A civil society demands from each of us good will and respect, fair dealing and forgiveness.

Some seem to believe that our politics can afford to be petty because, in a time of peace, the stakes of our debates appear small.

But the stakes for America are never small. If our country does not lead the cause of freedom, it will not be led. If we do not turn the hearts of children toward knowledge and character, we will lose their gifts and undermine their idealism. If we permit our economy to drift and decline, the vulnerable will suffer most.

We must live up to the calling we share. Civility is not a tactic or a sentiment. It is the determined choice of trust over cynicism, of community over chaos. And this commitment, if we keep it, is a way to shared accomplishment. . . .

Abandonment and abuse are not acts of God, they are failures of love.

And the proliferation of prisons, however necessary, is no substitute for hope and order in our souls.

Where there is suffering, there is duty. Americans in need are not strangers, they are citizens, not problems, but priorities. And all of us are diminished when any are hopeless.

Government has great responsibilities for public safety and public health, for civil rights and common schools. Yet compassion is the work of a nation, not just a government. . . .

Sometimes in life we are called to do great things. But as a saint of our times has said, every day we are called to do small things with great love. The most important tasks of a democracy are done by everyone. . . .

What you do is as important as anything government does. I ask you to seek a common good beyond your comfort; to defend needed reforms against easy attacks; to serve your nation, beginning with your neighbor. I ask you to be citizens: citizens, not spectators; citizens, not subjects; responsible citizens, building communities of service and a nation of character.

Americans are generous and strong and decent, not because we believe in ourselves, but because we hold beliefs beyond ourselves. When this spirit of citizenship is missing, no government program can replace it. When this spirit is present, no wrong can stand against it.

George W. Bush, Inauguration Speech, January 20, 2001.

DOCUMENT 3: UNITY IN A TIME OF DESPAIR

President Bush will be remembered as a president who helped to heal a nation. Addressing the country in its hour of grief on September 14, 2001, during a National Day of Prayer and Remembrance, President Bush said America's character had been shown to the world in acts of kindness, generosity, and bravery.

We are here in the middle hour of our grief. So many have suffered so great a loss, and today we express our nation's sorrow. We come before God to pray for the missing and the dead, and for those who love them. . . .

War has been waged against us by stealth and deceit and murder. This nation is peaceful, but fierce when stirred to anger. This conflict was begun on the timing and terms of others. It will end in a way, and at an hour, of our choosing. . . .

It is said that adversity introduces us to ourselves. This is true of a nation as well. In this trial, we have been reminded, and the world has seen, that our fellow Americans are generous and kind, resourceful and brave. We see our national character in rescuers working past exhaustion; in long lines of blood donors; in thousands of citizens who have asked to work and serve in any way possible.

And we have seen our national character in eloquent acts of sacrifice. Inside the World Trade Center, one man who could have saved himself stayed until the end at the side of his quadriplegic friend. A beloved priest died giving the last rites to a firefighter. Two office workers, finding a disabled stranger, carried her down sixty-eight floors to safety. A group of men drove through the night from Dallas to Washington to bring skin grafts for burn victims.

In these acts, and in many others, Americans showed a deep commitment to one another, and an abiding love for our country. Today, we feel what Franklin Roosevelt called the warm courage of national unity. This is a unity of every faith, and every background.

It has joined together political parties in both houses of Congress. It is evident in services of prayer and candlelight vigils, and American flags, which are displayed in pride, and wave in defiance.

Our unity is a kinship of grief, and a steadfast resolve to prevail against our enemies. And this unity against terror is now extending across the world.

America is a nation full of good fortune, with so much to be grateful for. But we are not spared from suffering. In every generation, the world has produced enemies of human freedom. They have attacked America, because we are freedom's home and defender. And the commitment of our fathers is now the calling of our time.

On this national day of prayer and remembrance, we ask almighty God to watch over our nation, and grant us patience and resolve in all that is to come. We pray that He will comfort and console those who now walk in sorrow. We thank Him for each life we now must mourn, and the promise of a life to come.

George W. Bush, Remarks at the National Day of Prayer and Remembrance, September 14, 2001.

DOCUMENT 4: THE MISSION AGAINST TERRORISM

On September 20, 2001, President Bush called a nation to defend its freedom. He addressed a joint session of Congress and the American people from the U.S. Capitol and gave evidence that al-Qaeda was the group responsible for the September 11 terrorist attacks on the United States.

On September the 11th, enemies of freedom committed an act of war against our country. . . .

Americans are asking: Who attacked our country? The evidence we have gathered all points to a collection of loosely affiliated terrorist organizations known as al-Qaeda. They are the same murderers indicted for bombing American embassies in Tanzania and Kenya, and responsible for bombing the USS *Cole.*

Al-Qaeda is to terror what the mafia is to crime. But its goal is not making money; its goal is remaking the world—and imposing its radical beliefs on people everywhere.

The terrorists practice a fringe form of Islamic extremism that has been rejected by Muslim scholars and the vast majority of Muslim clerics—a fringe movement that perverts the peaceful teachings of Islam. The terrorists' directive commands them to kill Christians and Jews, to kill all Americans, and make no distinction among military and civilians, including women and children.

This group and its leader—a person named Osama bin Laden—are linked to many other organizations in different countries, including the Egyptian Islamic Jihad and the Islamic Movement of Uzbekistan. There are thousands of these terrorists in more than 60 countries. They are recruited from their own nations and neighborhoods and brought to camps in places like Afghanistan, where they are trained in the tactics of terror. They are sent back to their homes or sent to hide in countries around the world to plot evil and destruction.

The leadership of al-Qaeda has great influence in Afghanistan and supports the Taliban regime in controlling most of that country. In Afghanistan, we see al-Qaeda's vision for the world.

Afghanistan's people have been brutalized—many are starving and many have fled. Women are not allowed to attend school. You can be jailed for owning a television. Religion can be practiced only as their leaders dictate. A man can be jailed in Afghanistan if his beard is not long enough.

The United States respects the people of Afghanistan—after all, we are currently its largest source of humanitarian aid—but we condemn the Taliban regime. It is not only repressing its own people, it is threatening people everywhere by sponsoring and sheltering and supplying terrorists. By aiding and abetting murder, the Taliban regime is committing murder.

And tonight, the United States of America makes the following demands on the Taliban: Deliver to United States authorities all the leaders of al-Qaeda who hide in your land. Release all foreign nationals, including American citizens, you have unjustly imprisoned. Protect foreign journalists, diplomats and aid workers in your country. Close immediately and permanently every terrorist training camp in Afghanistan, and hand over every terrorist, and every person in their support structure, to appropriate authorities. Give the United States full access to terrorist training camps, so we can make sure they are no longer operating.

These demands are not open to negotiation or discussion. The Taliban must act, and act immediately. They will hand over the terrorists, or they will share in their fate. . . .

Our war on terror begins with al-Qaeda, but it does not end there. It will not end until every terrorist group of global reach has been found, stopped and defeated. . . .

These terrorists kill not merely to end lives, but to disrupt and end a way of life. With every atrocity, they hope that America grows fearful, retreating from the world and forsaking our friends. They stand against us, because we stand in their way. . . .

Americans are asking: How will we fight and win this war? We will direct every resource at our command—every means of diplomacy, every tool of intelligence, every instrument of law enforcement, every financial influence, and every necessary weapon of war—to the disruption and to the defeat of the global terror network. . . .

Our response involves far more than instant retaliation and isolated strikes. Americans should not expect one battle, but a lengthy campaign, unlike any other we have ever seen. It may include dramatic strikes, visible on TV, and covert operations, secret even in success. We will starve terrorists of funding, turn them one against another, drive them from place to place, until there is no refuge or no rest. And we will pursue nations that provide aid or safe haven to terrorism. Every nation, in every region, now has a decision to make. Either you are with us, or you are with the terrorists. From this day forward, any nation that continues to harbor or support terrorism will be regarded by the United States as a hostile regime. . . .

This is not, however, just America's fight. And what is at stake is not just America's freedom. This is the world's fight. This is civilization's fight. This is the fight of all who believe in progress and pluralism, tolerance and freedom.

We ask every nation to join us. We will ask, and we will need, the help of police forces, intelligence services, and banking systems around the world. The United States is grateful that many nations and many international organizations have already responded—with sympathy and with support. Nations from Latin America, to Asia, to Africa, to Europe, to the Islamic world. Perhaps the NATO Charter reflects best the attitude of the world: An attack on one is an attack on all.

The civilized world is rallying to America's side. They understand that if this terror goes unpunished, their own cities, their own citizens may be next. Terror, unanswered, can not only bring down buildings, it can threaten the stability of legitimate governments. And you know what—we're not going to allow it. . . .

Great harm has been done to us. We have suffered great loss. And in our grief and anger we have found our mission and our moment. Freedom and fear are at war. The advance of human freedom—the great achievement of our time, and the great hope of every time—now depends on us. Our nation—this generation—will lift a dark threat of violence from our people and our future. We will rally the world to this cause by our efforts, by our courage. We will not tire, we will not falter, and we will not fail. . . .

I will not forget this wound to our country or those who inflicted it. I will not yield; I will not rest; I will not relent in waging this struggle for freedom and security for the American people.

The course of this conflict is not known, yet its outcome is certain. Freedom and fear, justice and cruelty, have always been at war, and we know that God is not neutral between them.

Fellow citizens, we'll meet violence with patient justice—assured of the rightness of our cause, and confident of the victories to come. In all that lies before us, may God grant us wisdom, and may He watch over the United States of America.

George W. Bush, Address to Congress and the American People, September 20, 2001.

DOCUMENT 5: MILITARY ACTION AGAINST THE TALIBAN

On October 13, 2001, President George W. Bush announced his order for the Armed Services to attack al-Qaeda terrorist training camps in Afghanistan. Bush stated that the British joined in the military operation, and he warned that each of the world's nations would have to take a stand against terrorism or become the enemy of those nations that would.

Good afternoon. On my orders, the United States military has begun strikes against al-Qaeda terrorist training camps and military installations of the Taliban regime in Afghanistan. These carefully targeted actions are designed to disrupt the use of Afghanistan as a terrorist base of operations, and to attack the military capability of the Taliban regime.

We are joined in this operation by our staunch friend, Great Britain. Other close friends, including Canada, Australia, Germany and France, have pledged forces as the operation unfolds. More than 40 countries in the Middle East, Africa, Europe and across Asia have granted air transit or landing rights. Many more have shared intelligence. We are supported by the collective will of the world.

More than two weeks ago, I gave Taliban leaders a series of clear and specific demands: Close terrorist training camps; hand over leaders of the al-Qaeda network; and return all foreign nationals, including American citizens, unjustly detained in your country. None of these demands were met. And now the Taliban will pay a price. By destroying camps and disrupting communications, we will make it more difficult for the terror network to train new recruits and coordinate their evil plans.

Initially, the terrorists may burrow deeper into caves and other entrenched hiding places. Our military action is also designed to clear the way for sustained, comprehensive and relentless operations to drive them out and bring them to justice.

At the same time, the oppressed people of Afghanistan will know the generosity of America and our allies. As we strike military targets, we'll also drop food, medicine and supplies to the starving and suffering men and women and children of Afghanistan.

The United States of America is a friend to the Afghan people, and we are the friends of almost a billion worldwide who practice the Islamic faith. The United States of America is an enemy of those who aid terrorists and of the barbaric criminals who profane a great religion by committing murder in its name.

This military action is a part of our campaign against terrorism, another front in a war that has already been joined through diplomacy, intelligence, the freezing of financial assets and the arrests of known terrorists by law enforcement agents in 38 countries. Given the nature and reach of our enemies, we will win this conflict by the patient accumulation of successes, by meeting a series of challenges with determination and will and purpose.

Today we focus on Afghanistan, but the battle is broader. Every nation has a choice to make. In this conflict, there is no neutral ground. If any government sponsors the outlaws and killers of innocents, they have become outlaws and murderers, themselves. And they will take that lonely path at their own peril.

I'm speaking to you today from the Treaty Room of the White House, a place where American presidents have worked for peace. We're a peaceful nation. Yet, as we have learned, so suddenly and so tragically, there can be no peace in a world of sudden terror. In the face of today's new threat, the only way to pursue peace is to pursue those who threaten it.

We did not ask for this mission, but we will fulfill it. The name of today's military operation is Enduring Freedom. We defend not only our precious freedoms, but also the freedom of people everywhere to live and raise their children free from fear.

I know many Americans feel fear today. And our government is taking strong precautions. All law enforcement and intelligence agencies are working aggressively around America, around the world and around the clock. At my request, many governors have activated the National Guard to strengthen airport security. We have called up Reserves to reinforce our military capability and strengthen the protection of our homeland.

In the months ahead, our patience will be one of our strengths— patience with the long waits that will result from tighter security; patience and understanding that it will take time to achieve our goals; patience in all the sacrifices that may come.

Today, those sacrifices are being made by members of our Armed Forces who now defend us so far from home, and by their proud and worried families. A commander in chief sends America's sons and daughters into a battle in a foreign land only after the greatest care and a lot of prayer. We ask a lot of those who wear our uniform. We ask them to leave their loved ones, to travel great distances, to risk injury, even to be prepared to make the ultimate sacrifice of their lives. They are dedicated, they are honorable; they represent the best of our country. And we are grateful.

To all the men and women in our military—every sailor, every soldier, every airman, every Coast Guardsman, every Marine—I say this: Your mission is defined; your objectives are clear; your goal is just. You have my full confidence, and you will have every tool you need to carry out your duty.

I recently received a touching letter that says a lot about the state of America in these difficult times—a letter from a fourth-grade girl, with a father in the military: "As much as I don't want my Dad to fight," she wrote, "I'm willing to give him to you."

This is a precious gift, the greatest she could give. This young girl knows what America is all about. Since Sept. 11, an entire generation of young Americans has gained new understanding of the value of freedom, and its cost in duty and in sacrifice. The battle is now joined on many fronts. We will not waver; we will not tire; we will not falter; and we will not fail. Peace and freedom will prevail.

Thank you. May God continue to bless America.

George W. Bush, "Bush Announces Military Action Against Terrorist Infrastructure and Taliban Regime in Afghanistan," *Congressional Quarterly Weekly,* vol. 59, no. 39, October 13, 2001.

DOCUMENT 6: WHAT HAS BEEN DONE AND WHAT CAN STILL BE DONE

With war under way in Afghanistan and an investigation of anthrax scares in the United States, President Bush spoke to the nation on November 8, 2001, to indicate America's progress against terrorism. While assuring the public that the nation was acting bravely in the face of adversity, Bush informed Americans that they all had a role to play in protecting and serving their country.

Tonight, many thousands of children are tragically learning to live without one of their parents. And the rest of us are learning to live in a world that seems very different than it was on September the 10th.

The moment the second plane hit the second building—when we knew it was a terrorist attack—many felt that our lives would never be the same. What we couldn't be sure of then—and what the terrorists never expected—was that America would emerge stronger, with a renewed spirit of pride and patriotism.

I said in my speech to a Joint Session of Congress that we are a nation awakened to danger. We're also a nation awakened to service, and citizenship, and compassion. None of us would ever wish the evil that has been done to our country, yet we have learned that out of evil can come great good.

During the last two months, we have shown the world America is a great nation. Americans have responded magnificently, with courage and caring. We've seen it in our children, who have sent in more than $1 million for the children of Afghanistan. We have seen it in the compassion of Jewish and Christian Americans who have reached out to their Muslim neighbors. We have seen it as Americans have reassessed priorities—parents spending more time with their children, and many people spending more time in prayer and in houses of worship.

We have gained new heroes: Those who ran into burning buildings to save others, our police and our firefighters. Those who battled their own fears to keep children calm and safe—America's teachers. Those who voluntarily placed themselves in harm's way to defend our freedom—the men and women of the Armed Forces.

And tonight, we join in thanking a whole new group of public servants who never enlisted to fight a war, but find themselves on the front lines of a battle nonetheless: Those who deliver the mail—America's postal workers. We also thank those whose quick response provided preventive treatment that has no doubt saved thousands of lives—our health care workers.

We are a different country than we were on September the 10th—sadder and less innocent; stronger and more united; and in the face of ongoing threats, determined and courageous.

Our nation faces a threat to our freedoms, and the stakes could not be higher. We are the target of enemies who boast they want to kill—kill all Americans, kill all Jews, and kill all Christians. We've seen that type of hate before—and the only possible response is to confront it, and to defeat it.

This new enemy seeks to destroy our freedom and impose its views. We value life; the terrorists ruthlessly destroy it. We value education; the terrorists do not believe women should be educated or should have health care, or should leave their homes. We value the right to speak our minds; for the terrorists, free expression can be grounds for execution. We respect people of all faiths and welcome the free practice of religion; our enemy wants to dictate how to think and how to worship even to their fellow Muslims.

This enemy tries to hide behind a peaceful faith. But those who celebrate the murder of innocent men, women, and children have no religion, have no conscience, and have no mercy.

We wage a war to save civilization, itself. We did not seek it, but we must fight it—and we will prevail.

This is a different war from any our nation has ever faced, a war on many fronts, against terrorists who operate in more than 60 different countries. And this is a war that must be fought not only overseas, but also here at home. I recently spoke to high school students in Maryland, and realized that for the first time ever, these seniors will graduate in the midst of a war in our own country. We've added a new era, and this new era requires new responsibilities, both for the government and for our people.

The government has a responsibility to protect our citizens—and that starts with homeland security. The first attack against America came by plane, and we are now making our airports and airplanes safer. We have posted the National Guard in America's airports and placed undercover air marshals on many flights. I call on Congress to quickly send me legislation that makes cockpits more secure, baggage screening more thorough, and puts the federal government in charge of all airport screening and security.

The second attack against America came in the mail. We do not know whether this attack came from the same terrorists; we don't know the origin of the anthrax—but whoever did this unprecedented and uncivilized act is a terrorist.

Four Americans have now died from anthrax, out of a total of 17 people who have been infected. The Postal Service has processed more than 30 billion pieces of mail since September the 11th, and so far we've identified three different letters that contained anthrax. We can trace the source of infection for all but one of the individuals, and we are still trying to learn how a woman who died in New York was exposed.

I'm proud of the way our health care and postal workers—and the American people—are responding with calm in the face of this deadly new threat. Public health officials have acted quickly to distribute preventive antibiotics to thousands of people who may have been exposed. The government is purchasing and storing medicines and vaccines as a precaution against future attacks. We are cleaning facilities where anthrax has been detected, and purchasing equipment to sanitize the mail. Thousands of law enforcement officials are aggressively investigating this bioterrorism attack—and public health officials are distributing the most accurate, up-to-date information we have to medical professionals and to the public.

To coordinate our efforts we've created the new Office of Homeland Security. Its director, my good friend and former Governor, Tom Ridge, reports directly to me—and works with all our federal agencies, state and local governments, and the private sector on a national strategy to strengthen our homeland protections. For example, the Coast Guard has taken on expanded duties to protect our shores and our ports. The National Guard has increased—an increased role in surveillance at our border. We're imposing new licensing requirements for safer transportation of hazardous material.

We've passed a new antiterrorism law which gives our law enforcement officers the necessary tools to track terrorists before they harm Americans. A new terrorism task force is tightening immigration controls to make sure no one enters or stays in our country who would harm us. We are a welcoming country, we will always value freedom—yet we will not allow those who plot against our country to abuse our freedoms and our protections.

Our enemies have threatened other acts of terror. We take each threat seriously. And when we have evidence of credible threats, we will issue appropriate alerts.

A terrorism alert is not a signal to stop your life. It is a call to be vigilant—to know that your government is on high alert, and to add your eyes and ears to our efforts to find and stop those who want to do us harm.

A lot of people are working really hard to protect America. But in the long run, the best way to defend our homeland—the best way to make sure our children can live in peace—is to take the battle to the enemy and to stop them.

I have called our military into action to hunt down the members of the al-Qaeda organization who murdered innocent Americans. I gave fair warning to the government that harbors them in Afghanistan. The Taliban made a choice to continue hiding terrorists, and now they are paying a price.

I'm so proud of our military. Our military is pursuing its mission. We are destroying training camps, disrupting communications, and dismantling air defenses. We are now bombing Taliban front lines. We are deliberately and systematically hunting down these murderers, and we will bring them to justice. . . .

After September the 11th, our government assumed new responsibilities to strengthen security at home and track down our enemies abroad. And the American people are accepting new responsibilities, as well. . . .

Many ask, what can I do to help in our fight. The answer is simple. All of us can become a September the 11th volunteer by making a commitment to service in our own communities. So you can serve your country by tutoring or mentoring a child, comforting the afflicted, housing those in need of shelter and a home. You can participate in your Neighborhood Watch or Crime Stoppers. You can become a volunteer in a hospital, emergency medical, fire or rescue unit. You can support our troops in the field and, just as importantly, support their families here at home, by becoming active in the USO or groups and communities near our military installations.

We also will encourage service to country by creating new opportunities within the AmeriCorps and Senior Corps programs for public safety and public health efforts. We'll ask state and local officials to create a new modern civil defense service similar to local volunteer fire departments, to respond to local emergencies when the manpower of governments is stretched thin. We will find ways to train and mobilize more volunteers to help when rescue and health emergencies arise.

Americans have a lot to offer, so I've created a task force to develop additional ways people can get directly involved in this war effort, by making our homes and neighborhoods and schools and workplaces safer. And I call on all Americans to serve by bettering our communities and, thereby, defy and defeat the terrorists.

Our great nation—national challenge is to hunt down the terrorists and strengthen our protection against future attacks. Our great national opportunity is to preserve forever the good that has resulted. Through this tragedy, we are renewing and reclaiming our strong American values. . . .

Above all, we will live in a spirit of courage and optimism. Our nation was born in that spirit, as immigrants yearning for freedom courageously risked their lives in search of greater opportunity. That spirit of optimism and courage still beckons people across the world who want to come here. And that spirit of optimism and courage must guide those of us fortunate enough to live here.

Courage and optimism led the passengers on Flight 93 to rush their murderers to save lives on the ground. Led by a young man whose last known words were the Lord's Prayer and "Let's roll." He didn't know he had signed on for heroism when he boarded the plane that day. Some of our greatest moments have been acts of courage for which no one could have ever prepared.

We will always remember the words of that brave man, expressing the spirit of a great country. We will never forget all we have lost, and all we are fighting for. Ours is the cause of freedom. We've defeated freedom's enemies before, and we will defeat them again.

We cannot know every turn this battle will take. Yet we know our cause is just and our ultimate victory is assured. We will, no doubt, face new challenges. But we have our marching orders: My fellow Americans, let's roll.

George W. Bush, Address to the Nation at the World Congress Center in Atlanta, Georgia, November 8, 2001.

DOCUMENT 7: A CALL FOR CORPORATE ETHICS AND REFORM

President Bush created a new Corporate Fraud Task Force to reform corporate integrity and introduce fiscal accountability after a series of management abuses made national headlines. In a speech delivered July 9, 2002, in the New York financial district, Bush summarizes the response of his administration to restore confidence in corporate America.

I've come to the financial capital of the world to speak of a serious challenge to our financial markets, and to the confidence on which they rest. The misdeeds now being uncovered in some quarters of corporate America are threatening the financial well-being of many workers and many investors. At this moment, America's greatest economic need is higher ethical standards—standards enforced by strict laws and upheld by responsible business leaders.

The lure of heady profits of the late 1990s spawned abuses and excesses. With strict enforcement and higher ethical standards, we must usher in a new era of integrity in corporate America. . . .

The American economy—our economy—is built on confidence. The conviction that our free enterprise system will continue to be the most powerful and most promising in the world. That confidence is well-placed. After all, American technology is the most advanced in the world. Our universities attract the talent of the world. Our workers and ranchers and farmers can compete with anyone in the world. Our society rewards hard work and honest ambition, bringing people to our shores from all around the world who share those values. The American economy is the most creative and enterprising and productive system ever devised. . . .

We've learned of some business leaders obstructing justice, and misleading clients, falsifying records, business executives breaching the trust and abusing power. We've learned of CEOs earning tens of millions of dollars in bonuses just before their companies go bankrupt, leaving employees and retirees and investors to suffer. The business pages of American newspapers should not read like a scandal sheet.

The vast majority of businessmen and women are honest. They do right by their employees and their shareholders. They do not cut ethical corners, and their work helps create an economy which is the envy of the world.

Yet high-profile acts of deception have shaken people's trust. Too many corporations seem disconnected from the values of our country. These scandals have hurt the reputations of many good and honest companies. They have hurt the stock market. And worst of all, they are hurting millions of people who depend on the integrity of businesses for their livelihood and their retirement, for their peace of mind and their financial well-being. . . .

I'm calling for a new ethic of personal responsibility in the business community; an ethic that will increase investor confidence, will make employees proud of their companies, and again, regain the trust of the American people. . . .

Self-regulation is important, but it's not enough. Government cannot remove risk from investment I know that—or chance from the market. But government can do more to promote transparency and ensure that risks are honest. And government can ensure that those who breach the trust of the American people are punished. . . .

Today, by executive order, I create a new Corporate Fraud Task Force, headed by the Deputy Attorney General, which will target major accounting fraud and other criminal activity in corporate finance. . . .

I'm also proposing tough new criminal penalties for corporate fraud. This legislation would double the maximum prison terms for those convicted of financial fraud from five to 10 years. . . .

Second, we're moving corporate accounting out of the shadows, so the investing public will have a true and fair and timely picture of assets and liabilities and income of publicly traded companies. Greater transparency will expose bad companies and, just as importantly, protect the reputations of the good ones. . . .

Third, my administration will guard the interests of small investors and pension holders. More than 80 million Americans own stock, and many of them are new to the market. Buying stock gives them an opportunity to build wealth over the long-term, and this is the very kind of responsible investment we must promote in America. To encourage stock ownership, we must make sure that analysts give honest advice, and pension plans treat workers fairly. . . .

The American system of enterprise has not failed us. Some dishonest individuals have failed our system. Now comes the urgent work of enforcement and reform, driven by a new ethic of responsibility. . . .

We will show that markets can be both dynamic and honest, that lasting wealth and prosperity are built on a foundation of integrity.

By reasserting the best values of our country, we will reclaim the promise of our economy.

George W. Bush, Remarks by the President on Corporate Responsibility, July 9, 2002.

DOCUMENT 8: THE UN MUST STAND AGAINST IRAQ'S DEFIANCE

On September 12, 2002, President Bush addressed the United Nations to gather a coalition of support to join the United States in forcing Iraq to comply with UN Security Council Resolutions from 1990. These resolutions called for Iraq to dispose of any weapons of mass destruction and permit UN inspectors to investigate Iraqi sites where such weapons could be made or stored. If Iraq refused to accede to these demands, Bush intimated that military action may be necessary to force Iraqi president Saddam Hussein's compliance.

The United Nations was born in the hope that survived a world war—the hope of a world moving toward justice, escaping old patterns of conflict and fear. The founding members resolved that the peace of the world must never again be destroyed by the will and wickedness of any man. We created the United Nations Security Council, so that, unlike the League of Nations, our deliberations would be more than talk, our resolutions would be more than wishes. After generations of deceitful dictators and broken treaties and squandered lives, we dedicated ourselves to standards of human dignity shared by all, and to a system of security defended by all.

Today, these standards, and this security, are challenged. Our commitment to human dignity is challenged by persistent poverty and raging disease. The suffering is great, and our responsibilities are clear. The United States is joining with the world to supply aid where it reaches people and lifts up lives, to extend trade and the prosperity it brings, and to bring medical care where it is desperately needed. . . .

Twelve years ago, Iraq invaded Kuwait without provocation. And the regime's forces were poised to continue their march to seize other countries and their resources. Had Saddam Hussein been appeased instead of stopped, he would have endangered the peace and stability of the world. Yet this aggression was stopped—by the might of coalition forces and the will of the United Nations.

To suspend hostilities, to spare himself, Iraq's dictator accepted a series of commitments. The terms were clear, to him and to all. And he agreed to prove he is complying with every one of those obligations.

He has proven instead only his contempt for the United Nations, and for all his pledges. By breaking every pledge—by his deceptions, and by his cruelties—Saddam Hussein has made the case against himself. . . .

Delegates to the General Assembly, we have been more than patient. We've tried sanctions. We've tried the carrot of oil for food, and the stick of coalition military strikes. But Saddam Hussein has defied all these efforts and continues to develop weapons of mass destruction. The first time we may be completely certain he has a—nuclear weapons is when, God forbid, he uses one. We owe it to all our citizens to do everything in our power to prevent that day from coming.

The conduct of the Iraqi regime is a threat to the authority of the United Nations, and a threat to peace. Iraq has answered a decade of U.N. demands with a decade of defiance. All the world now faces a test, and the United Nations a difficult and defining moment. Are Security Council resolutions to be honored and enforced, or cast aside without consequence? Will the United Nations serve the purpose of its founding, or will it be irrelevant?

The United States helped found the United Nations. We want the United Nations to be effective, and respectful, and successful. We want the resolutions of the world's most important multilateral body to be enforced. And right now those resolutions are being unilaterally subverted by the Iraqi regime. Our partnership of nations can meet the test before us, by making clear what we now expect of the Iraqi regime.

If the Iraqi regime wishes peace, it will immediately and unconditionally forswear, disclose, and remove or destroy all weapons of mass destruction, long-range missiles, and all related material.

If the Iraqi regime wishes peace, it will immediately end all support for terrorism and act to suppress it, as all states are required to do by U.N. Security Council resolutions.

If the Iraqi regime wishes peace, it will cease persecution of its civilian population, including Shi'a, Sunnis, Kurds, Turkomans, and others, again as required by Security Council resolutions.

If the Iraqi regime wishes peace, it will release or account for all Gulf War personnel whose fate is still unknown. It will return the remains of any who are deceased, return stolen property, accept liability for losses resulting from the invasion of Kuwait, and fully cooperate with international efforts to resolve these issues, as required by Security Council resolutions.

If the Iraqi regime wishes peace, it will immediately end all illicit trade outside the oil-for-food program. It will accept U.N. administration of funds from that program, to ensure that the money is used fairly and promptly for the benefit of the Iraqi people.

If all these steps are taken, it will signal a new openness and accountability in Iraq. And it could open the prospect of the United Nations helping to build a government that represents all Iraqis—a government based on respect for human rights, economic liberty, and internationally supervised elections.

The United States has no quarrel with the Iraqi people; they've suffered too long in silent captivity. Liberty for the Iraqi people is a great moral cause, and a great strategic goal. The people of Iraq deserve it; the security of all nations requires it. Free societies do not intimidate through cruelty and conquest, and open societies do not threaten the world with mass murder. The United States supports political and economic liberty in a unified Iraq. . . .

If we meet our responsibilities, if we overcome this danger, we can arrive at a very different future. . . .

We must choose between a world of fear and a world of progress. We cannot stand by and do nothing while dangers gather. We must stand up for our security, and for the permanent rights and the hopes of mankind. By heritage and by choice, the United States of America will make that stand. And, delegates to the United Nations, you have the power to make that stand, as well.

George W. Bush, Remarks by the President in an Address to the United Nations General Assembly, September 12, 2002.

DOCUMENT 9: IRAQ WILL BE HELD ACCOUNTABLE

Believing Iraq's use and development of weapons of mass destruction constitute a threat to America, President Bush addressed the nation. From the White House rose garden, Bush acknowledged the Congressional show of unity in favor of war with Iraq if it would ensure Iraqi disarmament or protect America from further terrorism.

On its present course, the Iraqi regime is a threat of unique urgency. We know the treacherous history of the regime. It has waged a war against its neighbors; it has sponsored and sheltered terrorists; it has developed weapons of mass death; it has used them against innocent men, women and children. We know the designs of the Iraqi regime. In defiance of pledges to the U.N., it has stockpiled biological and chemical weapons. It is rebuilding the facilities used to make those weapons.

U.N. inspectors believe that Iraq could have produced enough biological and chemical agent to kill millions of people. The regime has the scientists and facilities to build nuclear weapons, and is seeking the materials needed to do so.

We know the methods of this regime. They buy time with hollow promises. They move incriminating evidence to stay ahead of inspectors. They concede just enough to escape—to escape punishment, and then violate every pledge when the attention of the world is turned away.

We also know the nature of Iraq's dictator [Saddam Hussein]. On his orders, opponents have been decapitated and their heads displayed outside their homes. Women have been systematically raped as a method of intimidation. Political prisoners are made to watch their own children being tortured. The dictator is a student of [Soviet dictator Josef] Stalin, using murder as a tool of terror and control within his own cabinet, within his own army, even within his own family. We will not leave the future of peace and the security of America in the hands of this cruel and dangerous man.

None of us here today desire to see military conflict, because we know the awful nature of war. Our country values life, and never seeks war unless it is essential to security and to justice. America's leadership and willingness to use force, confirmed by the Congress, is the best way to ensure compliance and avoid conflict. Saddam must disarm, period. If, however, he chooses to do otherwise, if he persists in his defiance, the use of force may become unavoidable.

The course of action may bring many sacrifices. Yet delay, indecision and inaction could lead to a massive and sudden horror. By timely and resolute action, we can defend ourselves and shape a peaceful future. Together with the Congress, I will do everything necessary to protect and defend our country.

In accepting this responsibility, we also serve the interests and the hopes of the Iraqi people. They are a great and gifted people, with an ancient and admirable culture, and they would not choose to be ruled by violence and terror. The people of Iraq are the daily victims of Saddam Hussein's oppression. They will be the first to benefit when the world's demands are met. Americans believe all men and women deserve to be free. And as we saw in the fall of the Taliban [in Afghanistan], men and women celebrate freedom's arrival.

The United States will work with other nations. We'll work with other nations to bring Saddam to account. We'll work with other nations to help the Iraqi people form a just government and a unified country. And should force be required, the United States will help rebuild a liberated Iraq.

Countering Iraq's threat is also a central commitment on the war on terror. We know Saddam Hussein has long-standing and ongoing ties to international terrorists. With the support and shelter of a regime, terror groups become far more lethal. Aided by a terrorist network, an outlaw regime can launch attacks while concealing its involvement. Even a dictator is not suicidal, but he can make use of men who are. We must confront both terror cells and terror states, because they are different faces of the same evil.

I brought this issue to the attention of the world, and many, many countries share our determination to confront this threat. We're not alone. The issue is now before the United States Congress. This debate will be closely watched by the American people, and this debate will be remembered in history. We didn't ask for this challenge as a country, but we will face it, and we will face it together.

George W. Bush, "President, House Leadership Agree on Iraq Resolution," October 2, 2002.

DOCUMENT 10: SUPPORTING THE PRESIDENT

On October 2, 2002, Senator Joseph Lieberman commented on Congressional support of President Bush and why it passed the war resolution allowing President Bush the power to use military force against Iraq.

There is no more fateful, important, or difficult responsibility that the Constitution gives members of Congress than to decide when, whether, and how to authorize the President as Commander-in-

Chief to go to war. Mr. President, in your eloquent, powerful, and convincing statement this morning, you have reminded us, and I believe the American people, about why this is such a circumstance.

I have felt for more than a decade now that every additional day that Saddam Hussein is in power in Iraq is an additional day of danger for the Iraqi people, for his neighbors in the region, particularly for the people and military of the United States of America, and indeed for the people of the world. And that is why I am grateful for the opportunity to stand with my colleagues from both parties, and both Houses, and with you, Mr. President, in offering this resolution to authorize you to take military action to protect the region and the world from Iraq under Saddam Hussein, and to enforce the resolutions that are relevant of the United Nations.

There are those who say that this represents hurried or precipitous action, that we should give Saddam and the Iraqi government another chance. The record shows that for the last 10 years, we have tried—the world has tried—in just about every way—diplomatic, economic and otherwise, except military, in the end—to convince Saddam Hussein to live by the rules of international law and civilization. They've not worked.

The moment of truth has arrived. For Saddam Hussein, this is his last chance, and the best chance for the international community to come together behind the rule of law, and to show that resolutions of the United Nations are worth more than the paper that they are written on. . . .

And that, today, is the best hope for a stronger America and for a life for the American people that is safer.

Joseph Lieberman, Speech from "President, House Leadership Agree on Iraq Resolution," October 2, 2002.

DOCUMENT 11: LEAVE NO CHILD BEHIND

Listing education reform as a critical issue for America during his run for the presidency, George W. Bush was thrilled with bipartisan efforts to pass federal mandates on education in 2002. On January 8, 2003, Bush addressed the nation on the first anniversary of the No Child Left Behind Act. This landmark legislation made schools accountable to specific academic standards or face the loss of federal support funds.

[Today] marks the anniversary of an incredibly important legislative accomplishment. It was a year ago that I signed the No Child Left Behind Education Act. It was the most meaningful education reform probably ever. . . .

We can say that the work of reform is well begun. And that's— that's a true statement. The work will be complete, however, when every school—every public school in America is a place of high expectations and a place of achievement. That is our national goal.

Many schools in our country are places of hope and opportunity.

... Many schools ... are places where people can feel hopeful for the future. Unfortunately, too many schools in America have failed in that mission. The harm has been greatest in the poor and minority communities. Those kids have been hurt the worst because people have failed to challenge the soft bigotry of low expectations. ...

The time for excuse-making has come to an end. With the No Child Left Behind Act, we have committed the nation to higher standards for every single public school. And we've committed the resources to help the students achieve those standards. We affirm the right of parents to have better information about the schools, and to make crucial decisions about their children's future. Accountability of results is no longer just a hope of parents. Accountability for results is now the law of the land.

In return for receiving federal money, states must design accountability systems to measure whether students are learning to read and write and add and subtract. In return for a lot of money, the federal government, for the first time, is asking, are we getting the kind of return the American people want for every child. The only way to be sure of whether or not every child is learning is to test regularly and to show everybody, especially the parents, the results of the tests. The law further requires that test scores be presented in a clear and meaningful way, so that we can find the learning problems within each group of students. ...

Annual report cards are required to grade the schools, themselves, so parents can judge how the schools compare to others. Excellence will be recognized. It's so important for us to measure, so that we can praise the principals and teachers who are accomplishing the objectives we all hope for. And, at the same time, poor performance cannot be disguised or hidden.

Schools that perform poorly will be noticeable and given time, and given incentives, and given resources to improve. Schools that don't improve will begin to face consequences, such as that parents can move their child to another public school, or hire a tutor, or any other academic help. We will not accept a school that does not teach and will not change. ...

Some have claimed that testing somehow distracts from learning. I've heard this excuse since I was the governor of Texas—oh, you're teaching to test. Well, if a child can pass the reading test, the child has learned to read, as far as I'm concerned.

Other critics worry that high standards and measurement invite poor results. In other words, don't measure; you might see poor results, I guess is what they're saying. That they fear that by imposing clear standards, we'll set some schools up for failure, and that we'll identify too many failing schools. Well, the reasoning is backwards as far as I'm concerned, and a lot of other good people are concerned, as well. You don't cause a problem by revealing the problem. Accountability doesn't cause failure; it identifies failure. And only by acknowledging poor performance can we ever help schools to achieve. You can't solve a problem unless you first diagnose the problem. . . .

We've got to make sure the attitude changes. And the accountability systems within the No Child Left Behind Act insist that we have an attitude change in America. That's what this says.

One year ago, we met the first challenge of education reform. We passed the law. And now we've got another challenge, and that's the implementation of this law. . . . We look forward to a culture in America that understands every child can learn. And we look forward to the day that no child in this country is ever left behind.

George W. Bush, Speech on the First Anniversary of the No Child Left Behind Act, January 8, 2003.

DOCUMENT 12: A CASE FOR WAR

In his State of the Union Address to the American people on January 28, 2003, President Bush justified his case for involving the nation in a possible war against Iraq.

Twelve years ago, Saddam Hussein faced the prospect of being the last casualty in a war he had started and lost. To spare himself, he agreed to disarm of all weapons of mass destruction. For the next 12 years, he systematically violated that agreement. He pursued chemical, biological, and nuclear weapons, even while inspectors were in his country. Nothing to date has restrained him from his pursuit of these weapons—not economic sanctions, not isolation from the civilized world, not even cruise missile strikes on his military facilities.

Almost three months ago, the United Nations Security Council gave Saddam Hussein his final chance to disarm. He has shown instead utter contempt for the United Nations, and for the opinion of the world. The 108 U.N. inspectors were sent to conduct—were not sent to conduct a scavenger hunt for hidden materials across a country the size of California. The job of the inspectors is to verify that Iraq's regime is disarming. It is up to Iraq to show exactly where it is hiding its banned weapons, lay those weapons out for the world to see, and destroy them as directed. Nothing like this has happened.

The United Nations concluded in 1999 that Saddam Hussein had biological weapons sufficient to produce over 25,000 liters of anthrax—enough doses to kill several million people. He hasn't accounted for that material. He's given no evidence that he has destroyed it.

The United Nations concluded that Saddam Hussein had materials sufficient to produce more than 38,000 liters of botulinum toxin—enough to subject millions of people to death by respiratory failure. He hadn't accounted for that material. He's given no evidence that he has destroyed it.

Our intelligence officials estimate that Saddam Hussein had the materials to produce as much as 500 tons of sarin, mustard and VX nerve agent. In such quantities, these chemical agents could also kill untold thousands. He's not accounted for these materials. He has given no evidence that he has destroyed them.

U.S. intelligence indicates that Saddam Hussein had upwards of 30,000 munitions capable of delivering chemical agents. Inspectors recently turned up 16 of them—despite Iraq's recent declaration denying their existence. Saddam Hussein has not accounted for the remaining 29,984 of these prohibited munitions. He's given no evidence that he has destroyed them.

From three Iraqi defectors we know that Iraq, in the late 1990s, had several mobile biological weapons labs. These are designed to produce germ warfare agents, and can be moved from place to place to evade inspectors. Saddam Hussein has not disclosed these facilities. He's given no evidence that he has destroyed them.

The International Atomic Energy Agency confirmed in the 1990s that Saddam Hussein had an advanced nuclear weapons development program, had a design for a nuclear weapon and was working on five different methods of enriching uranium for a bomb. The British government has learned that Saddam Hussein recently sought significant quantities of uranium from Africa. Our intelligence sources tell us that he has attempted to purchase high-strength aluminum tubes suitable for nuclear weapons production. Saddam Hussein has not credibly explained these activities. He clearly has much to hide.

The dictator of Iraq is not disarming. To the contrary; he is deceiving. From intelligence sources we know, for instance, that thousands of Iraqi security personnel are at work hiding documents and materials from the U.N. inspectors, sanitizing inspection sites and monitoring the inspectors themselves. Iraqi officials accompany the inspectors in order to intimidate witnesses.

Iraq is blocking U-2 [spy plane] surveillance flights requested by the United Nations. Iraqi intelligence officers are posing as the scientists inspectors are supposed to interview. Real scientists have been coached by Iraqi officials on what to say. Intelligence sources indicate that Saddam Hussein has ordered that scientists who cooperate with U.N. inspectors in disarming Iraq will be killed, along with their families.

Year after year, Saddam Hussein has gone to elaborate lengths, spent enormous sums, taken great risks to build and keep weapons of mass destruction. But why? The only possible explanation, the only possible use he could have for those weapons, is to dominate, intimidate, or attack.

With nuclear arms or a full arsenal of chemical and biological weapons, Saddam Hussein could resume his ambitions of conquest in the Middle East and create deadly havoc in that region. And this Congress and the American people must recognize another threat. Evidence from intelligence sources, secret communications, and statements by people now in custody reveal that Saddam Hussein aids and protects terrorists, including members of al-Qaeda. Secretly, and without fingerprints, he could provide one of his hidden weapons to terrorists, or help them develop their own. . . .

Some have said we must not act until the threat is imminent. Since when have terrorists and tyrants announced their intentions, politely putting us on notice before they strike? If this threat is permitted to fully and suddenly emerge, all actions, all words, and all recriminations would come too late. Trusting in the sanity and restraint of Saddam Hussein is not a strategy, and it is not an option. . . .

The world has waited 12 years for Iraq to disarm. America will not accept a serious and mounting threat to our country, and our friends and our allies. The United States will ask the U.N. Security Council to convene on February the 5th to consider the facts of Iraq's ongoing defiance of the world. Secretary of State [Colin] Powell will present information and intelligence about Iraqi's illegal weapons programs, its attempt to hide those weapons from inspectors, and its links to terrorist groups.

We will consult. But let there be no misunderstanding: If Saddam Hussein does not fully disarm, for the safety of our people and for the peace of the world, we will lead a coalition to disarm him.

George W. Bush, State of the Union Address, January 28, 2003.

Document 13: Compassionate Conservative

George W. Bush describes himself and his political philosophy as compassionate conservative. Bush outlines this philosophy in an excerpt from a chapter in his book, A Charge to Keep.

We must close the gap of hope, but the answer is not found in yet another government program. The answer begins with each one of us assuming our responsibilities as parents and neighbors and citizens. I want to usher in the responsibility era, an era when every American knows with certainty that each of us is responsible for our actions, that each of us is responsible for our family and our community, that each of us is responsible for loving a neighbor as we would like to be loved ourselves.

During the more than half century of my life, we have seen an unprecedented decay in our American culture, a decay that has eroded the foundations of our collective values and moral standards of conduct. Our sense of personal responsibility has declined dramatically, just as the role and responsibility of the federal government have increased. . . .

The new culture said if people were poor, the government should feed them. If someone had no house, the government should provide one. If criminals are not responsible for their acts, then the answers are not in prisons, but in social programs. Every problem suddenly demanded a government solution.

Fathers moved out and Uncle Sam moved in. People became less interested in pulling themselves up by their bootstraps and more interested in pulling down a monthly government check. A culture of dependency was born. . . .

I am a conservative because I believe in the worth and dignity and power of each individual. My philosophy trusts individuals to make the right decisions for their families and communities, and that is far more compassionate than a philosophy that seeks solutions from distant bureaucracies. I am a conservative because I believe government should be limited and efficient, that it should do a few things and do them well. I am a conservative because I believe in a strong national defense to keep the peace. I am a conservative because I support free markets and free trade. I am a conservative because I believe government closest to the people governs best.

I am a fiscal conservative and a family conservative. And I am a compassionate conservative, because I know my philosophy is optimistic and full of hope for every American.

Compassionate conservatism outlines a new vision of the proper role for the American government. Government must be limited and focused, but it has an important job within its bounds. Government is too often wasteful and overreaching. But we must correct it and limit it, not disdain it. I differ with those who want to dismantle government down to the last paper clip—and with those who want to extend its reach. Government is neither the enemy nor the answer. The federal government has some compelling purposes: to defend our homeland, to help keep peace in the world, to help secure the retirement and health needs of our senior citizens, and to help our society confront human suffering. State and local government must educate children, put criminals behind bars, and maintain roads and basic services. But in some cases, the job is best done not by government itself, but by directing government resources to neighborhoods and parents and schools and faith-based institutions that shape values and change lives.

Compassionate conservatism is neither soft nor fuzzy. It is clear and compelling. It focuses not on good intentions but on good results. Compassionate conservatism applies conservative, free-market principles to the real job of helping real people, all people, including the poor and the disadvantaged. My vision of compassionate conservatism also requires America to assert its leadership in the world. We are the world's only remaining superpower, and we must use our power in a strong but compassionate way to help keep the peace and encourage the spread of freedom.

George W. Bush, *A Charge to Keep*. New York: William Morrow, 1999.

DISCUSSION QUESTIONS

CHAPTER 1

1. In his article, "Midland Influence," Nicholas D. Kristof discusses how the values George W. Bush absorbed growing up in west Texas are critical to understanding who Bush is. Describe how growing up in smalltown Midland, Texas, developed Bush's personal and political philosophies.

2. It has been noted that George Bush looks like his father but has the spirit of his mother, Barbara Bush. Provide examples of the influence she held over her son according to George Lardner Jr. and Lois Romano's article.

3. Joe Conason notes that by Bush's father's standards, Bush was impatient in beginning his own oil drilling company. Cite examples of how Bush's personal relationships became important to his survival in this business.

CHAPTER 2

1. Bush became a successful businessman as general managing partner of the Texas Ranger's ball club. Give examples of Bush's management style listed in Joe Nick Patoski's article. Do you think any of these skills have been useful to Bush as president of the United States? Explain using examples.

2. In Skip Hollandsworth's article, what was the struggle Bush had in the Texas gubernatorial race against Ann Richards, and how did he overcome it?

3. Evaluate Bush's success as a governor. Why did these successes prompt the Republican National Convention to nominate him as their presidential candidate for 2000?

CHAPTER 3

1. What evidence did Lee Edwards use to make his case that the 2000 presidential election was not as close as it seemed? According to Edwards, in what areas did Bush best Al Gore as a campaigner?

2. James W. Ceaser and Andrew E. Busch discuss the politi-

cal climate surrounding the 2000 presidential election. Describe the atmosphere of the time and indicate how these circumstances culminated in one of the closest and controversial elections of the century.

3. Andrew Phillips notes several hurdles that Bush had to overcome as a new president. Describe these obstacles and why Phillips considers the surmounting of them to be political triumphs for Bush.

CHAPTER 4

1. What skills did Bush demonstrate during the ten-day hostage standoff with China according to William Schneider? What did the American people learn about Bush during this incident?

2. According to Siobhan Gorman, why does Bush have a passion for education reform? Describe what Gorman says the real test of the Bush reform package will be.

3. According to Richard Cheney, what are some of the economic stimulants Bush put into practice to facilitate long-term economic growth in America?

CHAPTER 5

1. From Robin Wright's viewpoint, explain why international respect for Bush increased based on his handling of the terrorist attacks of September 11, 2001. Discuss why the Bush administration could face larger hurdles once initial retaliation in Afghanistan ceases.

2. The national agenda changed with the terrorist events of September 11, 2001, according to Jeffrey H. Birnbaum. Consider these changes and cite examples to support his view that the nation is headed in a new direction.

3. Jeffrey H. Birnbaum also explains how Bush's leadership style developed throughout initial terrorist attacks. Compare Bush's management style after September 11 to the presidential characteristics he displayed before September 11, 2001. What similarities and differences are apparent?

4. Using Tony Carnes's article, describe how Bush's faith and politics led the nation in healing from September 11, 2001, terrorist activity in America.

CHAPTER 6

1. Kenneth T. Walsh examines Bush's actions following the September 11, 2001, terrorist attacks against the United States and his plan to eliminate terrorist activity around the world. Explain what role Iraq, Iran, and North Korea play in Bush's plan.

2. T. Trent Gegax outlines Bush's approach to the war against terror. Once a plan was devised, what methods did Bush choose to explain his mission to the world?

3. Bush originally kept his administration at a distance from the Middle East conflict, according to Michael Duffy. Yet Bush eventually changed his mind over involving America in the conflict between Israel and the Palestinians. Describe the events that took place to make Bush reevaluate the situation and stake his presidency on peace in that region.

4. Why was the war with Iraq unprecedented? According to Kenneth T. Walsh, what was Bush's philosophy behind the coalition's attack?

CHRONOLOGY

1946

George Walker Bush is born in New Haven, Connecticut, on July 6.

1948

The Bush family moves to Odessa, Texas.

1953

Bush's sister, Robin, dies in October.

1961

Bush enters Phillips Academy in Andover, Massachusetts.

1964

Bush works as a campaign aide for his father's Senate race and enters Yale University in September.

1968

Bush joins the Texas Air National Guard on May 27 after graduating from Yale. On June 10 he leaves for one year of flight training at Moody Air Force Base in Georgia.

1973

Bush enters Harvard Business School.

1975

Bush graduates from Harvard and heads to Midland, Texas, to work in the oil industry.

1977

Bush organizes his first company, Arbusto, then runs for Congress. He meets and later marries Laura Welch on November 5.

1978

Bush wins the primary election for Congress but loses the general election.

1981

Bush's father becomes the vice president of the United States. Laura gives birth to twin daughters, Jenna Welch and Barbara Pierce Bush, on November 25.

1985

Bush discusses religion with the Reverend Billy Graham and finds renewed religious conviction in his personal life.

1988

George H.W. Bush becomes president of the United States.

1989

Bush purchases the Texas Rangers baseball club in April with a group of investors.

1994

Bush defeats Ann Richards in the Texas gubernatorial race.

1998

Bush is reelected governor of Texas.

1999

Bush enters the presidential race.

2000

Bush becomes the forty-third president of the United States.

2001

January: Bush is inaugurated on January 20.

April: Bush negotiates the release of twenty-four U.S. prisoners in China after the U.S. surveillance plane collided with a Chinese fighter; he implements a tax relief bill and issues refund checks to tax-paying Americans.

June: Bush introduces a patients' bill of rights, ensuring medical review; dedicates a D day memorial in Virginia; and visits Europe.

August: Bush approves federal funding of stem cell research only within federal limitations.

September: Bush proclaims a National Day of Prayer and Remembrance after planes crash into the World Trade Center, the Pentagon, and a field in Pennsylvania; he assembles an international campaign against terrorism.

October: Bush creates the Department of Homeland Security; he begins an antiterrorism war in Afghanistan.

2002

January: Bush passes Brownfield legislation, helping cities clean up industrial sites; he signs a landmark educational reform bill; he implements legislation to aid victims of terrorism.

February: Bush launches the USA Freedom Corps, an expansion of the Peace Corps serving and mentoring in local communities in America; he increases funding for bioterrorism research, defense, and test protocols; he meets with Israeli prime minister Ariel Sharon to discuss peace in the Middle East and eliminating world terrorism.

March: Bush signs the Corporate Responsibility Act, requiring business leaders to adhere to a code of ethics.

May: Bush signs a treaty with Russian president Alexander Putin to reduce nuclear arsenals to their lowest levels in decades.

September: Bush addresses the UN General Assembly, challenging it to enforce disclosure and destruction of weapons of mass destruction for Iraq according to Security Council resolutions from 1991.

October: Bush gets the House's approval to use force to impel Iraq to comply with UN Security Council resolutions to eliminate weapons of mass destruction.

2003

January: Bush assembles a multinational coalition to force Iraq to adhere to UN Security Council resolutions from 1991.

February: Bush attends memorial services for *Columbia* astronauts killed in flight; he sends Secretary of State Colin Powell to address the UN, requiring it to enforce previous mandates against Iraq.

March: After giving Iraqi leader Saddam Hussein forty-eight hours to leave power, Bush authorizes a military strike against Iraq. War with Iraq ensues.

April: Bush declares the United States has military control of Iraq; he addresses the Iraqi people by radio, promising the return of the country's power to the people.

May: Bush announces that combat operations in Iraq are over; he removes sanctions imposed by the United States against Iraq under Saddam Hussein; Bush signs the Jobs and Growth Tax Relief Reconciliation Act offering tax relief.

June: Bush signs an agreement with the EU to stop the proliferation of nuclear, biological, and chemical weapons; he outlines am agenda for U.S.-African relations.

July: Bush travels to Africa offering terrorism, education, and AIDS initiatives.

FOR FURTHER RESEARCH

BY GEORGE W. BUSH

George W. Bush, *A Charge to Keep.* New York: William Morrow, 1999.

BOOKS ABOUT GEORGE W. BUSH

Frank Bruni, *Ambling into History: The Unlikely Odyssey of George W. Bush.* New York: HarperCollins, 2002.

Barbara Bush, *Barbara Bush: A Memoir.* New York: Charles Scribner's Sons, 1994.

George H.W. Bush, *All the Best, George Bush.* New York: William Morrow, 1999.

David Frum, *The Right Man: The Surprise Presidency of George W. Bush.* New York: Random House, 2003.

Bill Minutaglio, *First Son George W. Bush and the Bush Family Dynasty.* New York: Time Books, 1999.

Bill Sammon, *The War on Terrorism from Inside the Bush White House.* Washington, DC: Regnery, 2002.

Bob Woodward, *Bush at War.* New York: Simon and Schuster, 2002.

BOOKS ON THE 2000 ELECTION

James W. Ceaser and Andrew E. Busch, *The Perfect Tie: The True Story of the 2000 Presidential Election.* Lanham, MD: Rowman & Littlefield, 2001.

E.J. Dionne Jr. and William Kristol, *Bush vs. Gore: The Court Cases and the Commentary.* Washington, DC: Brookings Institution, 2001.

Martin Merzer and the Staff of the *Miami Herald, Democracy Held Hostage.* New York: St. Martin's, 2001.

Dana Milbank, *Smashmouth: Two Years in the Gutter with Al Gore and George W. Bush—Notes from the 2000 Campaign Trail.* New York: Basic Books, 2001.

New York Times, Thirty-Six Days: The Complete Chronicle of the 2000 Presidential Election Crisis. New York: Henry Holt, 2001.

Richard Posner, *Breaking Deadlock: The 2000 Election, the Constitution, and the Courts.* Princeton, NJ: Princeton University Press, 2001.

Jeffrey Toobin, *Too Close to Call.* New York: Random House, 2001.

PERIODICALS

Michael Beschloss, "How Bush Rates: Does He Measure Up to Other Wartime Presidents?" *Time*, December 31, 2001.

Jeffrey H. Birnbaum, "Bush's Growth Spurt: George W. Has Found His Presidential Authority and Voice Since September 11th," *International Economy Publications*, 2001.

Robert J. Bresler, "Bush, War, and Iraq," *USA Today*, November 2002.

Tony Carnes, "Bush's Defining Moment," *Christian Reader*, March 2002.

Joe Conason, "Notes on a Native Son," *Harper's*, February 2000.

Michael Duffy, "After Several False Starts, George W. Bush Commits Himself Fully to Ending the Bloodshed in the Middle East. The Inside Story of His About-Face, and the Risks He Confronts," *Time*, April 12, 2002.

Lee Edwards, "The Closest Presidential Election Ever—Bush Won, Barely, by Offering a Slightly to the Right, Limited-Government Presidency," *World & I*, February 2001.

T. Trent Gegax, "Bush's Battle Cry: Drawing on Prayer and a Sense of Personal Mission, W Becomes a War President," *Newsweek*, October 1, 2001.

Nancy Gibbs, "Person of the Year: George W. Bush," *Time*, December 17, 2000.

Siobhan Gorman, "Bipartisan Schoolmates," *Education National Journal*, 2002.

Fred Greenstein, "The Contemporary Presidency: The Changing Leadership of George W. Bush: A Pre- and

Post-9/11 Comparison," *Presidential Studies Quarterly*, June 2002.

Skip Hollandsworth, "Born to Run: What's in a Name? How About the Republican Nomination for Governor," *Texas Monthly*, May 1994.

Nicholas D. Kristof, "A Boy from Midland: A Philosophy with Roots in Conservative Texas Soil," *New York Times*, May 21, 2000.

George Lardner Jr. and Lois Romano, "At Height of Vietnam, Bush Picks the Guard," *Washington Post*, July 28, 1999.

———, "Bush Earned Profit, Rangers Deal Insiders Say," *Washington Post*, July 31, 1999.

———, "Bush Name Helps Fuel Oil Dealings," *Washington Post*, July 30, 1999.

———, "Bush's Life-Changing Year," *Washington Post*, July 25, 1999.

———, "Bush's Move Up to the Majors," *Washington Post*, July 31, 1999.

———, "So-So Student but a Campus Mover," *Washington Post*, July 27, 1999.

———, "Tragedy Created Bush Mother-Son Bond," *Washington Post*, July 26, 1999.

———, "Young Bush a Political Natural, Revs Up," *Washington Post*, July 29, 1999.

Ryan Lizza, "White House Watch—Future Tense," *New Republic*, September 2, 2002.

Dana Milbank, "What 'W' Stands For," *New Republic*, April 26, 1999.

Adam Nagourney, "White House Power Grows Under Bush," *Seattle Times*, December 22, 2002.

Joe Nick Patoski, "George Bush's Career Running the Texas Rangers," *Texas Monthly*, June 1999.

Andrew Phillips, "Victory at Last," *Maclean's*, December 25, 2000.

Ramesh Ponnuru, "Bush at One Year," *National Review*, January 28, 2002.

———, "The Front-Runner: Is It George W. Bush Already?" *National Review*, December 1997.

Harold C. Relyea, "The Law: Homeland Security; the Concept and the Presidential Coordination Office—First Assessment," *Presidential Studies Quarterly*, June 2002.

Jon Sawyer, "President's Leadership Gets High Marks, but Test Looms," *St. Louis Post-Dispatch*, December 28, 2002.

William Schneider, "Bush Wins 'Let's Make a Deal,'" *National Journal*, April 21, 2001.

Kathryn Dunn Tenpas, "The Bush White House, First Appraisals," *Presidential Studies Quarterly*, September 2002.

Michael Waller, "A Wartime Window of Opportunity," *Insight on the News*, September 2, 2002.

Kenneth T. Walsh, "W, as in War," *U.S News & World Report*, February 25, 2002.

WEBSITES

Republican Party, www.georgewbush.com. This site highlights George W. Bush and his presidency. Information on Bush, his 2000 election campaign, and where he stands on current issues are some of the topics offered.

Texas, http://gotexas.about.com. This site focuses on information on Texas. Search "George W. Bush" to find family history, biographies, his role as president, and his campaign and work as governor of Texas. Photos and links to other sites are provided.

Texas Monthly, www.texasmonthly.com. This site keeps archives of George W. Bush, especially his life as governor, his biography, and information about his life in Texas and his family.

Washington Post, www.washingtonpost.com. This site has archives that focus on George W. Bush and issues at large during his presidency.

The White House, www.whitehouse.gov. This site provides information on George W. Bush as president. Speeches by Bush as well as photos, press releases, presidential time lines, and links to other sites are available.

INDEX